Oraon Christian's Way of Life

Christian Heritage Rediscovered - 83

Oraon Christian's Way of Life

Interaction of Faith and Culture

Clare Purakary HM

CWI

Christian World Imprints

First Published in 2019 by

Christian World Imprints
Christian Publishing & Books from India
C-3, Shop No. 14, Ground Floor
Wazirpur Industrial Area, **Delhi-110052**
cwidelhi2017@gmail.com
www.ChristianWorldImprints.com
Phone: +91 11 41526079

ISBN: 978-93-5148-360-1

Printed in India.

CONTENTS

FOREWORD

The author of the book: *Oraon Christian's Way of Life: Interaction of Faith and Culture* Sr. Clare Purakary of the Handmaids of Mary (HM), introduces the reader into one of the fast growing Churches, not by chance but by integrating Christian values in its way of life, especially in its very way of thinking and celebrating. Perhaps, it would be better to say that the Kurukh (Oraons), who are one of the major communities to embrace Christianity, found in Christianity complementary meaning to their existing expressions of Beliefs, Festivals and Rites. In the language of the Kurukh themselves, they have found in Christianity a good spouse for their marriage.

The anthropologists have classified the Kurukh in items of indigenous or primitive culture, meaning they are not civilized yet and are away from the main-stream philosophy. This detailed study on the Beliefs, Festivals and Rites of the Kurukh would enlighten the readers in understanding that these people have been responding to the same questions, which every religion asks: What is man? Who is God for them? Where does the suffering and sin come from in the world? What is the final destination of man? In other words, the Kurukh were fully human in their search for meaning of their own life.

The study on 'Beliefs' shows that the Kurukh call God '*Dharmes*', who is 'Father' to them: Creator, caretaker and Protector of life. The similar affectionate filial relationship with God is found also in Christianity, which has made their bond easier. The concept of 'good spirit' and 'evil spirit' is found in the traditional thinking of the Kurukh as well as in Christianity with some variations, but the struggle to fight against the evil in the world is a reality in both religions; *Kurukh* as well as Christianity. Finally, the 'Life after death' continues in both religions, though in different forms. The celebrations of Festivals and Rites emerge from the same basic belief-system, which prove the integrity of their total expression as a distinct Kurukh-culture.

As a scholar, Sr. Clare first and foremost has explored the life of the Kurukh and their historical background for the readers, foreign to Extended-Jharkhand, which was known as Chotanagpur during the time of the British Raj in India. Then, she narrates how Christianity arrived in the territory of the Kurukh. In short, the search for true Liberation was already there among the Kurukh, which the Church understood and responded, both in the form of human liberation as well as spiritual redemption. Theologically speaking this mutual-relationship is known as 'inculturation', an official approach of the Catholic Church towards any other culture, as explained by the author.

The detailed study of Beliefs, Festivals and Rites of Passage of the Kurukh is praiseworthy. Sr. Clare has also proposed on how far they are compatible with the Christian way of life, and where there are needs of further understanding. The responses with signs and symbols are different, but the answers are not contradictory. Thus, without losing their traditional festivals and rites, some of the Kurukh have embraced Christianity, for it has respected them and their way of life.

The book should be especially enlightening for those who would like to work among the people of Chotanagpur; the present Jharkhand, Odisha, West Bengal and Chhattisgarh. It should also illumine those who seek to understand people only from the anthropological or sociological point of view, and are unable to see the minds and hearts of the Kurukh's belief-system.

The testimony of this research is an example of how one culture meets other cultures and how religious aspirations of people is not limited to any one religion, as defined in rituals and festivals. The transcendental Nature of Man is unlimited, due to which every culture tends to grow by embracing the values of other cultures as well as of other religions, in so far a particular community is able to integrate or assimilate them personally. Thus, education for discernment is the only way to make every culture more Universal and International; the true nature of Man.

Fr. Linus Kujur, S.J.
Pontifical Gregorian University, Rome

ARCHBISHOP'S HOUSE
9/16, Satyanagar
Bhubaneswar- 751 007, Odisha, India
Mobile: (91) 9437390428
E-mail: abjohnb@gmail.com

PREFACE

This book is first of its kind; in an analytical and descriptive way the author has placed before us the interaction between Oraon culture and Christian Faith. Chotanagpur which is also called "Lievens Mission" (religious unit) is a very promising Mission area, in spite of the fact that Christianity is just one hundred and thirty four years old. Yet, Oraons have proved to be one of the fast growing communities who have accepted Christian faith and enjoying the transformative power of the Gospel.

Sr. Clare Purakary HM belongs to a Congregation which is born in this soil and her experiences with the people of Chotanagpur enkindled in her the interest to bring forth this book which would serve as a source for developing a theology for Oraon Culture in view of evangelization through Inculturation. In her book, she has beautifully brought out the concept of God and the myth of creation which has got similarities with Christianity, which helped the Oraons to experience the liberative power of the Gospel in their life's struggles. The use of holy water, medals, and rosaries encouraged them as materials which would enable them to resist the attack of evil spirits. The Ancestor worship has made meaningful the veneration of Saints as intercessors and patrons of the community. Thus, they found their basic questions answered in Christianity, which they were looking for, they also found that their new religion gave them meaning and purpose in life.

No culture is perfect; culture is a medium for human beings to express their faith. In the life of Oraons dance and music has a prominent place. They communicate through songs and dance rhythmically what they believe, feel and experience. Festivals and celebrations of important events of nature as well as of life are very much part of their life. They are people profoundly in love with nature, collaborators with the Creator God, and it is clear from the creation story.

In this age of technology and mind blogging, in a culture where there is a transition from oral tradition to written tradition, this book is a challenge as well as an eye opener to the future generations, that there is much more to explore in the Oraon culture, there is much to appreciate and to feel great.

Most Rev. John Barwa SVD
Archbishop of Cuttack - Bhubaneswar

INTRODUCTION

At the threshold of the third millennium Christians look afresh at the mysteries of their faith and dedicate themselves anew to the service of the Gospel. "God is opening before the Church the horizons of a humanity more fully prepared for the sowing of the Gospel."[1]

Already the Second Vatican Council had opened a new path in the history of the Church with its promulgation on the Declaration on the relationship of the Church to the Non-Christian Religions. It is significant because after many years of reflection and discernment the Church has invited her members to see the hidden goodness in these religions foregoing the attitude of superiority, ignorance and incomprehension.[2] The conciliar declaration speaks that there is an awareness of a hidden power which surpasses the daily events of human history, and leads the people to a profound religiosity, with the recognition of a Supreme Being or even more of a Father.[3] Even though the Church has arrived at the realisation of the "ray of Truth which enlightens all men"[4] in non-Christian religions it speaks explicitly of the two great world religions: Hinduism and Budhism. The declaration does not say anything clearly about the religions of the pre-literate peoples. Yet one can presume that the Church does not oppose any thing that displays Truth when she says,

"The Catholic Church rejects nothing that is true and holy in these religions. She regards with sincere reverence those ways of conduct and of life, those precepts and teachings which, though differing in many aspects from the ones she holds and sets forth, nonetheless often reflect a ray of that Truth which enlightens all men."[5]

---

[1] RM 3.

[2] Cf. H.R. SCHLETTE, "The Plurality of Religions," in K. RAHNER (ed.), *An Encyclopedia of Theology, Sacramentum Mundi*, V (London: Burns & Oates, 1970), 282.

[3] Cf. NA 2.

[4] NA 2.

[5] NA 2.

Some rays of Truth or seeds of Word are found in all the religions and cultures and the Word reveals himself to peoples of various religious traditions in many ways. And from experiences it is proven that the followers of the traditional religions are more open to Christianity than the followers of Hinduism and Budhism. This is also true with the Oraons of Chotanagpur.

The relationship between Gospel and culture is a difficult but important matter to understand and to practice. With the revival of nationalism and the renaissance of indigenous cultures it has become a burning issue in our days in the field of evangelisation. Inculturation was one of the central points in Pope Paul VI's apostolic exhortation *Evangelii Nuntiandi* (on the Evangelization of Peoples). Pope John Paul II also sees the urgency of inculturation in bringing faith to peoples. He says that "there is an organic and constitutive link between Christianity and culture" and that "the synthesis between culture and faith is not just a demand of culture, but also of faith. A faith that does not become culture is a faith which has not been fully received, not thoroughly thought through, not fully lived out."[6]

Christianity is born and alive when people accept its message, when this message touches their hearts and finds expression in their culture. As Pope Paul VI says:

"Evangelization loses much of its force and effectiveness if it does not take into consideration the actual people to whom it is addressed, if it does not use their language, their signs and symbols, if it does not answer the questions they ask, and if it does not have an impact on their concrete life."[7]

Thus, the ecclesial documents speak of the need of inculturation, for it is of vital importance and inseparably tied up with Evangelisation. India is a country with a very large proportion of tribal population.[8] Among the tribals of India, those of the Chotanagpur in the central belt of India popularly known as the Adivasis[9] (especially the Oraons, Mundas, and Kharias), and the tribals of North East India, have shown positive responses to the Christian message. Missionary efforts in India are mainly concentrated in these areas.

Christianity in India has given a relatively wrong impression of itself in its efforts of evangelisation during the early days of its existence. Acceptance of faith was considered as an alienation of one's socio-cultural life. Christians were considered as aliens to their fellow men. Christianity in Chotanagpur too had more or less a similar fate. Oraon Christians differed from non-Christian Oraons, not only by faith itself, but also in the forms and ways to express their worship.

---

[6] JOHN PAUL II, *Letter to Cardinal Agostino Casaroli*, Secretary of State, 20th May 1982, quoted in *L'Osservatore Romano*, English edition, 28th June 1982, 7-8.

[7] EN 63.

[8] About 60 million.Statement by the Indian Council of Indigenous and Tribal Peoples at the United Nations Working Group on Indigenous Peoples at the 9th Session: July 22 to August 2, 1991. See the sixth paragraph of the statement, also the covering letter on page 2.

[9] Adivasis means the original settlers of the place.

Hence, they became 'strangers' to their fellow Oraons. Religion and culture are living realities connected with people. Religion and culture influence each other, and so the Gospel touches and transforms both. Exactly here one has to pay attention. Acceptance of faith means surrendering oneself to Christ and to his cause. It is not the Church but Christ who demands a radical change in a person which will be expressed explicitly in life.[10] Therefore, efforts must be made for an authentic evangelisation of Oraon culture so that the Good News may touch the lives and concrete life situations of its hearers, and find meaning in their expressions of faith bringing a transformation in their lives. "They (cultures) have to be regenerated by an encounter with the Gospel. But, this encounter will not take place if the Gospel is not proclaimed."[11] Hence, inculturation is inevitable, necessary and fruitful for an authentical evangelisation of Chotanagpur: Oraons are meant to become Christians without losing their identity either as Oraons or as Christians where one may be expressing one's faith using the same cultural expressions which are redeemed and assimilated.[12]

It is not enough to announce the Word, calling people to faith and conversion, to gather them in worship, but the Church needs to inculturate herself to the milieus and traditions, the cultural and religious expressions of the people. The Word of God passes through the human word; and this should be meaningful to the recipient when it is expressed in concrete cultural forms.[13] And such faith expressions embedded in a cultural garb give cohesiveness to the group as well as identity and self-image.[14] But above all, culture itself through its symbolic aspects and concrete elements becomes a real road on which the Gospel with its transcendent values reaches the very centre of the human heart. The Word event should induce a continual and ever more radical conversion and transformation which will be translated into daily life thus becoming a new creation in Christ.[15] This is what the Church aims at by the inculturation of the Christian faith in Chotanagpur. In fact, inculturation should be part and parcel of the very process of evangelisation.

I am delighted to be a member of the active missionary Congregation of Handmaids of Mary which was born on the soil of Chotanagpur in order to evangelise this region. I had ample opportunities to be in the field of direct evangelisation. By adoption I too am an Oraon, for the past thirty years I have

---

[10] Cf. J. DINH DUC DAO, "Evangelization and Culture in Asia: Problems and Prospects", in *Omnis Terra* (English edition, February 1994), 74.

[11] EN 20.

[12] Cf. J. DINH DUC DAO, "Evangelization and Culture in Asia: Problems and Prospects", op. cit., 76.

[13] Cf. G.M. SOARES PRABHU, "From Alienation to Inculturation," in T.K. JOHN (ed.), *Bread and Breath: Essays in Honour of Samuel Rayan* (Anand: Gujarat Sahitya Prakash, 1991), 79-80.

[14] Cf. A. YVON, "Culture: Liberating or Alienating?," in *Jeevadhara,* 22 (1992), 28.

[15] Cf. F.A.B.C. Papers No. 41, 15.

become an inhabitant of Chotanagpur. Therefore, it is my personal identification with the charism of my congregation, and my special interest in the people of Chotanagpur which gave me the thought to select this topic. From the results it is desired to seek further towards the formation of a suitable Oraon (tribal) theology.

For my work, I have collected material from the official documents of the Magisterium, and other ecclesial texts. I have tried to explore all possible and available books and articles which speak directly or indirectly about evangelisation and inculturation, and about the Oraon traditional religion. Hence, one may come across some books and articles in the bibliography which I have not quoted but that have served as background information. I have to mention that there are not many written records particular for the Chotanagpur context, which is understandable especially in a culture that relies mostly on oral transmission. Thus there is the possibility of a situation that keeps on changing and it is difficult to find any original form. The main sources I have used in this context are mostly from the earlier periods of contact between people from Chotanagpur and outsiders. These notes were the work of the administration officials (Hindus) employed by the British government at the beginning of this century. For the completeness of their researches they depended on Belgian missionaries to collect information about the Oraons of Chotanagpur because the missionaries knew the language of the people. Unfortunately, later authors have used these not very reliable writings as their main source material. Therefore, I had to depend much on my personal experience as a sister working in this area and also on the knowledge I gained through my discussions and interviews with Oraons.

The method used is mainly analytic-descriptive for understanding the facts, but partially also interpretative and propository in view of a missionary application. The relevant biblical passages, Church documents, books and articles are quoted and cited. Indications regarding the references to documents, books and articles are presented in the footnotes on each page. The full information regarding the written material used in my work is given in the bibliography. To facilitate easy reading and understanding of the use of Oraon or Hindi words a glossary is included.

The entire work is structured into four chapters, followed by a conclusion, and each chapter is further divided into various sub-divisions for convenience of study. The first chapter speaks of the geographical and ethnological, cultural and religious contexts of the Oraons of Chotanagpur. It displays a brief history of the Catholic faith in Chotanagpur narrating the situation which made the Oraons to seek for and cling to the Gospel message, the various upheavals which prompted the spread of the faith. At any rate today the Oraon church is a self-evangelising church, which has reached a state of growth and maturity that enables her to send her sons and daughters as evangelisers both to and out of India as convinced and convincing witnesses of faith.

The second chapter draws our attention to inculturation in evangelising Chotanagpur, studying the importance of interactions of faith and culture in the teachings of the Magisterium and in the theology. This chapter explores further various aspects of inculturation and evangelisation on a national level and particularly in Chotanagpur, thus opening up the way for the study of basic beliefs of the Oraons of Chotanagpur.

Therefore the third chapter is dedicated to the basic beliefs of Oraon traditional religion which can be grouped into three main sub-divisions, i.e., the world of supernatural spirits with *Dharmes* as the Supreme Being, followed by a chain of ancestral and other spirits; the myths of the creation of the world and man, with special attention to the concept of man; and the ideas of sin and salvation. The myths are narrated and analysed, underlying meanings are interpreted in the light of Christian faith, seeking out some possibilities for the integration of Christian faith in the framework of a given tradition.

In the fourth chapter we concentrate our study on the cyclic festivals of the Oraon community and the transitory rites of the individuals. All the important festivals are critically studied with the scope of inculturation. Therefore, here too descriptive, analytic, and interpretative methods are followed which lead to certain points of convergences and divergences. This sort of comparison is used with the scope of understanding the meaning of traditional religious expressions, which are then interpreted in the light of the Gospel, thus opening a way for a meaningful and effective evangelisation.

There are some clearly converging values but at times appear also diverging view points in the Christian and Oraon traditional religion. This offers a lot of challenges for meaningful inculturation thereby an effective evangelisation. It also renders immense possibilities for further studies which would display a wide open path for an enriching interaction of Oraon traditional religion and Christian faith. In fact, it is through inculturation of the Gospel in a given context that evangelisation has now become truly effective in Chotanagpur.

Chapter 1

CHOTANAGPUR-THE LAND OF ORAONS

Introductory Remarks

This chapter gives an account of the historical background of the Catholic Church in Chotanagpur by looking at it as characterized by its geographical and ethnological, cultural and religious contexts. The Catholic faith was sown in this soil in an opportune time. In its growth process it went through periods of struggles and upheavals which, in one way, facilitated the progress of the Church within a remarkably short period of time. The church in Chotanagpur has become a viable and vibrant local Church.

1.1. Geographical Description

The Chotanagpur[16] is not a well-defined area. It covers an area of 6,000 square miles. Chotanagpur plateau is surrounded by Bihar in the north, Odisha in the south, West Bengal in the east and Madhya Pradesh in the west. Centuries ago Aryans called it Jharkhand, i.e., forest Tract, as to indicate that forests were the dominant feature of this plateau. The name Jharkhand survived during the Muslim and Moghul rule (in the 15th century) in India.[17]

---

[16] There are conflicting opinions regarding the name 'Chotanagpur'. Due to lack of written sources these opinions remain as mysteries. According to J.H. Hewitt a historian, *Nagbansi* family who conquered this region coined this name. *Nag* means cobra snake, and *pur* denotes realm or kingdom. They were worshipers of the cobra snake. Therefore *Nagbansi* family added the prefix '*Chota*' which meant for them (mother of *nagas*). However Chotanagpur literally means small nagpur as Chota is small and *pur* means land or country (of *nagas*) in Hindi. (Cf. M. BANAERJEE, *An Historical Outline of Pre-British Chotanagpur* (Ranchi: Educational publications, 1989), 2-5).

[17] Cf. A. A. KUJUR, *The Oraon habitat, A Study in Cultural Geography* (Ranchi: the Daughters of St Ann, 1989), 11.

The geography of Chotanagpur is marked by its geological features that belong to some of the old parts of the earth. It forms the eastern end of the Vindhyan ranges and it contains one of the richest mineral deposits[18] of India. The surface soil is characterised by a red brown texture covered with distinct deciduous vegetation dominated by the *Sal*[19] tree (Shorea robusta) which has become an object of worship for the people of this area.[20]

The land can be divided into three plateaus, the north-west plateau has an elevation of 2500 feet, the central plateau an average height of 2,000 feet, and the extreme southern and eastern parts, the third plateau, have lofty hill ranges. The area counts for numerous streams and small rivers, and is studded with low rocky hills and isolated peaks of base igneous rocks.[21] Important but not navigable rivers like Sankh, Brahmani, south Koel, North Koel, Mahanadi, Narmada, and the Ib with their tributaries flow through Chotanagpur.

Most of these rivers are almost dry except during the rainy season. There is no natural lake. The Chotanagpur in the past was a land of dense forests. The famous Saranda jungle and the Netarhat range of mountains stand out.[22]

This region is full of forest resources such as timber, fruits, various medicinal plants, roots and flowers, providing good environment for wild animals, birds and snakes. In general the region is immensely rich with natural resources and possibilities for power generation and industrialisation. "Because of the plateaus, hills, mountains and rivers, this region provides the best resources for generating hydropower."[23] Out of the six major steel plants in India three are located in this area.The Jharkhand area is famous for its iron and steel industry.

There are three distinct seasons-winter, summer, and a rainy period. Life and occupation of the people are patterned on these seasons. The annual rainfall varies

---

[18] The main minerals of Chotanagpur are iron, ferro manganese and coal. The other metals and minerals that are found in this region are mica, copper, lime-stone, sand-stone, laterite, graphite, clay, iron-stone, magnetic and titaniferous iron ores, lead-ores, chalk, nickel, gold, quartz, feldspar, beryl, schortcassiterpite (tin-stone) lepidolite, apatite lead, zinc, blende, galena diabese gneisses, granites, soap-stone and bauxite. (M. BANAERJEE, *An Historical Outline of Pre-British Chotanagpur* (Ranchi: Educational publications, 1989), 35).

[19] *Sal* tree (Shorea robusta) is the most common tree in Chotanagpur. It is the sacred tree for the tribals, even though it is felled and turned into timber for the construction of their houses. *Sal* leaves are used for making cups and plates which are made use of on occasions of feasts and festivals, also sold in the market. Its' leaf is used, to give few drops of water into the mouth of a person at the moment of his / her death. When his /her body will be laid to rest, *Sal* billets will form a chamber with in the grave to further safeguard him / her from evil spirits. Its fruit is edible, when it is dry oil is extracted from it. Incense is also bled from the bark of Sal tree.

[20] Cf. R.D. MUNDA, "The Bases of Cultural Identity of Chota Nagpur" in *Religion and Society*, 36 (June 1989), 25

[21] Cf. L. CLARYSEE, *Father Constant Lievens, S. J.* (Ranchi: Satya Bharati, 1984), 80.

[22] M. BANAERJEE, *An Historical Outline of Pre-British Chotanagpur*, op. cit., 30.

[23] M. MINJ, " Mission in the Context of Diversity: Mission in Tribal Context", in Religion and Society, 36 (March 1989), 8.

from 40 inches to 60 inches. During the rainy season crops like rice, millet, oil seeds are cultivated. Except during monsoon (June- September) the country enjoys sunny weather throughout the year. The climate affects the life style of the people both in respect to agriculture and health.[24] Politically Chotanagpur includes six administrative districts. The Ranchi (comprising the districts of Lohardaga and Gumla), Hazaribagh, Girindi, Palamau, Singbhum and Dhanbad.[25] Chotanagpur is not a political unit but Catholic missionaries have treated it as a unit due to the similarities of culture, habits, and life style of the Adivasis, the original inhabitants in this region. Although now up to 60% of the population are non-Adivasis and non-Christians, I deal with the region as a unit as my interest is focussed on the Catholic mission among the Adivasis known as the ' Lievens Mission.'[26]

1.2. People of Chotanagpur

Chotanagpur is the home of Adivasis belonging to many tribal communities.[27] Till recent centuries, Chotanagpur was inhabited by numerous Pre-Aryan and

---

[24] Cf. A. A. KUJUR, *The Oraon Habitat,* op. cit., 20-21.

[25] Cf. A. A. KUJUR, *The Oraon habitat,* op. cit., 11.

[26] Father Constant Lievens, S.J. (1856-1893) came to India in 1880. He was a student of theology (2nd year) at the diocesan Major Seminary at Brugge, when he joined the Society of Jesus in 1878, with an ardent desire to be sent to the Missions. On arrival at Calcutta, he was sent to Asansol to complete his theological studies. He was ordained priest by Archbishop Goethals of Calcutta on 14th January 1883. He taught for one year at St. Xavier's college, Calcutta before completing his theology in March, 1885. The Superior of the mission, Fr. S. Grosjean who had already destined young Lievens for Chotanagpur mission sent him there immediately after completing his theology. From March till November 1885 Lievens toured extensively in the Munda districts of Ranchi before establishing himself at Torpa. In August 1888 he was made director of the Lohardaga Mission and took up residence in Ranchi. He returned to his home country Belgium in 1892 when he was sick. He died at Leuven on November 7th 1893. (Cf. L. CLARYSEE, *Father Constant Lievens, S. J.*, op. cit.).

The Ranchi Archdiocese was erected in 1927 from where many other dioceses came into existence in the following years. The diocese of Sambalpur in the state of Odisha was erected in 1951 which was again divided into Rourkela and Sambalpur in 1979. Raigarh-Ambikapur in the state of Madhya Pradesh was erected in 1951, which was again divided into Raigarh and Ambikapur in 1977. The diocese of Jamshedpur was erected in 1962 and the diocese of Daltonganj was erected in 1971. The diocese of Dumka was founded in 1962, which was divided into Dumka and Raiganj in 1978. The diocese of Raiganj now belongs to the ecclesiastical province of Calcutta.The dioceses of Gumla and Simdega were erected in 1993. These are the dioceses which belong to the Chotanagpur area known as 'Lievens Mission'. (Cf. O TANGHE, "Father Constant Lievens, Apostle of Adibasis of Chotanagpur (India)," in *Omnis Terra* (English Edition, Nov. 1993), 456).

[27] There are twenty-nine tribes. They are Asur, Baiga, Bangra, Bathudi, Bedia, binjhia, Birhor, Birjia, Bhumiji, Chero, Chik-Baraik, Gond, Gorait, Ho, Karmali, Kharia, Kharwar, Kisan, Kora, Korwa, Lohara, Mahli, Munda, Mal Pharias, Oraons, Pahariya, Santal, Sauria Paharia, and Savar. (Cf. N. PRASAD, *Land and People of Tribal Bihar* (Ranchi: Bihar Tribal Research Institute, 1961), 15-16.

non-Aryan tribes who had never been completely subjugated either by the early invaders or by any outside power until the advent of the British in the year 1765.

"Tribe, in cultural anthropology, can be considered as a theoretical type of human social organization based on small groups defined by traditions of common descent and having temporary or permanent political integration above the family level and a shared language, culture and ideology."[28]

Other authors express the same reality in different, yet similar words, for instance, "even though there are various definitions, in India a tribe is defined as a collection of families bearing a common name, speaking a common dialect, and claiming a common territory. They are the indigenous, autochthonous people of the land who were here long before the Aryans arrived. They are the ancient settlers, the adivasis- the aboriginal peoples of India."[29]

There are various Hindustani or Indian terms referring to them, such as *Adivasi* (dwellers from the beginning), *Vanvasi* (dwellers of the forest), *Pahari* (hill dwellers). Among the people themselves the preferred term is *Adivasi* because it expresses something of their origin and dignity. Besides it promotes a fellow feeling among them.[30] Although Chotanagpur is the dwelling place of twenty -nine tribal communities, the most numerous tribes among these are the Oraons, who followed by Mundas, Ho and Santal.[31] This study is limited to the Oraons, who have a major role in shaping the history of evangelisation in this region.

1.2.1. The Oraons

"The Oraons are a Dravidian tribe who live mostly in the west, north-west and centre of the Ranchi district, and also in the adjoining areas of Jhaspur, Surguja and Gangpur."[32] They are also found scattered in other districts of Bihar, e.g. Shahabad, Champaran, Darbhanga, Bhagalpore, Saharsa, Purnea, Santal Pargana, Hazaribagh, Dhanbad, Singbhumand the neighbouring states of Odisha and Madhya Pradesh. Many have migrated to West Bengal, Assam and Andaman and Nicobar Islands due to poverty, loss of land and over population.

From various traditions,[33] legends, we come to know about their history prior to their settlement in Chotanagpur. "According to tradition the Konkan

---

[28] No Author, "Tribe", in P.W. GOETZ, (ed.), The *New Encyclopaedia Britannica,* Micropaedia Vol. XI (Chicago: University of Chicago, 1985), 918.

[29] R. E. HEDLUND, "Missiological issues in the study of Christianity in Tribal areas" in *Ishvani Documentation and Mission Digest,* XV (1997), 94

[30] Cf. E. DE MEULDER,*They Have Not Spoken Yet* (Raigarh: Catholic Ashram, 1963), 56

[31] Cf. N. PRASAD, *Land and People of Tribal Bihar,* op. cit., 16.

[32] S.T. DAS, *Indian Tribes* (New Delhi: Gian Publishing House, 1989), 28.

[33] Oraon scholars are of the opinion that the Oraons have come from Konkan in Decan.They might have lived in the Pandya kingdom of Karnataka. Following the western coast, then Narmada river they might have proceeded to the East. They crossed the Vindhyas and came to the valley of the Sone river in the Amarkantak forest ranges. From Sone Valley they migrated to the Bihar plateau of Shahabad.This thesis is supported by Oraon legends about ancestors' sojourn. The legends mention

is said to be the original home of the Oraons. Owing to overpopulation and external pressure they migrated from the west cost of India to northern India."[34] Travelling through river valleys they settled down in the Shahabad district of Bihar as agriculturists and land owners around 270 B.C. When further driven by successive hordes of newer races they took shelter on the Rohtas Plateau (Rohtasgarh), which they fortified.

Driven from Rohtas by Kurus[35] the tribe split in to two. "One of these followed the course of the Ganges, and finally settled in the Rajmahal Hills, where their descendants are now known as Ma-le; while the other ascended the sone into Palamau, and turning eastward along the Koel, took possession of the north-western portion of the Chotanagpur plateau."[36]

There are more sources still which give some hints about olden times; "Ptolemy, who was living in 175 A.D., refers to a certain Indian diamond-river, the source of which he clearly indicates in Kokkonage or Kokrah. Now, Kokrah is to this day the Oraon name Chutia Nagpur.[37] The word is an almost evident derivation from Kurkha, and means "the Oraon Land." Hence the natural inference that, in the second century after Christ, the Oraons were already recognised occupants of the soil in Chutia Nagpur."[38]

The Oraons do not belong to the caste system (Brahmin, Ksatriya, Vaisya, Sudra) nor are they out-castes. They stand on their own, independent of Hinduism and Islam which are not only the dominant religions in India but also largely responsible for social organisation. For the origin of the Oraons as well as the racial and linguistic affinities one has to look to Southern India. "The Oraons are both linguistically and ethnologically a Dravidian tribe."[39] Their language is

---

the names of Nandagrah, Piprigarh, or Garhpipra which may correspond to the present day villages of Pipla and Hardinagar in Gujarat. (Cf. B.TIRKEY, *The Smiling Oraon, A people on Move*, (Patna: Navjyoti Niketan, 1989), 7.), S. C. ROY, *The Oraons of Chotanagpur, their History, Economic Life and Social Organization* (Ranchi: Catholic press, 1915, reprinted 1984), 19-22.), (E. DALTON, *Descriptive Ethnology of Bengal* (Calcutta: Studies Indian, 1973), 280).

[34] R.O. DHAN, *These are my Tribesmen: The Oraons* (Ranchi: G.E.L. Church Press, 1967), 6.

[35] A powerful dynasty who gave shelter to the Oraons during their wandering. In the beginning the Kurus were friendly but when they saw the fortified Rohtas and the flourishing life of Oraons' they attacked them (Cf .F.A. GRIGNARD," The Oraons and Mundas from the time of their settlement in India", in *Anthropos*, IV (1909), 12).

[36] P. DEHON, "Religion and Customs of the Uraons", in *Memoirs of the Asiatic Society of Bengal*, 1 (1906), 121.

[37] Chotanagpur

[38] (Cf. F.A. GRIGNARD, "The Oraons and Mundas from the time of their settlement in India", in *Anthropos*, IV (1909), 17.

[39] S. C. ROY, *The Oraons of Chotanagpur, their History, Economic Life and Social Organization*, op. cit.17.

'Kurukh'. The Oraons[40] are known by different names such as *Kurukh, Dhangers, Kodas, Modis, Kols.* The latter four names are employed by the Hindus to describe the Oraons and have a pejorative meaning. The Oraons in their language call themselves *Kurukh*[41] and they are proud of being called by this name. Today they are known as Oraons, a name which was probably given to them by the neighbours after their settling in Chotanagpur and coming in contact with Mundas. So *Kurukh* is the Original and older name than Oraon. Because of the fact that they live mostly by agriculture, they are called '*Kisan*' (farmer) in some parts of the state of Odisha.

"Among the purely aboriginal tribes of Chotanagpur plateau, the Oraons appear to occupy the first rank in intelligence and social progress as they stand foremost in numerical strength."[42] Self-reliance with co-responsibility can be counted as one among their many outstanding qualities.

There is another feature by which others can know that one belongs to Oraon tribe. This is the practice of 'Totemism.'[43] The whole tribe is divided into number of gotras or clans. The Totemism has special as well as religious significance. It unites a person with a specific social group and gives a 'religious' and social identity. "It expresses a range of associations that link the individual with the ancestors, spirits and deities."[44]

---

[40] S. C. Roy holds the opinion that Hindus seeing the Oraons as a prolific people compared them to the progeny of the legendry monster- king Rawana of Ramayana fame.They called them Rawana *put* (progeny of rawana). Thus from rawana, pronounced with an arrested 'O' sound at the beginning gives us the present form O-rawan or Oraon. (Cf.S. C. ROY, *The Oraons of Chotanagpur, their History, Economic Life and Social Organization,* op. cit.14-15). Others like F. Hahn and S. Konow say that the name Oraon may have come from the Urapai, Urapo, and Urang, which in the Dravidian dialects of Kaikadi and Burgandi mean "man". In this case Oraon would be an ethnocentric auto-designation of the people calling themselves "men". (Cf. F. HAHN, *Grammar of the Kurukh Language*, Introduction, XII).

[41] According to S. C. Roy the name *Kurukh* has been traced to one of the mythical hero-kings called Karukh. He was king of Karus-des which roughly comprised what is now the district of Shahabad, a former home of the Oraons, before the arrival at Chotanagpur. The Oraons in order to keep up the remembrance of their king, also to distinguish themselves from other tribes might have assumed this name *Kurukh. Kurukh* also has a close resemblance to the Sanskrit root 'Krs' which means to plough. This interpretation goes well with names '*Dhangar*' and '*Kisan*' by which at times they are called. Therefore S. C. Roy concludes "that the Oraons of Chotanagour came to call themselves the *Kurukhs* in the triple sense of 'man' of the tribesmen of the traditional hero-king Karukh, and also in the sense of a tribe of agriculturists *Kisan* or *Kurukhar*" (S. C. ROY, The *Oraons of Chotanagpur,* op. cit.9-11).

[42] S. C. ROY, *The Oraons of Chotanagpur,* op. cit., 8.

[43] "Totemism is a social institution, through which divisions of a tribe (totem groups) are systematically and permanently associated with species, usually of animals but sometimes of plants or inanimate objects, that are their totems". (R.M. BERNDT, " Totemism" in *Catholic Encyclopedia* (St. Louis: New York, McGraw-Hill Book Company, 1967), 212).

[44] S.K. TOPPO, "Totemism (Gotra Pratha) in Chotanagpur", in *Sevartham* , 4 (1979), 144.

"Oraons are considered to be good cultivators. The striking feature of their character is their joviality. When they are together they always laugh in most excellent spirits. Their cheerfulness makes them swallow many a bitter pill with a light heart, and they appear to be happy even under the most trying circumstances."[45]

1.2.2. Religion of the Oraons

Religion of the Oraons can be understood as a system of beliefs, and sacrifices offered to supernatural powers. Anthropologists have classified the religion of Oraons in traditional terminology as animism or spiritism. We can define "animism as the belief in personalised supernatural beings."[46] Its manifestations range from the Supreme Being to innumerable spirits, ancestral spirits and spirits in natural objects. Belief in these spirits evokes in them an attitude to communicate with them by offering sacrifices in order to ward off evil, to remove calamity or to insure well-being.[47]

The Oraons worship a Supreme Being whom they call *Dharmes.*[48] They acknowledge him as the master of the universe, creator and provider, giver of life and prosperity. They consider him as a perfect being.[49] Attitude of fear, submission, dependence, etc. plays a major role in their relationship with the Divine.

"In religion proper, the attitude of Oraon society,...towards the supernatural is one of reverential fear in the presence of certain mysterious supernatural powers and beings, and dependence on and conciliation and propitiation of prayerful submission to them, and the result expected is averting the ill-will and securing the good will of the supernatural beings, and good luck to man in crops and cattle, health and progeny."[50]

Worship and sacrifices are given only to this Supreme being. "God is absolutely supreme: he has no consort, he does not share his godhead with the spirits. The Oraon religion is clearly monotheistic. Only God is prayed to and he has mastery not only over all humans, but overall spirits and over all forces of nature."[51]

It is important to note that the flora of the place play a central role in the religion of the Oraons. There is mutual relationship between the environment and the religion of the Oraons. There are many environmental features in their

---

[45] P. DEHON, "Religion and Customs of the Uraons", op. cit., 169.

[46] M. DHAVAMONY, *Phenomenology of Religion* (Rome: Gregorian University press, 1973), 51.

[47] Cf. M. DHAVAMONY, *Phenomenology of religion*op. cit., 51.

[48] *Dharmes* means Virtuous, Honourable, Righteous, Just, etc. (A. GRIGNARD, *Oraon-English Dictionary* (Vienna: St. Gabriel, Administration of "Anthropos", 1924), 203.

[49] Cf.S. C. Roy, *Oraon Religion and Customs* (Calcutta: Editions Indian 1928, reprinted 1972), 14.

[50] S. C. Roy, *Oraon Religion and Customs,* op. cit., 2.

[51] A. BRUGGEMAN, "Worship: Sarna and Christian", op. cit., 49.

religion. "These features are considered as the residence of spirits and are foci of ritual worship. Such common features in Oraon religion are the sacred grove of some trees, a mountain, a hill, a river, a tank, a well and a stone. The symbolic fire, sacred colour, direction, position, sound number, time and motion are also involved in Oraon religion."[52]

It is wrong to consider that Oraons are idol worshippers. They do not adore the trees, stones, and pools, nor do they worship the spirits dwelling in them. They venerate them and pray to them to intercede with *Dharmes,* the Supreme Being. Hence the religion of Oraons is characterised by their belief in and the cult of the Supreme Being, and a multitude of spirits who are subordinate to this Supreme Being. Belief in the ancestral spirits is also part of their religious system.[53]

Having built no temples and shrines of stone or clay, the Oraons of Chotanagpur worship in groves of *Sal*, known as *Sarna.*[54] At the foot of a chosen tree they prepare *Sarna*, the place of worship. *Sarna* is believed to be the dwelling place of the spirit of their progenitor *Chala Pachho* (mother of the tribe).

"*Sarna* worship belongs to very ancient religious traditions. It is a form of worship of God via nature. Man is also part of nature and hence great events in man's life are also occasions for worship."[55] Not only no temples or shrines but also no images of the spirits are made. They believe that those important spirits are visualised in the form of certain human beings, animals etc. For example the progenitor *Chala Pachho* or the *Sarna Burhia* (Old lady) invariably appears as an old woman with matted locks of snow white hair. They establish harmonious relationship with the ancestral and other disembodied souls, nature spirits through their supplications and prayers at times through offerings and sacrifices.[56]

In the Oraon tradition we do not find anything such as pilgrimages to the holy places, sacred books, holy vestments etc. Their religion is as simple as their life, but closely connected with nature. They consider their ancestors as part of their life and as their protectors. Hence they express their gratitude to the ancestral spirits by offering them sacrifices.[57] Prayers are spontaneous invocations without fixed formulas addressed to all entities whenever they venerate them. These prayers relate to all needs and desires and may include moral and spiritual values.

---

[52] A. A. KUJUR, *The Oraon Habitat*, op. cit., 166.

[53] Cf. ibid., 166.

[54] *Sarna* is a Kurukh word meaning "Sacred grove".This grove can be of *sal* trees or cluster of any trees where the spirits of nature dwell. By extension, the word *Sarn*a is used to designate the ancestral religion of Chotanagpur for which they have no specific term.The followers are known as *Sarna* people or people of *Sarna Dharma* (*Sarna* religion)

[55] A. BRUGGEMAN, "Worship: Sarna and Christian", in *Sevartham*, 7 (1982), 55.

[56] Cf. S. C. Roy, *Oraon Religion and Customs,* op. cit., 2.

[57] Cf.A. BRUGGEMAN, "Worship: Sarna and Christian", op. cit., 55.

1.2.3. Socio-economic and Political Situation

The Socio-economic system of the Oraons mainly depends on land and agriculture. When they came to Chotanagpur they occupied some area of jungle and cleared it and began to cultivate it. The pioneer families were *bhuinhars* which means the original settlers of the land. The land cleared by them is *bhuinhari* land belonged to the families that cleared it. The land became their property. Gradually it was considered as the bond between ancestors and the family. The head of the family was responsible for safeguarding this bond.[58] "He cannot sell or pledge the land as it is considered as a sacred trust from the ancestors."[59]

"A typical Oraon village consists of the Bhuinhars, subsequent Oraon settlers (called Jethraiyats or ordinary raiyats, according as they are earlier or later settlers) and a Gorait family (a village drudge), one or two Ahir families (who graze and look after the cattle of the villagers), a Lohar family (blacksmith), and sometimes also a family of Kumhars (potters)."[60]

In the course of time this *Bhuinari Khunt* (lineage) split up to the *Mahato khunt* and *Pahan Khunt. Mahato* (village leader) or the secular headman manages the secular affairs of the village and acts as an intermediary between the villagers and government authorities. *Pahan* (village Priest) offers sacrifices to the village spirits at the *Sarna* or sacred grove, or other public places of worship, although each clan has its own separate clan-spirit and each family has its own family spirits, or ancestral spirits to whom sacrifices are individually offered.[61]

Only the sons inherited the land, daughters have no right to inherit their father's property. Daughters by their marriage pass out of their father's family. Thus women do not have the rights, duties and privileges which the male members enjoy. For instance they are not bound to offer or to take part in the sacrifices offered to deceased ancestors, village deities of her father's house.[62]

The Oraons consider that the living and the dead members of the same exogamous clan of any particular village form one large family. The deceased ancestors of the same clan live together in the underworld. "These spirits are believed to derive nutrition from offerings made by their male descendants before every meal, periodically at certain sacrificial feasts, and annually at the bone-burial festival when the remains of those who died during the year were buried."[63]

Thus we come across certain fundamental rules of their society like "property must not pass out of the clan nor be inherited in absolute right by a woman."[64]

---

[58] Cf. F. DE SA, *Crisis in Chotanagpur*, (Bangalore: A Redemptorist Publication, 1975), 26.

[59] R.O. DHAN, *These are my Tribesmen: The Oraons*, op. cit., 24.

[60] S. C. ROY, *The Oraons of Chotanagpur*, op. cit., 68.

[61] Cf. R.O. DHAN, *These are my Tribesmen: The Oraons*, op. cit., 23-24.

[62] Cf. S. C. ROY, *The Oraons of Chotanagpur*, op. cit., 213.

[63] F. DE SA, *Crisis in Chotanagpur,* op. cit., 26.

[64] S. C. ROY, *The Oraons of Chotanagpur*, op. cit., 213.

Such rules are based partly on religious and partly on sociological aspects. Oraon families are patrilineal and patrilocal. They live in close unity with the members of their community. There is no room for individualism. Tribal social structure in Chotanagpur has to some extent neutralised the caste and hierarchical notions found elsewhere in the country. Tribal societies to this day are by and large castles.[65] "The tribe appears as the temporal organisation which directs all political, social and economic activities. Through its clan's wise exogamy the tribe remains in one single large family united and stable."[66]

The economic system of the Oraons is mainly based on agriculture. Over the years they were alienated from their fertile lands by later coming non-tribal people which in the beginning they had occupied in Chotanagpur. This alienation continues even today. There is the uprooting of an entire village area thus to make it available for public and private sector industries.[67] The land they are forced to cultivate today is infertile and lacks any means of irrigation and modern technology. It cannot be anything more than just sufficient for survival. These are bad omens for their socio-economic system. According to A. Van Exem "the tribals (Oraons) rightly vaunt their attachment to the land, but neither do they protect it from intruders, nor do they treat it well. While other economic attitudes impede their progress, their attitude towards landed property imperils their survival."[68]

Forests are another source of their sustenance. The forest offers many resources which would give them employment and trade. "Oraons are not manufacturing people."[69] They believe that each day will take care of itself, hence do not venture for new opportunities. At times they may engage themselves, especially the women, in making mats, rain caps, *Sal* leaf plates and cups. Their economic intentions are different from comparable attitudes in modern economy and they do not easily adapt themselves to changing situations. They do not want to be rich, but to have enough to satisfy their immediate needs.[70]

Politically the Oraons were a self-governed society. They have organised their village on a pure monoclan basis. There is no general administrative organisation; "There is no recognised headman of the whole tribe, and the authority of any man does not reach beyond the limits of his own village. The only organisation

[65] Cf. R.D. MUNDA, "The Bases of Cultural Identity of Chotanagpur", op. cit., 26.

[66] A. VAN EXEM,"The Crisis and the Sarna", in *Sevartham*, 2 (1978), 36.

[67] 50,000 Adivasi families were uprooted during the first three year plans. Cf. S. FUCHS, "Liberation Movements among the Tribals of India", in P. PUTHANAGNADY (ed.), *Towards an Indian Theology of Liberation* (Bangalore: N.B.C.L.C., 1986), 200-201.

[68] A. VAN EXEM, *Basic Socio-Economic Attitudes of Chota Nagpur Tribals*, (Ranchi: The Catholic Co-operative Society, 1992, 2 ed.), 17.

[69] S. C. ROY, *The Oraons of Chota Nagpur*, op. cit., 110.

[70] Cf. A. VAN EXEM, *Basic Socio-Economic Attitudes of Chota Nagpur Tribals*, op. cit., 18.

to safeguard the customs of the tribe is a general 'panchayat[71]' of chief men of a group of villages."[72]

Formerly the authority of *Panchayat* or *Panch* was paramount among the Oraons. In every important affair before beginning their deliberations they say "*Upare Dharmes, Hete Panch*" which means: after *Dharme*s (God), the *panch* is the highest authority.

Practically, in cases where the modern type civil or penal law does not interfere, the *Panchayat* remains the traditional law giver. In short it is the authority which regulates the internal order of the Oraon community. "They can settle land disputes, difficulties about inheritance, marriage questions, adultery cases, and any infringement of the customs of the tribe."[73] The *Panch* was selected in a democratic process and it also functioned democratically. "Their social system represents one of the most ancient democracies of India. Tribal *panchayat*s are among India's most ancient democratic institutions."[74]

Inter-village disputes such as those regarding precedence at the *Jatra* festival[75] or the right to game, cases arising out of the violation of certain taboos affecting the *Parha* or tribe as a whole, are settled by the *Parha panchayat.*[76]

The advent of the British with their written code of laws and regulations in the Oraon land had disrupted this efficient system of self-government. But in

---

[71] *Panchayat* is an assembly of the *panch* (a body of five men) or the five elderly people of the village elected by the people to discuss a question or to settle difficulties that arise in the community. (Cf. A.A. KUJUR, *The Oraon Habitat*, op. cit., 180).

[72] P. DEHON, *Religion and Customs of the Uraons*, op. cit., 157.

[73] P. DEHON, *Religion and Customs of the Uraons*, op. cit.,158.

[74] E. DE MEULDER, *They Have not Spoken yet*, op. cit., 76.

[75] In *Kurukh* language jatra denotes gatherings. *Jatra* festivals are annual meetings of the neighbouring *parhas* held at convenient centres. At these *jatra*s outstanding disputes between the *parhas* are settled by *parha panchayat* or *parha* council. (Cf. A.A. KUJUR, *The Oraon Habitat*, op. cit.,183).

[76] Cf. S. C. Roy, *The Oraons of Chota Nagpur*, op. cit., 235. *Parha* is an administrative unit grouping a number of villages, i.e. five, seven, nine, eleven, twenty one, or twenty five. One of the villages is called the *Raja* (King) village, another the *Dewan* (Prime minister) village, a third the *Panrey* (Clerk of the Crown) village, a fourth the *Kotwar* (Bailiff) village and so on. Such villages which have no such denominations are known as *praja* (subject) villages. The *Raja* village is the head village of the *Parha*, the headman of this village presides at meetings of the *parha panchayat.* Villages of a *parha* were like members of one family. The evolution of the *parha* system signifies a great achievement of the Oraons in the field of efficient village administration. (Cf. S. C. Roy, *The Oraons of Chota Nagpur*, op. cit., 235). A. A. KUJUR , an Oraon scholar, is of opinion that the number of villages is always uneven."A unique feature of the *Parha* is their grouping in uneven numbers seven, five, twenty-one etc., because an even number is considered inauspicious". (A.A. KUJUR, *The Oraon Habitat*, op. cit., 134).

recent years there was the introduction of *Panchayati-Raj*[77] by the government of India.

1.3. A Situation Open to the Liberating Gospel Message

The Chotanagpur Oraons had a well-organised village government (*panchayat*), under its elected leader, a tribal *Raja* (king).[78] As far as we know they seem to have lived in peace and harmony until the Muslim invasion in the 16th century.[79]

"It was in 1585 A.D., for the first time, that the Raja of Chotanagpur (then called Khukra) was reduced to the position of a Malguzar (tributary) of Moghul emperor of Delhi. The necessity of raising the tribute which Muhammadan Emperors or their Subadars or viceroys demanded from him may have first suggested to the Raja and his advisers the necessity of converting the periodical supplies or aids hither to obtained by him from the Oraon and the Munda village communities into regular payments in the nature of revenue."[80]

In 1616, Durgan Sal, the *Raja* of Chotanagpur was imprisoned by Moghul emperor Jahangir, as the *Raja* was unable to pay a tribute of rupees 15,000. On his return from the prison in 1628, he began to promote new ideas and practices in his territory. He introduced Brahmin priests, Rajput courtiers and warriors and other caste-Hindus from outside Chotanagpur. Marriage alliances were contracted between the Chotanagpur *Raja* family and neighbouring Hindu ruling families, especially Bengal and Bihar. These innovations provoked a change in the traditional way of life of the *Adivasis.*[81] "The new government officials were given some right for supplies from the villagers who used to pay a certain rent as well as service to the king. The new system of service grants (*jagir*) and its new beneficiaries (*jagirdars*) were a burden to the people"[82]

The traditional owners of land were reduced to mere rent-paying tenants and cultivators of the land. Generally the service grants were interpreted as property rights. The Moghuls did not interfere with the internal administration of the

---

[77] It is a decentralised democratic pattern for administration. Here the local government plays an important role. It has the responsibility for all that it can do on its own without the assistance of the higher ones. The higher ones came into the picture only in so far as their assistance is required and asked for by the local authority. In the section on the Directive Principles of State Policy the Constitution of India has made a provision for the creation of the *Panchayati Raj* system in the Country. Thus Article 40 says: "The State shall take the steps to organise village *panchayat*s and endow them to function as units of self-government". (S.L RAJ, "People's Power through Panchayati Raj", (editorial), in *Social Action*, Vol. 47 (1997), III-IV). Attempts to introduce *Panchayati Raj* system was being done from 1985 onwards.

[78] The headman of the administrative unit of the Oraons.

[79] Cf. S. C. Roy, *The Oraons of Chota Nagpur*, op. cit., 29.

[80] Ibid., 29.

[81] Cf. S. C. Roy, *The Oraons of Chota Nagpur*, op. cit., 30.

[82] A. KANJAMALA, *Religion and Modernization of India* (Indore: Steyler Verlag, St. Augustin / Ishvani, Satprakashan, 1981), 56.

tribal Raja (king), who was free to act as he liked. The tribal Raja introduced temporary *thikedars* or lease-holders, who too joined the *jagirdars* in exploiting the people. This was the beginning of a landlord system which systematically robbed the ancestral property of the Oraons. "In 1765, the Moghul Emperor, Shah Alam II, was defeated and Chotanagpur nominally came under the British with the grant of Diwani (tribute paying district) of Bengal, Bihar and Orissa to East India Company."[83]

Although this affected the tribal population socio-economically to a large extent, the internal administration of the tribes continued to be the responsibility of the Tribal *Raja* (king) until 1834. But he had been asked by the British to establish police stations and police officers in Chotanagpur already in 1806 (the so called *zamindari* police system). Naturally these officers were non-Chotanagpurians, and they favoured the landlords, in a well-organised way, by eliminating the proprietary rights of the Adivasis. The rapacious *zamindars*[84] grabbed vast areas of land unlawfully, and became eventually the self-styled landlords.[85]

"The prolonged and systematic exploitation of the people of Chotanagpur reduced the majority to the status of tenants. The landlords regularly collected rent, but often refused to give a receipt for the rent received so that they could demand rent two or three times over. When the people were unable to pay due to poverty, natural calamities or to other valid reasons, their land was taken away. Further many landlords extracted 60-70 days of work per year from the tenants as unpaid labour (*bethbegari*). In case of unwillingness on the part of the tenants, often they were brutally man-handled or taken to courts where the legal system and police worked in favour of the rich."[86]

Thus the Adivasi peasants were mercilessly exploited in every way. Step by step they were dispossessed of their ancestral land. For the tribals, however, this loss of their ancestral land meant not only the loss of their livelihood and material welfare, but also the disintegration of their social structure and, in fact, of their whole traditional culture. They lost their value systems and their identity.

The Adivasi peasant "found himself to be a savage, a beast of burden, made to carry his lord oppressor, and being beaten by him."[87] The Oraons felt that the religion of their forefathers would no more support them, for their God was silent and helpless when all sorts of difficulties befell them. The tribals fought vigorously for the preservation of their culture and identity, but it was in vain. "Their traditional beliefs in benevolent spirits were weakened, for these spirits on

---

[83] A. KANJAMALA, *Religion and Modernization of India*, op. cit., 56.

[84] Originally a revenue collector. The British regarded him as a landlord. Hence the term was used for landlords.

[85] Cf. A. KANJAMALA, *Religion and Modernization of India*, op. cit., 56-57.

[86] Ibid., 57.

[87] A. VAN EXEM, "The Crisis and the Sarna", op. cit., 38.

whom they relied for good weather, good harvest, health, continuation of family and clan seemed powerless to protect their land from the intruders."[88]

Moreover their own religious specialists, the *pahan* (village priest) and *deonra* (soothsayer) were not able to explain the roots of their illnesses. "Thus the very *Sarna* beliefs forced the tribals to call more and more non-tribal *sokhas* (ministers of witchcraft) to divine the causes of their illness."[89] They were attacked in their deepest self. They were desperate and frightened. They hated their invaders, they hated foreign spirits. When they were defeated by the invaders they turned to religion and magic.

A religious revivalistic movement called *Kabirpanthi*[90] came into existence and worked in full swing. The magicians and soothsayers instilled a deep dread of the evil spirits.

Having lost their belief systems and their social and economic security they gave up all struggle but perhaps not all hope. When the creed of the *Sarna* religion came to weigh down on the Oraons they searched for liberation, justice and peace. They found no solace and protection in *Sarna*. Neither the *Kabirpanthi Gurus* nor the magicians could offer them the religious and social identity they were searching.[91]

It was in such a desperate situation that the Christian missionaries came in with *Susamachar* (Good News) to them. *Susamachar* brought in the glad tidings of liberation from their spiritual and socio-economic crisis and offered them a new identity.

1.4. Birth of the Christian Faith in Chotanagpur

The first ever Christian missionaries to enter Chotanagpur were the German Evangelical Lutherans of Berlin, who arrived in Chotanagpur in 1845. These

---

[88] A. KANJAMAL A, *Religion and Modernization of India*, op. cit., 58.

[89] A. VAN EXEM, "The Crisis and the Sarna", op. cit., 40.

[90] The *Kabirpanthis* is a Hindu sect enjoying the patronage of the Oraons.This movement was promulgated by a man called Kabir. The increasing dissatisfaction among the Oraons with their cult of the spirits and a growing aspiration to be freed from the invaders, made them followers of this revival movement. Their belief and rites differ slightly from those of the other movements as *Tana Bhagat* and *Birsa*. The *Kabirpanthi Gurus* act not only as spiritual teachers but as priests.Their ministrations are obligatory for the religious service that must be performed at important occasions as birth, marriage and death.The Oraons who joined the movement did not completely abandon their tribal customs. Their regular ceremonies were performed, either before or after the *Kabirpanth* rites.The vacillating Oraons could not comply to the tenet of the movements. There were many tenets which a member must observe. Here are some of them: Abstention from worship of idols and other visible symbols of divinity; abjuration of intoxicating drink and its use for libation, prohibition of blood sacrifices and of the eating of beef, pork, and fowl's meat; no worship of spirits and minor deities; belief in a single personal God; etc. (Cf. S.FUCHS, The *Rebellious Prophets: A Study of the Messianic Movements in Indian Religions* (Bombay: SVD Anthropological Institute, 1965), 61).

[91] A. VAN EXEM, "The Crisis and the Sarna", op. cit., 41.

men were members of the Missionary Society founded by John Baptist Gossner.[92] It in Calcutta that the interest of the Lutheran missionaries was aroused in the Aboriginals of Chotanagpur.

"On the streets of the city they saw tribals working as 'coolies' and were impressed by their gaiety and their simplicity. Friends told them of the opportunity of missionary work in Chotanagpur, and the missionaries decided to go there. Four members of the Gossner Evangelical Society established themselves at Ranchi, the first Christian mission among the Mundas and Oraons."[93]

They went out to the villages and markets and preached in the open and invited people to Sunday services in the Church. They distributed medicines to the sick and opened schools for the children. Their work produced no results for five years. Finally on June 9, 1850, four Oraons were baptised in Ranchi, where had come for court cases. The conversions, once begun, went on increasing rapidly. The four Oraon Christians returned to their villages, and spread the news about the mission. Many people came to the missionaries to talk, to attend the Church services, to be instructed and baptised. By the end of 1855, there were 400 baptisms and another 800 registered their names, asking for instruction in the Christian religion.[94]

The missionaries along with the preaching and catechising also assisted the people with their court cases. When the Adivasis won a few court cases, with the help of the missionaries, they said to themselves, "let us give up demon worship, become Christians and be instructed, that assisted by the Padris, we may be saved from the unjust oppression of the Hindus and regain the land that we have been deprived of."[95]

Before the Sepoy Mutiny in the middle of 1857,[96] already 500 were baptised and nearly 2,000 expressed their willingness to become Christians. During the Mutiny, the missionaries were forced to leave the area, and the new converts were forced by the landlords to leave the place and this oppression, helped them to

---

[92] John Baptist Gossner was born in Bavaria (Germany) in 1773. he was ordained a Catholic priest in 1796, but he left the Catholic Church in 1826. In 1836 he founded this Missionary society known as the Gossner Missionary Society.

[93] A.TIRKEY, "Father Constant Lievens, S.J., The Missionary", in *Indian Missiological Review*, 2 (1985), 110.

[94] Cf. L. CLARYSEE, *Father Constant Lievens, S.J.*, op. cit., 110.

[95] A. KANJAMALA, *Religion and Modernization of India*, op. cit., 61.

[96] Sepoy is a native of India employed as a soldier by a European Power. (Cf. WEBSTER'S COLLEGIATE DICTIONARY (USA Springfield: G & C Merriam Co., Publishers 1946), 907)." Mutiny and Revolt of 1857 in several parts of India shook foundations of British rule in the country, and resulted in the British crown taking over the government of India from the East India company in 1858. The troubles ignited by the Sepoys, spread also to Chota Nagpur, where unlike many other places all over North India, the civilian population did not join the revolt." (L. CLARYSEE, *Father Constant Lievens, S.J.*, op. cit., 104).

escape into the interior regions and spread the news about the missionaries were lending.[97]

By the end of October 1857, order was restored in Chotanagpur and the missionaries returned. They found the converts loyal in spite of their sufferings. The Sepoy Mutiny was a blessing in disguise for it helped the spreading of Christianity.

Meanwhile an internal crisis with in the Lutheran Church confused the new converts. In 1868, six of the Lutheran missionaries joined the Anglican church. They were ordained as priests by the Anglican bishop of Calcutta. They came to Chotanagpur as a new mission group. Some of the converts followed them as their old missionaries.

The split came at an unfortunate time for mission of Chotanagpur. It was a year of change in the region and had brought more and more people to the missionaries for advice and assistance in their court cases and many other needs. it was a time of the investigation and consequently promulgation of the *Bhuinari* Survey and Settlement Act of 1869, which would give tribals the legal right to their land.[98]

1.4.1. The Infant Catholic Church

The Portuguese who landed on the West coast of India in 1498 were followed by Catholic missionaries. Although Catholic communities existed in the Southern parts of India, it was with the efforts of St. Francis Xavier (1540-1550) that a real missionary movement began. The contact of Jesuit missionaries with the Moghul emperor at Agra near Delhi, had not much noticeable effect. Thus the whole of India was a mission land, when Belgian Jesuit Province took charge of 'Bengal mission.'[99]

The Jesuit missionaries began to work in Chotanagpur when Father Stockman settled down in Chaibasa, the capital of Singhbhum on July 10, 1869. After four years of preaching and teaching, the first group of Chotanagpur tribals became Catholics. This group, consisting of 24 adults and four infants from seven villages, was baptised in November 1873. Along with the new converts some former Lutherans joined them. The mission had a slow progress. By the year 1882 there were only 371 Catholics.[100]

"The mission stations...were situated in what was called the "forest area". Although the missionaries knew of the disputes between the landlords and tenants, they decided to keep clear of these troubles and stay in the forest region where

---

[97] Cf. A. KANJAMALA, *Religion and Modernization of India*, op. cit., 61.

[98] Cf. L. CLARYSEE, *Father Constant Lievens, S.J.*, op. cit., 112.

[99] Bengal mission was the vicariate of Calcutta which consisted of the whole of West Bengal and most of Chotanagpur. Later the vicariate of West Bengal became the Archdiocese of Calcutta with Mgr. Goethals as its first Archbishop.

[100] Cf. L. CLARYSEE, *Father Constant Lievens, S.J.*, op. cit., 119.

there were fewer opponents for such disputes. Hidden in this region, and reluctant to help the people against oppression, the missionaries had little influence on the people and conversions were very few. To get involved in land disputes and court cases, they considered to be outside the scope of their apostolate and proper missionary work."[101]

The real change came when missionaries began to commit themselves to the actual needs of the tribals. It is noticeable that there was a considerable number of conversions when the missionaries helped the tribals in their land disputes. Young missionaries, especially Müllender and Fierens spent a lot of time in visiting the people and getting aware of their problems. however the most spectacular mass conversion took place in the time of a young Flemish Jesuit missionary: Father Constant Lievens, known as the *Apostle of Chotanagpur.*

The young Lievens, *Libin Sahib* as people called him, arrived in the land of tribals in March 1885. It was not hard for him to adapt himself to the surroundings, circumstances and people of Chotanagpur. After a few months of search and exploration, he settled at Torpa. "He assimilated easily what was native to the soil, language, thoughts, manners and custom. He knew the land, the people, their way of living, and so opened the way for them to have easy access to him."[102]

Young Lievens had a special charism to draw people to himself by his friendly talks. Thus it was during one of his conversations with his friend, Biseshwar Dayal, the *Jamadar* (a Hindu, in charge of the Police station) that he discovered the key to his success. Biseshwar Dayal advised the missionary, "If you really desire the conversion of the natives, you have only to undertake the defence of their interest, especially in connection with the question of their rights regarding land tenure and landlord service, and you will have as many Christians as you desire."[103]

He followed this advice and had its results too. He took pain to study the laws governing the land tenure, the traditional rights of the tribals, also the limitations of the rights of the landlords (*zamindars*). He kept himself in touch with lawyers and government officials and gained adequate knowledge regarding the rights and obligations of the oppressed tribals. Then he helped the people in their land disputes through legal channels, without offending the government.[104]

As soon as a few tenants won their cases with the help of Libin Sahib, the news spread like wild fire among the Adivasis. Day by day the number of people gathering around him increased. The zealous missionary, in the course of winning their court cases, found an opportune moment to preach the Good News (*Susamachar*). It was the Good News of Justice and liberation and the people were in search of it. Those who expressed their desire to become Catholic, he gave them

[101] Cf. L. CLARYSEE, *Father Constant Lievens, S.J.*, op. cit., 120.

[102] L. CLARYSEE,"Lievens and the Missionary", in *Indian Missiological Review*, 7(1985), 20.

[103] A. KANJAMALA, *Religion and Modernization of India*, op. cit., 63.

[104] Cf. L. CLARYSEE, *Father Constant Lievens, S.J.*, op. cit., 141-142.

proper instructions and baptised them; and the number kept growing every day. By 1891 the number of Catholics was 35,786, in Chotanagpur it became 73,265 in 1893, when father Lievens died at the age of 38 in his country Belgium.[105]

Those were the initial stages of the Church in Chotanagpur. The heroic zeal, transparent sincerity, infinite patience and utter selflessness of Father Lievens acted like a magnet and won thousands of poor, oppressed tribals to the Catholic faith. His whole energy and time was spent for the people, by helping them in their troubles. However within these missionary activities he continued to be a man of prayer. He believed that "only a man of prayer could accomplish God's work. He spent the evenings in prayer which followed his exhausting rounds, his teachings or his talks."[106]

"I am not a saint", he would often say, "to work like St. Francis Xavier and perform miracles to bring souls to the Church; my method is to help people in their difficulties, and God desires me to save them in this manner."[107]

1.4.2. Methods Used to Evangelise Chotanagpur

Conversion is a divine gift. It is God who takes the initiative and he conveys his offer through human agencies. Fr. Lievens, after understanding the socio-economic situations of the tribals, did not want to preach the Gospel directly.

"The people were in such a state of economic exploitation that direct preaching and instruction about God and his love for man, about Jesus Christ and his saving work would have no effect on them, and would be a sheer waste of time and energy. People's attention was wholly concentrated in simple survival."[108]

Fr. Constant Lievens developed his own methods to sow the seeds of faith in the soil of Chotanagpur. He was an enthusiastic missionary with a strong determination. He wanted the whole of Chotanagpur to be evangelised. He worked tirelessly for this cause.

Fr. Lievens learned from experience that direct contact with the people through the visits of a missionary to the villagers had a tremendous influence in the life of the people. Since he was an excellent horseman, he went around the villages visiting the people far and wide. "The people seeing the missionary in their midst could feel his interest and sympathy, and regarded him as a friend and protector."[109] People were impressed by the life witness of Fr. Lievens, who was totally dedicated to them. They came to him to tell their woes, their pains. Lievens, as he attended to their immediate problems, made use of this opportunity to implant in them the trust and confidence in a God who loves them, who wants

---

[105] Cf. A.TIRKEY, "Father Constant Lievens, S.J., The Missionary", in *Indian Missiological Review*, (April 1985), 141-142.

[106] O. TANGHE, "Father Constant Lievens", op. cit., 455.

[107] F. BOWEN, *Father Constant Lievens, SJ, The Apostle of Chotanagpur* (London: 1936), 86.

[108] L. CLARYSEE, *Father Constant Lievens, S.J.*, op. cit., 141.

[109] F. DE SA, *Crisis in Chotanagpur*, op. cit., 128.

their welfare, and liberty. He explained to them the implications of a discipleship of Jesus. People were ready and eager to get away from their bondages, material, social, and spiritual. "Those who aspired were given intensive instruction and learning. When they could show that they knew their prayers and the chief truths of the faith they were baptised."[110]

A noble characteristic of Lievens' approach was the introduction of the laity for evangelisation. He selected influential and intelligent Lutheran converts and trained them as catechists. These catechists spread the news about the help given by the missionary to the people. Many came to him to discuss their problems. He received them gently and offered them guidance and help. Gradually many accepted the Catholic religion.[111]

In spite of various trying and challenging situations, Fr. Lievens was strong and firm in his missionary methods. He knew that the missionary activities should correspond to the needs and aspirations of the people. Therefore he tried to present the Gospel in a way acceptable to them.

Although in *Sarna* religion the Supreme being is understood by the Oraons as benevolent he is also considered as someone who is unrelated to their daily life and its problems. He appeared less influential in their life, and they paid more attention to innumerable spirits whom they feared, and offered various sacrifices to placate them on every important occasion of their life as well as in the search of a solution to their problems. But with his charismatic personality, Father Lievens, preached a God who is a loving father, who is all powerful and who is very close to them and who knows every one of his children by name. He gave us his son, Jesus Christ, who shared the human condition especially of the poor, marginalised, oppressed, and who befriended everyone whom society rejected, and helped all to remove their barriers, thus to become his brothers.[112] "The teaching that death of his son Jesus Christ on the Cross was a sacrifice for the sins of his friends was an idea very familiar to the Oraons who offered various animal sacrifices."[113] The Oraons experienced in the new religion a God who is benevolent and who is related to their life and their problems. It was easy for them to accept his teachings and commandments. Since singing and dancing were part and parcel of their daily life the prayers were taught in the form of songs which the people found easy to learn and memorise.

There is a *Sarna* proverb which means "The world is full of spirits as the tree is full of leaves."[114] Father Lievens instructed the fearful Oraons about the help and protection of guardian angels and of saints, who guard them against the power of evil spirits. He taught them that by baptism they became children of

---

[110] L.CLARYSEE, *Father Constant Lievens, S.J.*, op. cit., 155.

[111] Cf. Ibid., 154.

[112] Cf. A. KANJAMALA, *Religion and Modernisation*, op. cit., 86.

[113] Ibid., 85.

[114] Ibid., 86.

God and their bodies temples of the Holy Spirit. Hence no evil spirit has power over them. He gave them scapulars, medals, and rosaries. He asked them to wear those symbols as a sign of their new faith but also as an armour against the evil spirits or powers. He himself wore the rosary around his neck and insisted his catechists to wear rosaries. He was convinced of the idea which Pope Paul VI expresses in *Evangelii Nuntiandi*; "Modern man listens more willingly to witness than to teachers."[115]

The Oraons gave their progenitor, the female principle (*Chala Pachao*) a prominent place in their life. "A stone under a *Sal* tree represented her and reminded the people of her presence in their midst."[116] Fr. Lievens substituted this female principle with Mother Mary. It was easy for him to cultivate in them the devotion to Mother Mary, for he himself was a great devotee of Mary. Remembering and praying for souls in the purgatory, also celebrating the Holy Eucharist for the deceased helped them to continue their cult of ancestor veneration. The new religion did not impose any thing on them, instead gave them renewed dignity, courage, freed them from all enslavement.[117]

Thus we see that already a century ago the Apostle of Chotanagpur found the way of transmitting the Gospel message in accordance with the people's culture, without separating them from their roots. He purified the rich values of their culture and helped them to worship a God in a way which gave meaning to their life. "In the light of God's presence in the world, it is evident that what is determinative in the apostolate, are not the methods or pastoral projects but the Spirit that guides the apostle in his use of methods and in planning and carrying out the apostolate."[118]

1.4.3. A Period of Trials

The conversions to Christianity alarmed both the landlords and British officers. The missionaries were involved in peoples' struggles in order to obtain their rights. Therefore the missionaries were often accused of leading the people to rebellion against the law and order of the region. Such accusations were not pleasing to their ecclesiastical authorities and their religious superiors. Thus the missionaries had to face many objections and criticisms from them. Moreover the untimely death of Father Lievens too disheartened the people as well as his co-workers. The inspiration and drive which he had set in motion disappeared slowly. The missionaries struggled valiantly to stem the tide of defection and to strengthen what needed consolidation. Religious revival movements like the *Birsa movement* and *Tana Bhagat movement*, put the tribals into much confusion and

---

[115] EN 41.

[116] A. KANJAMALA, *Religion and Modernisation*, op. cit., 86.

[117] Cf. Ibid., 87.

[118] J. DINH DUC DAO, "Present–Day Situations of the Mission "ad gentes" at the Service of the Poor", in *Omnis Terra* (English edition, April 1993), 288.

fright. Added to these, the famine in 1897, the cholera epidemic in 1898 and a severe drought in 1899 worsened the miseries of the tribals and the Church of Chotanagpur found herself in an extremely difficult situation.[119]

1.4.3.1. Birsa Movement

In 1895, a man called *Birsa Munda*[120] started a rumour that God had appeared to him with a message for the people of his tribe-Munda. Although this was a Munda agitation its proceedings had a great influence on the Oraons. Mundas were to abandon *bongas* or spirits. They were to observe certain rules of ritual purity by putting on the sacred thread of the Hindus, to abandon alcoholic beverages and to quit eating meat. He predicted the end of the world and said that only those who would gather round him would be saved while all the rest would perish. He forbade his followers to pay any rent to the government and told them to stop ploughing the fields and let the cattle be loose. He also asked all his followers to buy slates and pencils from the shops but never to go to school as the knowledge would come to them without going to schools. As most tribals had difficulties with the land ownership, paying taxes, spirits' worship, Birsa gained numerous followers and was called by the followers *Dharti Abba* signifying 'Father of earth'.

People credited him with miraculous powers multiplying rice, curing the sick or even raising the dead. Birsa considered himself as the saviour of the tribals and he had 12 disciples, perhaps in imitation of Christ and his apostles. He was arrested on 25th August 1895. When he and his followers manhandled a deputed constable who collected the proceedings of Birsa, he was condemned to one and half year of imprisonment.[121]

When he was arrested, he assured his followers that he would be back after three days. Just as he was being led into jail, a torrential shower of rain brought down a shed in the jail compound. This was interpreted as a divine intervention of Birsa. Together with many others, Birsa was released from jail a little before the end of his prison term on the occasion of the diamond jubilee of Queen Victoria. His followers interpreted this as Birsa's early escape from jail by divine intervention.[122]

After his release from jail, Birsa started reorganising his followers. As the people were suffering from famine, cholera, oppression from landlords, etc., they

---

119 Cf. P. EKKA, "Messianic Movements among the Chota Nagpur Tribes", in *Sevartham*, 4 (1979), 27.

120 Birsa Munda was born on 15th November 1875 at Bahamba in Tamar Thana (Police station) and was christened Daud Purti at the Lutheran Church of Burju. His father Sugna Purti was the Catechist of Bahamba. In 1890, Birsa left school and was employed as a domestic servant by Anand Panr of Kandir who taught him the art of sorcery. (Cf.P. EKKA, "Messianic Movements among the Chota Nagpur Tribes", op. cit., 26).

121 Cf. S. FUCHS, "Messianic and Chiliastic Movements Among Indian Aboriginals", in AAVV., *Hinduism* Studia Missionalia, XIII (Romae: Pontificiae Universitatis Gregorianae, 1963), 89.

122 Cf. P. EKKA, "Messianic Movements", op. cit., 27.

had little strength left to withstand their misery. Birsa found it easy to incite his followers to revolt. On Christmas eve 1899, he ordered a general massacre of the *Rajas, Zamindars, Hakims* (officials) and the Christians, who had left him on the advice of the missionaries. There was a great chaos among the tribals of Chotanagpur and thousands of innocent poor tribals lost their lives.

Birsa was arrested on 4th February 1900 with 67 of his followers of whom some were deported to *Kala Pani* or the Andaman isles. Birsa died on 9th June 1900 in a Ranchi jail allegedly of cholera and his body was publicly cremated close to the spot where Ranchi distillery stands today.

Peace returned finally to the tribals when, on the advice of Father J. Hoffman, the British Government undertook the survey and settlement of the *khuntkatti* (originally forest land cleared by the tribals) between the years 1902 and 1908. It was also Father Hoffman who drafted the Chotanagpur Land tenancy Act which was passed by the Government in1908 to safeguard the *khutkatti* and *bhuinari* (orginal settlers of the village) rights of the Adivasis. But by then much of the *khuntkatti* land had been lost to the alien *zamindars* and the landlords.[123]

These years of confusion, oppression and natural calamities were a dark period for the Church. Hardly any conversions took place. The British Government, afraid of the tribals getting organised against them, did not support the missionaries. Hence, many tribals, who had already accepted faith did not know what to do and left their faith; thus the Church lost many of her children during those years.

1.4.3.2. Tana Bhagat Movement

In April 1914 a certain Jatra Oraon of Chingri village close to the Bishunpur circle, Gumla Thana (Police station), Ranchi district, proclaimed that in a vision of God *Dharmes* he had received a revelation for the Oraons. He got an enthusiastic following, mostly from the Oraons since they were quite unable to have their wrongs redressed by recourse to law. The law courts were not only too distant, but also too expensive and incomprehensible to the illiterate Oraons. Jatra proclaimed that it was God's order that the Oraons should adore God alone through prayers and *bhakti* (devotion) and that they should completely abandon the worship of the *bhuts* or spirits, and do away with animal sacrifice. It was also God's command that they should lead an ascetic life and give up meat, alcoholic drinks, traditional songs and dances and showy ornaments. They ought further to stop ploughing the fields and paying rent to the landlords and should refuse to engage themselves as labourers to any non-Oraons.

Jatra taught his followers what he claimed were divinely inspired prayers and incantations for exorcising spirits, curing diseases and for neutralising the evil spell of witches. He warned them that those who did not follow him would soon

[123] Cf. S. FUCHS, "Messianic and Chiliastic Movements", Op. cit., 89-90.

perish, that foreigners would soon be expelled from the country, that the Tribal-*Raj* (tribal kingdom) would be established and that he would be its first king.[124]

In the year 1915, the new cultists not only abandoned the worship of the *bhuts* or spirits, but they expelled them from the country with a mass exorcism. They marched across the country sweeping the land with branches, chanting incantations, loudly calling on all the benevolent powers known to them, including the name of Birsa, to come to their aid and expel the spirits. From their endless repetition of *tana baba tana* (pull out, father, pull out) in their exorcism hymns, the new cultists came to be nicknamed *Tana Bhagats.*

The rumours of a coming massacre of the non-Oraons and Christians frightened the people so that they fled to the towns as well as to the jungles for safety. But a prompt posting of the police force at all likely trouble spots forestalled any outbreak of violence. The belief in the coming deliverer became at one time quite strong in *Tana Bhagats.* It was said that very soon, either God himself or an envoy of his such as Birsa Munda would come and set the people free. In order to facilitate the entry of the messiah into their homes, they even took off some rows of tiles from roofs.[125]

From 1920, most of the *Tana Bhagats* joined the main political party, the Indian national Congress, and played a prominent part in the "non- co-operation movement" launched by Gandhiji. They went to jail for refusing to pay their rents and for boycotting locally made liquor and foreign goods. They are very much attached to the cause of the Congress party. But they had not yet completely abandoned their dream of an eventful advent of the Tribal-*Raj* (tribal kingdom) and many of them resolutely refused for a long time to pay their rent to the state Government just as they had done to the British Government.[126]

These religious revivalist movements were also called messianic movements because they originated in order to liberate the people from the oppressive structures. Birsa Munda called himself saviour of the Munda tribe and Jatra Oraon similarly for the Oraons.

So each of them tried to keep their identity, by destroying the people of other tribes. Both imitated Christians by adopting their monotheism and assemblies of prayer, and imitated Hindus by adopting their sacred thread, and the vegetarian diet. Thus it was a great block to new evangelisation and also to existing Christianity. Christians found themselves maltreated by their non-Christian fellow tribals, and oppressed by their landlords. It was a situation in which they had to hope beyond hope.[127]

With these movements the young Church of Chotanagpur suffered very much. Those who had embraced the faith found themselves in a confused

---

[124] Cf. P. EKKA, "Messianic Movements", op. cit., 30.

[125] Cf. P. EKKA, "Messianic Movements", op. cit., 31.

[126] Cf. P. EKKA, "Messianic Movements", op. cit., 91.

[127] Cf. S. FUCHS, "Messianic and Chiliastic Movements", op. cit., 91-92.

situation. By and by those movements lost their vigour and strength though to this day there are still a few followers. When peace was finally restored, the people turned to the missionaries with even more enthusiasm and conviction. Referring to the way the tribals finally turned to Christianity, bishop Philip Ekka writes,

"It is natural, when all pragmatic means fail, to turn to God for help. Even in the traditional culture, the Mundas and Oraons try to placate the bongas and nads (spirits) in order to avoid suffering, sickness and death, but if all these fail them, they turn to God as their final refuge; akkuganinimr'day; O God, now you are our final refuge; just as the Israelites did of God."[128]

1.5. The Church Today

"Evangelisation will never be possible without the action of the Holy spirit."[129] "The Holy Spirit is indeed the principal agent of the whole of Church's mission."[130]

It is evident that the young Church of Chotanagpur had to face many critical situations on her way to growth. From this experience it is clear that the seeds which the missionaries sowed, fell in different types of ground as it is said in the parable of the Sower (cf. Lk. 8:5-15). It is a matter of great joy to note that much of the seed fell on good ground and is producing 100, 60, 30 fold. In 1985, the faithful celebrated the centenary of their Church, an event which coincided with the memory of Father Constant Lievens' arrival a 100 years ago. Although missionaries went into the region before the arrival of Lievens, it is with his arrival that the Church started taking roots in Chotanagpur.

"A hundred and eight years ago, when the Catholic Missionaries entered the Chotanagpur region, there were less than 50 Catholics. The mass conversion movement that was set in motion by the young Jesuit missionary Constant Lievens made history by converting nearly 75,000 Adivasis, mostly Mundas, Oraons and Kharias, during a short period of seven years."[131]

In spite of the struggles and trials the Church of Chotanagpur grew steadily. Today it is one the most dynamic Churches in India.

Today the Chotanagpur Catholic Tribals have extended themselves into many parts of India and abroad. They number close to ten lakh faithful. They certainly are better educated and have more professionally placed members than their non–Christian tribal brethren. Catholic aboriginal families supply the Church of India with many fervent vocations to religious life and priesthood. Tribal missionaries serve not only nationally but internationally as well. There have been to date one

[128] P. EKKA, "Messianic Movements", op. cit., 32.

[129] EN 75.

[130] RM 37.

[131] A. KANJAMALA, "The Future of the Mission in the Hindi Belt", in *Vidyajyoti*, 5 (May 1992), 264.

tribal Cardinal, three tribal archbishops over a dozen bishops, hundreds of priests and thousands of religious sisters and brothers.[132]

In spite of the continuous oppression and dispossession of their ancestral land by injustice, Chotanagpur Catholics moved forward, facing the difficulties with cheerful courage and celebrating the gift of life and goodness of God. Chotanagpur mission history bears witness to the transforming power of the Gospel both in the life of the individuals as well as of society. The local traditions and cultures were preserved to such an extent that the Church can consider herself truly indigenous.[133] Hopefully this transforming power of the Gospel will continue to work in them in the years to come, ever producing richer harvests. "The Mission work in Chotanagpur during the last hundred years has resulted in a very vibrant and nearly self-sufficient church in that area. The Catholics were account for 9% of the total Catholic population of India."[134]

1.5.1. Church Personnel and Institutions

"The Church is missionary by its very nature."[135] All Christians by virtue of their baptism, share the same life with Christ and are also responsible for the spread of faith. Although it is so, Christ selects certain people from his followers "whom he desires, to be with him, and to send them to preach" (Mk. 3: 13) to the nations. It is a special vocation, because Jesus calls them that they may have communion with him in a particularly profound way and that they may share their experience with others, and also bring others to this communion. Therefore this vocation is a gift or a charism, with a responsibility to preach Good news to others. Among those who have been involved in the spread of the 'Gospel' the missionaries occupy a particular place because of their special vocation.[136] The one who is called in such a way is meant to become another Christ, continuing his mission.

Mission is marked by the action of the Holy Spirit. Jesus presents himself as one sent by the Father and led by the Holy Spirit. A missionary is 'bound' by the Spirit. His/her vocation is for the service of other persons. Thus in the Chotanagpur Church, in addition to lay missionaries, there are 'professional' missionaries such as diocesan priests, religious priests, as well as religious brothers and sisters. Many of them are from the local Church itself and others are from different parts of India and a small number from outside India. All of them work in close collaboration with the diocesan bishops. There are religious institutes like "Handmaids of Mary" and the "Divine Word Missionaries" who are directly involved in primary evangelisation. For instance, the local Congregation of the

---

[132] CATHOLIC BISHOPS' CONFERENCE OF INDIA, National Catechetical Directory of India (Bangalore: C.B.C.I. Commission for Christian Life and N.B.C.L.C, 1990), no.165, 18.

[133] Cf. A. KANJAMALA (ed.) *Paths of Mission in India Today* (Mumbai: St.Paul's, 1996), 248.

[134] Ibid., 247.

[135] AG 2.

[136] Cf. AG 23.

Handmaids of Mary, founded by Father Edmund Harrison, SJ in 1944, works to evangelise this region with the help of local vocations. Whatever may be the different charisms of the Religious Institutes, all of them should work as heralds of the Gospel, understanding the signs of the times, also being aware of the various dimensions of the mission of Christ Jesus. Hence their special vocation "is manifested in a total commitment to evangelisation, a commitment which involves the missionary's whole person and life, and demands a self-giving without limits of energy or time."[137]

Like in the past, missionary work (evangelisation) in this region continues to be very challenging. The life of a Chotanagpur missionary is not easy. There are various obstacles from the part of political leaders and from the Hindu revival movements like *Arya Samaj,Hindu Mahasabha*, *Rastriya Swayam Sevak Sangh* and *Ram Samaj Parishad*. Though the Constitution of India offers religious freedom, tolerance etc., evangelisation is often blocked in different ways. Hence the Church in Chotanagpur cannot hope to aim at mass conversions; instead she offers ways and means to all God's people to live as free children of God. The first and most fundamental step is a conversion of heart to the God in whom each one believes. Therefore the Chotanagpur missionary is a pastor to all, to the Catholics as well as non-Catholics.[138]

1.5.2. Lay Missionaries

"The Church, born of the evangelising activity of Jesus and the twelve Apostles, is in her turn SENT to continue the evangelising mission of Jesus. Entrusted with the mission and power to proclaim the good news, she is also entrusted with the mission and power to build up and deepen continually the gift of faith that has been accepted and ratified at Baptism, confirmed at Confirmation and continually nourished at the Eucharistic table. This obligation to evangelise and catechise belongs to every member of the body of Jesus."[139]

Thus every Christian is a missionary and on mission, called to witness in word and deed. It is no longer the exclusive work of the official Church personnel but it has become the task of every baptised Christian, to be in the service of the Church, and through her to the whole human society, to bear witness to the Gospel. "From the very origins of Christianity, the laity as individuals, families, and entire communities shared in spreading of faith."[140]

The family, especially the parents, have an important role to play, to build up local Church. The parents are in the ideal case the first missionaries who are always in touch with their children. In fact, some parents by their very way of life give a

---

[137] RM65.

[138] Cf. A. KANJAMALA (ed.) *Paths of Mission in India Today*, op. cit., 216.

[139] CATHOLIC BISHOPS' CONFERENCE OF INDIA, *National Catechetical Directory of India*, op. cit., no. 5285, 74.

[140] RM 71.

profound testimony of love and faith to their children. Therefore it is the duty of every parent to cultivate the seeds of faith, also to help and guide their children towards living faith. Nothing can entirely replace the concrete example and living witness of parents praying together with their children, praying together as a couple. Habits of prayer formed from early childhood will make their impression for life. Unfortunately in Chotanagpur region family prayer is sometimes taught merely as a duty and not always as the loving and willing homage of adoration, thanksgiving, praise and petition to a personal God who loves, cares for, and is concerned about every one of his children.[141]

Right from the initial stages of Church in Chotanagpur, when the number of priests was so small, when there was not much facilities for travelling, and the territory to be covered was so vast the Catechists played a major role in the evangelisation and pastoral work of the Church. And today too their service is very essential for the spread of the Gospel. They serve as link between the people and the priests and religious. They are the most important co-ordinators of all the activities of a local Church. Theirs is a noble task and an explicit vocation.[142] A dedicated missionary catechist is always at the service of his fellow men, without counting the cost as Vatican II says

"Worthy of praise is that army of catechists both men and women to whom missionary work among the nations is so indebted, who imbued with an apostolic spirit make an outstanding and absolutely necessary contribution to the spread of faith and the Church by their great work."[143]

Each Chotanagpur village, besides the village catechist, has a *sirpanch* (head leader) and other *panches* (leaders) and every group of ten families has a leader who is in charge of their spiritual welfare. He visits these families, thus he is aware of their needs, drawbacks etc.. It is his responsibility to help them when they are sick or in any other needs, to find means and ways for the material as well as spiritual uplift of the family. Head leaders (*sirpanch*) have also got almost the same responsibility. The village catechist primarily attends to religious matters. But he is part of the village leadership, responsible for the religious formation of the whole village. This kind of organisation is seen in large villages. When the village is small, there may be only the need of one person, probably the catechist.[144]

It is the duty of the village catechist to conduct the Sunday services in his village Church. He takes his responsibilities as his vocation and helps his fellow Christians in their journey towards the Heavenly Jerusalem, without counting costs. *Panches, sirpanches*, village catechists work together as faith-formators in their own way, by their life witness. Much of the catechising of children and

---

[141] Cf. A. VAN EXEM, *Evangelisation Today, A Local Church Reflects* (Ranchi: Ranchi Jesuit Society, 1975), 38-39.

[142] Cf. Ibid., 38.; Cf. L. CLARYSEE, *Father Constant Lievens, S. J.*, op. cit., 175.

[143] AG17 (a).

[144] Cf. A. VAN EXEM, *Evangelisation Today, A Local Church Reflects*, op. cit., 36.

adults for various sacraments etc. is done by the catechists. Catechism classes for the children are also given by one of them. They guide the villagers in their evening prayers, and devotional life and celebration of feasts. They are spiritual leaders as well as lawyers too. They help the villagers in settling their disputes. This represents a well-organised village system (*panchayat*) which can be seen from the very beginning of the tribals' existence in India.

Many of the parishes have a *munshi*, a kind of a parish clerk, a man of great inside knowledge and influence, without whose help it would be hard to do all the detailed work of a well organised parish. He keeps the baptismal and other registers along with great files listing all the members and families of the parish.[145]

Many religious movements and pious organisations do their part in the evangelisation efforts of the Church. For example the women leaders of the *Ayo Sangat* (Mother's Sodality) are also messengers of the Good News in their own way. They do help their fellow ladies to lead an exemplary life after the model of Mary. They organise evening prayers together, thus help to have a living faith.

These all are lay missionaries who are in general good and faithful servants and friends ready at any time, waiting and keeping watch with their flock and leading them to green pastures.

1.5.3. Present Day Evangelisation in Chotanagpur

Indian culture testimony has a transforming value. The witness of a Christian life is the first and irreplaceable form of mission; Christ, whose mission we continue, is the "witness" par excellence (Rev. 1:5; 3:14) and the model of all Christian witness. The Holy Spirit accompanies the Church along her way and associates her with the witness he gives to Christ (cf. Jn. 15: 26-27). The first form of witness is the very life of the missionary, of the Christian family, and of the ecclesial community, which reveal a new way of living.[146]

The Christian Oraons living among their non-Christian fellow men are like lamps that light up a dark place. Every baptised Oraon is theoretically an evangeliser. By living a life worthy of his Christian vocation he attracts practically his non-Christian *Sarna* brethren to worship God and to be away from evil and its consequences. "The prophetic role of the Christian faith is to enlighten, interpret, develop and carry on the work of God among all peoples."[147]

Personal contact has proved to be one of the best methods of evangelisation in Chotanagpur. If the missionary visits the villagers, it helps him to start a relationship and also to strengthen the existing relationship between the people and him. He is a friend and a guide to all people in the village, Christians as well as non-Christians. People's concern are his concerns, their struggles his. He cares for their material and spiritual needs. Through daily conversations about various

[145] Cf. A. FLEMING (ed.) *Golden Harvest* (Rourkela: Bishop's House, 1958), 15.

[146] Cf. RM 42.

[147] A. PARAPULLIL, "Tribal Theology", in *Sevartham*, 2 (1979), 28.

concerns, the missionary draws the people to something greater and supreme, the care and concern of God. The Oraons have a fairly clear notion of God (*Dharmes*), the creator and provider of everything, but somehow he seems to be far away. There is a need to deepen and develop this concept of God so as to present him in a tangible way. With a growing Christian understanding, the Oraons have experienced God as a liberator, a saviour who listened to their cry of despair and hopelessness. What they have experienced, they have shared with their friends and relatives in the family, in the village gatherings and the market places.[148]

Up to recent times, the sharing of their faith experience was part of their everyday conversation. They sang devotional songs as they worked in the fields. In the midst of all modern means of communication person to person communication seems to be the most effective. "Thus person to person transmission of the gospel continues to be valid and important."[149] Jesus communicated to us a personal God in a very personal way and thereby became one with us. Evangelisation is ultimately a sharing of one's own belief with others. After all there is no other convincing way of evangelising than transmitting to another person one's own experience of faith.[150]

During the season of lent and advent there is usually an organised visit of the missionary to the village, accompanied and well informed by a catechist. This is a special occasion of grace for individuals as well as for the community. Sacraments of the Holy Eucharist and Confession are celebrated, catechetical instructions are given. Individual and community problems are settled. Each family is visited. The sick are given the sacraments. The whole community, together with the priest, visits the village cemetery and renew the bond with the ancestors.

"Then of course after the missionary left the village it was these men who incarnated more deeply the faith by their being on the spot to interpret all situations of life in the light of faith, to form a community of the faithful, and to organise their prayer and Christian living so that faith was grasped more deeply and lived out more generously."[151]

Another effective method is the adaptation of the existing social organisation that is *Adivasi Panchayat* system, for the organisation of village Churches. Here the catechist acts as a religious head with other socio-economic authorities. "By becoming a part of the religious administrative system the traditional village *panchayat* and its authority was given further justification on the basis of their

[148] Cf. A. VAN EXEM, *Evangelisation Today, A Local Church Reflects*, op. cit., 3-5.

[149] J. SALDANHA, "A Fresh Impluse for Evangelisation in our Times", *in Indian Missiological Review*, 1 (1979), 36.

[150] Cf. Ibid., 36.

[151] M. DULLARD, "Ignatian Spirituality and Chotanagpur Mission", in *Indian Missiological Review*, 7 (1985), 13.

new religion. A catechist in a village carried out most of the functions of a catholic priest except administering a few sacraments specially reserved for priests."[152]

Catholic Sabha (Catholic meeting) is an Adivasi Movement. It is an organisation which works in the parish and diocesan level as an advisory body. Meetings are held every month in the parish, and according to the need on a diocesan level, where the decisions are made for the needs of the Church by the community itself. The main concern of this organisation is faith formation.[153]

There is catechetical instruction which aims at strengthening and forming patterns of Christian living. Seminars, Bible classes and retreats are organised for various groups on the village, parish and diocesan levels. Small Christian communities play an active role in living out the gospel values and thus enforce effective evangelisation. Popular religiosity includes expressions of the search for God and for faith commitment. It offers much scope for evangelisation. "It fosters generosity, patience, detachment, even heroic sacrifice. It is truly the religion of the people."[154]

The liturgy is also a means of evangelisation. "The form of community prayer should be adapted that it reflects and creates in the community a sense of belonging and communion with the neighbourhood that has to be evangelised."[155] Much effort has been made to adapt the Eucharist and other sacraments to the tribal cultures. With this view, the Holy Eucharist is celebrated many times, adapting many of the symbols taken from the given culture. Tribal music and dances have become part of the liturgical celebrations. Traditional tribal festivals are being Christianised. However these efforts stand on the surface level even though inculturation is an effective way of evangelisation. Therefore this study is aimed to seek out the possibilities of meaningful inculturation in this region especially through the celebration of liturgy. These liturgical celebrations at times provide opportunities even for the non-Christians to experience the Divine in a unique way. This is possible through the constant and continuous way of interactions of their faith and the gospel. Inculturation seeks relevance. Christ and his message is being incarnated into tribal culture, thereby enabling the people to recognise the Christian God as their God. Their personal and community experience of Christ enables them to enflesh the gospel ever more deeply into their own lives.

Chapter summary

This study on the historical background of the Christian faith in Chotanagpur enabled us to look into the socio-economic and political realities along with

---

[152] A. KANJAMALA, *Religion and Modernisation of India*, op. cit., 95.

[153] Cf. R. TOPPO, *The Role of the Oraons in the work of Evangelisation in Chotanagpur*, Doctoral dissertation (Rome: Pontificia Universitas Urbaniana, 1987), 208-209.

[154] J. SALDANHA, " A Fresh Impulse for Evangelisation in our Times", op. cit., 36.

[155] P. PUTHANAGADY, "A Missionary Approach to Liturgy", in *Indian Missiological Review*, 1 (1979), 244.

the religion of the Oraons. We have found that socio- economic conditions are intimately linked with their religion. The seed of faith was sown in this area by Fr. Constant Lievens in an appropriate time, when the Oraons were under the yoke of non-tribals who exploited the illiterate Oraon landowners, reducing them to tenants. In their misery, the Oraons found their faith in their innumerable spirits as impotent, for they could not help them in their misfortune that alienated them from their ancestral land. The zealous missionary helped them to liberate themselves from their spiritual and material bondages. Within a short time Lievens learned the essence of their culture and offered the people faith in a new form without demolishing the cherished aspects of their culture.

"Unless a wheat grain falls into the earth and dies, it remains only a single grain; but if it dies it yields a rich harvest" (Jn.12:24). Despite many trials and difficulties on her way, the Chotanagpur Church shows tremendous growth towards maturity; as a Church that cares not only for her own members but for entire people. It has been living out a life of inculturation from the very beginning of its existence. Perhaps, it is this way of encounters between culture and faith which has made evangelisation possible for this church at a time when even knew the term "inculturation". By adapting to the people's way in mentality and culture, the church has proved to be effective in her evangelising mission.

All in all, the vitality of the Church stems from the fact that it is an inculturated Church from its origin. Faith was introduced to them through their own cultural categories and socio-economic realities. The Church became part of the real life of the people and eventually revealed herself as an evangelising Church. In fact, inculturation is an important sign of hope and a permanent challenge to the Church in her life as well as in her mission. In this sense, Chotanagpur is a striking example as we will see in the next chapter.

Chapter 2

INCULTURATION IN EVANGELISING CHOTANAGPUR

Introductory Remarks

Having examined the socio-cultural and religious background of the people of Chotanagpur, also the birth and growth of the Christian faith in this area, we now step further, by studying the inculturation of Christian faith. Hence, in this chapter we come across the interaction of faith and culture by considering its importance in the teaching of the magisterium, its theological importance, etc.. We then look at the insertion of the Gospel message into the life of Chotanagpur whereby, we discover the relevance of inculturation in the auto evangelisation of the Chotanagpur Church herself as well as in her outreach towards the non-Christian society in the Chotanagpur region.

2.1. Key Word- "Inculturation"

In the Council texts of Vatican II, the second chapter of the Constitution on the Church in the Modern World gives us a rather good description of culture and its proper development:

"The word "culture" in the general sense refers to all those things which go to the refining and developing of man's diverse mental and physical endowments. He strives to subdue the earth by his knowledge and his labour; he humanizes social life both in the family and in the whole civic community through the improvement of customs and institutions; he expresses through his work the great spiritual experiences and aspirations of men throughout the ages; he communicates and preserves them to be inspiration for the progress of many, even of all mankind."[156]

---

[156] GS 53.

Therefore man expresses himself fully - his material, social and spiritual life - through culture. According to some North American ethnologists, (e.g. M.J. Herskovoits) inculturation or better enculturation in its anthropological sense is that "process by which a child or every human being acquire from the social surrounding both social and cultural behaviour that are necessary in an automatic way for a normal life in a society."[157]

This learning of one's own culture begins at birth and is a continuous process lasting all through life, yet it remains at a purely human level. Our interest here is not in this type of enculturation in the anthropological perspective but in the typically Christian concept of inculturation in the theological perspective. As mentioned above, man expresses himself fully through culture; then religious beliefs or faith expressions are also manifested in cultural terms. 'Faith', in its broadest understanding is an on-going search for a valid response to the Divine; and so when one accepts a new faith he also has to deal with an interaction between the existing culture and the new faith.

"A term that is frequently used in this connection is 'message.' Thus inculturation is said to be a dialogue between the Christian message and a human culture."[158] Religion and culture go hand in hand. Christian religion is not something abstract which consists of certain books, doctrines and myths; but in a concrete sense it consists in the adherence to and life through the person Jesus Christ, the Word of God made flesh. Hence, in the last analysis, the subject matter of inculturation is Jesus himself. He is the manifestation of God's self-communication to us, his chosen people all over the world; therefore God's message must take root in human cultures and should transform them.[159] This is what we mean by inculturation:

"Inculturation is the incarnation of Christian life and of the Christian message in a particular cultural context, in such a way that this experience not only finds expression through elements proper to the culture in question, but becomes a principle that animates, directs and unifies the culture, transforming and remaking it so as to bring about a "new creation."[160]

Although there are many possible ways to present meaningful descriptions of content, we shall use the term "inculturation" with approximately the following significance, the effort the Church makes to present the message and the values of the Gospel that are incarnate in the forms and words proper to each culture, in such manner that the faith and the Christian life of each local Church is

---

[157] V. L. GROTTANELLI, *Dinamica Culturale e Dialettica Etnologica* (Roma: Urbaniana University Press, 1964), 29. The original text is in Italian and the translation is mine.

[158] A. SHORTER, *Toward a Theology of Inculturation* (London: Geoffrey Chapman, 1988), 59.

[159] Cf. A. SHORTER, *Toward a Theology of Inculturation*, op. cit., 59-60.

[160] P. ARRUPE, "Letter on Inculturation to the Whole Society of Jesus", in *Indian Missiological Review*, 1 (1979), 88.

integrated into its own cultural frame, in the most intimate and profound manner possible.[161]

In Jesus Christ we have a perfect example of inculturation. "The Word became flesh and dwelt among us" (Jn. 1:14). Jesus, the personification of God's message, communicated this Divine message by becoming one like us, and we call it incarnation. Therefore "the most directly theological word to express the meaning of inculturation is incarnation."[162] In Christ the two natures divine and human, are united yet remain distinct. And yet there are not two persons, for the two natures, are united in the unity of a single person: the Word made flesh. "It incorporates the human without losing the divine, it assumes whatever is good, true, beautiful, valid and positive in the human and integrates it with divine grace, it redeems the human and elevates it to the divine."[163]

Cultures are more than passive receptacles for universal Christian faith; they have within them positive elements, seeds of the Word (LG. 11) within which the Word of God can develop. Missionary activity therefore imitates "the plan of Incarnation" (AG. 22).[164]

"Go therefore and make disciples of all nations, baptising them in the name of the Father and of the Son and of the Holy Spirit" (Mt. 28:19). This is the mandate the Church has received from her founder and this command the Church had been carrying out through her missionary activities, encountering different peoples and cultures, also becoming involved in the process of inculturation. Pope John Paul II emphatically speaks about inculturation in his recent Encyclical letter *Redemptoris Missio*:

"Through inculturation the Church makes the Gospel incarnate in different cultures and at the same time introduces peoples, together with their cultures, into her own community. She transmits to them her own values, at the same time taking the good elements that already exist in them and renewing them from within. Through inculturation the Church, for her part, becomes a more intelligible sign of what she is, and a more effective instrument of mission."[165]

Hence the Church, as she continues the mission of the Incarnate Word, helps herself and others to become incarnate and to be transformed. St. Paul calls incarnation (perfect inculturation) of Christ as 'self-emptying' (cf. Phil. 2:5-11), because Christ renounced so to speak his own divinity, while inserting himself fully and totally into the human culture in which he was born. As Pedro Arrupe puts it:

---

[161] P. GIGLIONI, *Inculturation and Non-Christian Religions* (Roma: The P.M.U. International Secretariat, 1983), 4.

[162] P. SCHINELLER, *A Handbook on Inculturation* (Mahwah: New York, Paulist Press, 1990), 20.

[163] A. REBELLO, "Inculturation and Education", in *Euntes Docete* XLVII (1994), 171.

[164] F. E.GEORGE, *Inculturation and Ecclesial Communion* (Rome: Urbaniana University Press, 1990), 50-51.

[165] RM 52.

"The Incarnation of the Son is the primary motivation and perfect pattern for inculturation. Just like him, and because he did so, the Church will become incarnate as vitally and intimately as it can in every culture, being enriched with its values and offering it the unique redemption of Christ, his message and the resources for a new life."[166]

2.2. Biblical Perspectives

God has been communicating himself from the very moment of creation. In human history he has revealed himself in different forms, through various people, first to his chosen people Israel and then to us, the new Israel, through his son Jesus Christ - his most personal communication. The Bible presents fascinating accounts of the encounter between the Divine and human cultures. The creation itself shows the interaction between the Divine and human.[167] "In the beginning was the Word, the Word was with God, and the Word was God. He was in the beginning with God; all things were made through him" (Jn. 1:1-3). The whole creation is the epiphany of God's effective Word. He uttered his Word and everything came into being. "The logos is God's agent in creation."[168]

It is a common opinion that the Bible is culturally ethnocentric because its dominant theme is that of God's action towards a particular people, the Jew. Although the Jews were not free from the temptation of ethnocentrism particularly in later Old Testament times, such a generalisation is, in fact, very far from the truth. The Jewish culture was but one component in a historical process of interaction between many cultures. The 'fertile crescent' of the Middle East was a veritable cross road of culture from the earliest times. The Jewish people and their traditions were, humanly speaking, the product of this remarkably varied cultural interaction, and were themselves contributors to the on-going intercultural process.[169]

Between the Exodus event and the Exile, Israel had to contend with the various forms of Canaanite culture encountered in the promised land. It was a cultural conglomerate of varied origins. Israel's faith - faith in the God of Abraham, Isaac and Jacob got to some extent inculturated with the customs and traditions of Canaanites. This was the Canaanite inculturation, perhaps the most outstanding instance of inculturation in the Old Testament.[170] "The Old Testament, especially the Psalms, adopted so many images from other peoples, that it prompted O. Keel

---

[166] P. ARRUPE,"Letter to the Whole Society", quoted in P. SCHINELLER, *A Handbook on Inculturation,* op. cit.,20.

[167] Cf. A. SHORTER, *Toward a Theology of Inculturation*, op. cit., 76.

[168] Ibid., 77.

[169] Cf. I. HUNT, "Excursus: Israel and her Neighbours", in *Jerome Biblical Commentary*, Vol. 1, 211-214.

[170] Cf. J. SALDANHA, *Inculturation* (Bombay: St. Paul Publications, 1987), 17.

to remark that Israel's experiences and conceptions of God were `rounded out by those of neighbouring peoples."[171]

Thus OT gives us a God who communicates himself and his designs for man through creation, through the historical events of the Jewish people. And finally God's self-communication or revelation is made manifested in Christ Jesus fully and totally. "God so loved the world, that he gave his only Son" (Jn. 3:16a). The Father willed to share his divine life with his children. Thus the incarnation of Christ is the final step of "God's inculturation" with human beings. Jesus was born, lived and died in a particular context and culture. "Christ himself in virtue of his incarnation, bound himself to the definite social and cultural conditions of those human beings among whom he dwelt."[172] And Samuel Rayan says " in coming to dwell among us, among his people, he was being himself there as the concrete saving presence and self-giving of God to them."[173]

By his incarnation Christ became one with the people of his time. Thus we see him participating in the religious feasts of the Jewish tradition, and we see him living in accordance with the piety of his people. By taking up the religious traditions of his people, he was able to avail himself of the opportunity to offer them a new and full significance.[174]

Jesus not only lived in accordance with the piety of the people, he strongly challenged certain aspects of the culture which he had inherited. He stood against the established order so as to prepare the new order willed by his Father. He questioned the regulations of the Sabbath day rest (cf. Mt. 12:8). He condemned the ritual observances of the law, but insisted on the spirit of the law (cf. Mt. 5:21-40). He opposed the punishment that was due to the woman caught in adultery (cf. Jn. 7: 53). In short he purified all those rigid practices, rules and regulations through his compassion and forgiving love, thus he opened a way to an interior transformation of the heart which can be expressed in their every day living.[175]

The incarnation of Jesus and the preaching of the Good News was addressed to all, but it was especially directed towards the poor, the needy, the sick and the sinners. Christ taught in parables, with imageries taken from their daily life experiences; this made him to draw many people to himself, giving them the experience of the Father who cares for his children, who shares his life with them. Thus Jesus enters into dialogue with each and every type of persons and recognises the good in them. He marvels at the centurion's faith and said "not even in Israel have I found such faith" (Mt. 8:10). He converses with the Samaritan woman and

---

[171] J. SALDANHA, *Inculturation*, op. cit., 17.

[172] THE INTERNATIONAL THEOLOGICAL COMMISSION, *Faith and Inculturation*, 1988, 7.

[173] S. RAYAN, "Flesh of India's Flesh", in *Jeevadhara*, VI (1976), 260.

[174] P. GIGLIONI, *Inculturation and non-Christian Religions,* op. cit., 4.

[175] Cf. P. GIGLIONI, "Inculturazione e Missione", in *Chiesa Locale e Inculturazione* (Roma: Urbaniana University Press, 1987), 83.

speaks to her of a time when true worshippers will "worship the Father in spirit and truth" (Jn. 4:23). Jesus thus opens a new horizon, far beyond the old and local.[176]

The inculturation of Christ finds its climax in the resurrection, a truly intercultural as well as transcultural event. The Resurrection enabled Christ to transcend the physical limitations of an earthly life bounded by time, space and, of course, culture. The intercultural contacts of the earthly Jesus were necessarily limited. After the Resurrection, Christ belonged to every culture at once.

The Resurrection made it possible for him to identify explicitly with the cultures of every time and place, through the proclamation of the Gospel to every nation. The Resurrection made possible the release of the Spirit to the people of every culture, and this was effectively symbolised by what happened at Pentecost, when people of diverse languages heard and understood the one language of faith. The Paschal Mystery, then, is intimately linked to the inculturation process itself. It is precisely because of the resurrection that we can become members of Christ, and that Christ in his members, can become African, Indian, American and so on.[177]

Incarnation points out our responsibilities. As followers of Christ we need to identify ourselves with the people with whom and among whom we work, so that we may be persons who help the people to identify and to realise the positive values that are hidden in their culture, thereby bringing a transformation into the life of the people. As St. Paul spells it out:

To the Jews I became a Jew, in order to win Jews; to those under the law I became as one under the law - though not being myself under the law - that I might win those under the law. To those outside the law I became as one outside the law - not being without law toward God but under the law of Christ - that I might win those outside the law. To the weak, I have become all things to all men, that I might by all means save some. I do it all for the sake of the Gospel, that I may share in its blessings (1 Cor. 9:20-23).

St. Paul was well aware of the meaning of inculturation in its proper sense, that he adapted himself to the cultures which made him an effective missionary of the time. This basic biblical model[178] remains valid also for the missionaries of our times.

---

[176] Cf. M. AMALADOSS, "Inculturation and Tasks of Mission", in *East Asian Pastoral Review*, XVII (1980), 119.

[177] A.SHORTER, *Towarda Theology of Inculturation,* op. cit., 83.

[178] Although there are many other personalities like St. Paul, he is the most obvious and well known missionary figure in the Bible. This dissertation is not a complete elaboration of these topics but aims only at giving a few hints which indicate the direction for further research. More information on this vast topic in the Bible can be found, for instance, J. H. Kane, E. Testa, D. Senior, C. Stuhlmueller, etc. in the following works. J. H. KANE, *Christian Missions in Biblical Perspective* (Grand Rapids: Baker Book house 1976), E. TESTA, *L'Evangelizzazione nelle Sacre*

2.3. Meaning of Inculturation According to the Magisterium

The term inculturation is only a few decades old; the real break-through for its common use in the Church came with the 32nd General Chapter of the Jesuits.[179] The Church always encounters various religions and cultures in her path of evangelisation. As we glance through the evangelising history of the Church in modern times it is clear that from the second half of the 19th century onwards there were efforts made to inculturate the Gospel. The Church was aware of the need to insert the Christian message into the cultures of the peoples.

During the pontificate of Pope John XXIII, there occurred some changes in the Church in relation to Church and the world. The Church became more and more aware of the importance of various traditions and cultures which added beauty and enrichment to her universality and catholicity. It was Vatican II which made a bold step towards inculturation though it did not use this word explicitly.[180] The Church realises her duty to present the Gospel message to all the peoples in an acceptable form, grafting it to the values of a people's culture and customs so that the revelation of God in Jesus is understood well and "conceptualised, expressed in worship, formulated in propositions, assimilated, lived, proclaimed and witnessed to in a specific manner and with varying emphasis."[181]

2.3.1. Conciliar Documents

The process whereby the mystery of Christ becomes indigenised in thought and expression is a gradual one. But, unless it is initiated and set on its way towards fulfilment, the mission of the Church will not have been fully accomplished. Drawing inspiration and insights from the mystery of incarnation, the Church in her infancy set this inculturation process into motion at the Council of Jerusalem. It began with the declaration of Peter that all men, whether Jews or Gentiles, were called to salvation by one and the same God, and that, although called in different ways to profess their faith in Christ, yet God made no distinction between the one and the other (cf. Acts. 15:7ff).[182]

Scritture (Roma: P.U.U., 1977); D. SENIOR and C. STUHLMUELLER, *The Biblical Foundations for Mission* (New York: Orbis Books, 1983).

[179] This General Chapter took place between December 1st, 1974 and April 7th 1975. In two places, the texts issued after this meeting speak of inculturation: in the numbers 36 and 53 to 56 of the Fourth Decree (on "Our Mission Today") and in the short Fifth Decree, which is specially dedicated to this: "On promoting the work of Inculturation of faith and Christian Life." (A. R. CROLLIUS, "Inculturation: Newness and Ongoing Process," in J. M. WALIGGO and others, *Inculturation: Its meaning and Urgency* (Kampala: St. Paul Publications, 1986), 32).

[180] Cf. L. J. LUZBETAK, *Church and Cultures, New Perspectives in Missiological Anthropology* (Maryknoll: New York, Orbis Books, 1980), 109.

[181] S. KAROTEMPREL, "Inculturation and Missionary Formation", in *Indian Missiological Review*, 7 (1985), 246.

[182] Cf. P. SCHINELLER, *Handbook on Inculturation*, op. cit., 29-30.

"According to Karl Rahner, Vatican II was the most historically significant Council since the Council of Jerusalem. Both councils marked a clear break in church history."[183] The fathers of the Second Vatican Council were well aware of the fact that the history of the Church bore witness to the innumerable times, that she adopted or adapted from other peoples not only their laudable customs and traditions, festivals and seasons, languages and art forms, but also their signs, symbols, gestures and other cultural and cultic elements. As a result, the Council presented the Church's views on adaptation in a welcoming spirit of ecumenism and dialogue. It states:

"God who "wills that all men be saved and come to the knowledge of the truth" (1 Tim. 2:4),... sent His Son, the Word made flesh, anointed by the Holy Spirit, to preach the gospel to the poor, to heal the contrite of heart to be a bodily and spiritual medicine: the Mediator between God and man. For His humanity united with the person of the Word was the instrument of our salvation."[184]

The Church, when incarnated in the local cultural context of a given Christian community, is said to be the local Church. The local Christian community is the principle agent of inculturation, for there is much communion, creativity, spontaneity which can enrich the universal Church. The Church can fulfil her mission only by being local and incarnated, and she will express herself and operate through the social, cultural, religious realities of the place, time and population.

"The Church, the visible community of Christ's disciples, the Body of Christ, the embodiment of His Spirit, the historical and social prolongation of Jesus Christ in time and space has no other mission than that of Christ, namely, of recapitulating, reconciling and unifying all men and all things making them all belong to God so that God may be all in all (LG 1; Eph. 1: 3 and 14; Col. 1: 15-20; 1Cor. 3: 23; 15: 20-28). The Word through whom all things were made and who has been present through history is made flesh and dwelt among us (Jn.1:12). Everything that was created needs to be saved, and nothing is saved unless it is taken up by the Word. Hence the Church and Christ should gather and assume all and everything in the Word Incarnated, purify and redeem them, fulfil and unify them, and lead and consecrate them to God. This mission of recapitulation includes not only all men but also all the cultures and religions."[185]

Inserted into human history the Church has been influenced by the various cultures of her members. She has used those cultures for the effective proclamation of the Gospel and thus has led the faithful to feel at home with Christian worship and life styles.

"The Church or people of God in establishing that kingdom takes nothing away from the temporal welfare of any people. Rather she fosters and takes to

---

[183] L. J. LUZBETAK, *The Church and Cultures*, op. cit., 109.

[184] SC 5.

[185] D. S. AMALORPAVADASS, *Gospel and Culture* (Bangalore: N.B.C.L.C., 1978), 34.

herself, in so far as they are good, the abilities, the resources and customs of peoples. In so taking them to herself she purifies, strengthens, elevates them."[186] "Whatever good is found sown in the minds and hearts of men, or in the rites and customs of peoples, these not only are preserved from destruction, but are purified, raised up and perfected for the glory of God, the confusion of the devil and the happiness of man."[187]

We have already seen that the second chapter of the Constitution on the Church in the Modern World gives a clear account of the development of culture. The text then explains the relationship between culture and the Good News of Christ, pointing out the self-revelation of God the Father which has found its fulfilment in his Incarnate Son, and how the Church has `used' the cultures in order to proclaim the Incarnate Word.

"There are many links between the message of salvation and culture. In his self-revelation to his people culminating in the fullness of manifestation in his incarnate Son, God spoke according to the culture proper to each age. Similarly the Church has existed through centuries in varying circumstances and has utilized the resources of different cultures in its preaching to spread and explain the message of Christ, to examine and understand it more deeply, and to express it more perfectly in the liturgy and in various aspects of the life of the faithful."[188]

God became man. He thus adapted himself to human nature in order to elevate the human beings to the level of the divine that they have a share in his very life. This is the focal point of inculturation. Prompted by this awareness, working on the renewal of Sacred Liturgy, Council fathers proposed radical adaptation for mission countries.

"Even in the liturgy, the Church does not wish to impose a rigid uniformity in matters which do not involve the faith or the good of the whole community. Rather does she respect and foster the qualities and talents of the various races and peoples. Anything in these peoples' way of life which is not indissolubly bound up with superstition and error she studies with sympathy, and, if possible, preserves intact. She sometimes even admits such things into the liturgy itself, provided they harmonize with its true and authentic spirit."[189]

Ad gentes, the Decree on the missionary activity of the Church, also presents the relation between evangelisation and culture. The Church's missionary activity is the manifestation and the realisation of God's salvific will in the world. Missionary activity is addressed to people who are closely linked to their culture. Holy Eucharist is the centre of all missionary activities. It enables people to purge negative elements and to value the positive elements.[190] "So whatever goodness is

---

[186] LG 13.

[187] LG 17.

[188] GS 58.

[189] SC 37.

[190] Cf. AG 9.

found in the minds and hearts of men, or in the particular customs and cultures of peoples far from being lost is purified, raised to a higher level and reaches its perfection, for the glory of God,...and the happiness of man."[191]

Ad Gentes (cf. AG 22) outlines a whole gamut of programmes to be covered by inculturation. The image of 'seed' is shown as the symbol of the Gospel proclamation. As the seed absorbs from the soil and the atmosphere the necessary elements for its growth and development, so too the Gospel message will grow when it is allowed to take root in the surrounding culture.

"The seed which is the word of God grows out of the soil watered by the divine dew, it absorbs moisture, transforms it, and makes it part of itself, so that eventually it bears much fruit. So too indeed, just as happened in the economy of the incarnation, the young Churches, which are rooted in Christ and built on the foundations of the apostles, take over all the riches of the nations which have been given to Christ as an inheritance (cf. Ps 2, 8). They borrow from the customs, traditions, wisdom, teaching, arts and sciences of their people everything which could be used to praise the glory of the Creator, manifest the grace of the saviour, or contribute to the right ordering of Christian life."[192]

The Church recognises that human sciences, achievements and cultures, however good, beautiful and true they may be, are not absolutely perfect, without the mark of sin and evil. All of them stand in need of purification, need to pass through death in order to rise in Christ to a new life. The Church wants to communicate the salvation which is offered in Christ Jesus to all peoples. Today there are more than four billion people who have not even heard the gospel message, and this number is on the increase as each day there is an increase of population. These people "constitute large and distinct groups united by enduring cultural ties, ancient religious traditions, and strong social relationships."[193] The Church cannot ignore the plan of salvation. Therefore the document throws light on the importance of inculturation.

While speaking of the Church's presence among peoples who have not yet heard or just barely heard the Message, the Council document stresses Christian witness too. Preaching of the Word is oral proclamation, whereas life witness is an effective way of proclaiming the Good News.

"All Christians by the example of their lives and witness of the word, wherever they live, have an obligation to manifest the new man which they put on in baptism, and to reveal the power of the Holy Spirit by whom they were strengthened at confirmation, so that others, seeing their good works, might glorify the Father (cf. Mt. 5:16) and more perfectly perceive the true meaning of human life and the universal solidarity of mankind. In order to bear witness to Christ, fruitfully, they should establish relationships of respect and love with those

---

[191] AG 9.

[192] AG 22a.

[193] AG 10.

men, they should acknowledge themselves as members of the group in which they live, and through the various undertakings and affairs of human life they should share in their social and cultural life. They should be familiar with their national and religious traditions and uncover with gladness and respect those seeds of the Word which lie hidden among them."[194]

A Christian community is a Christ centred group of people imbued with the Spirit, transformed by him, and led by him. The values of the Gospel, and the Kingdom or the reality of the new era and new creation, are to be translated in an embodiment and communicated to others by visible and concrete media. The transformational encounter between the living Gospel, as it is understood and practised by the Church in a living culture, and the everyday realities of the people - this process is called inculturation. Hence there is no preaching of the Gospel without inculturation. As Vatican II says,

"If the Church is to be in a position to offer all men the mystery of salvation and the life brought by God, then it must implant itself among all these groups (people of various cultures and religious traditions) in the same way that Christ by his incarnation committed himself to the particular social and cultural circumstances of the men among whom he lived."[195]

Even though *Evangelii Nuntiandi* is not a Council text, some years later, Pope Paul VI again emphasises this same idea in it.[196]

2.3.2. Missionary Encyclicals

The first mission encyclical in the proper sense of the word was the Apostolic letter *Maximum Illud* of Pope Benedict XV, dated 30 November 1919. Appearing, as it did, a year after the first World war, the main thrust of this encyclical was to strengthen and co-ordinate the Catholic missionary effort. The Pope wants to foster the effectiveness of the preaching of the Gospel. In order to achieve this the Pope asked the heads of the missions to collaborate and co-operate with one another (eventually to form episcopal conferences).[197] "It was a precondition for a common cultural policy in newly formed colonial states and establishing the identity of a local Church."[198] Another important precondition for an eventual

---

[194] AG 11.

[195] AG 10.

[196] "What matters is to evangelise man's culture and cultures (not in a purely decorative way as it were by applying a thin veneer, but in a vital way, in depth and right to their very roots), in the wide and rich sense which these terms have in *Gaudium et Spes*, always taking the person as one's starting-point and always coming back to the relationship of people among themselves and with God" (EN 20). Many more references can be found in various Council texts. Unfortunately in this study we must limit ourselves to a few important points central to the topic we are dealing with.

[197] Cf. A. SHORTER, *Toward* a *Theology* of *Inculturation,* op. cit., 179-180.

[198] Ibid., 180.

dialogue between faith and culture can be noticed when the Pope insists on the training of an indigenous clergy. He explains:

"Nor should the indigenous priest be trained for the sole purpose of assisting foreign missionaries in a subordinate ministry, but he must be fitted for his divine task and rendered able one day to undertake with credit the administration of his own people."[199]

The Pope exhorted the missionaries to have a profound knowledge of the language and culture of the people and not to despise the people. He strongly opposed every attitude of cultural domination.

"The Missionary should bear in mind that he is the ambassador not of his own country but of Christ, he should so comport himself that everyone can recognise in him a minister of a religion which embraces all men who adore God in spirit and truth, is a stranger to no nation."[200]

"As a result, there is no longer any distinction between Gentiles and Jews, circumcised and uncircumcised, barbarians, savages, slaves and free men, but Christ is all, Christ is in all" (Col. 3:11).

Seven years later, in 1926, another document was published on promoting the sacred missions: *Rerum Ecclesiae.* It was the encyclical letter of Pope Pius XI, called the Pope of the Missions. Here again the Pope agrees with his predecessor Benedict XV for the promotion of an indigenous clergy. He says:

"Since the native priest,... by birth, temper, sentiment, and interests is in close touch with his own people, it is beyond all controversy how valuable he can be in instilling the Faith into the minds of his people. The native priest understands better than any outsider how to proceed with his own people. Such being the case, he can often gain access to places where a foreign priest would not be permitted to enter."[201]

The Pope was concerned about the establishment of seminaries, native religious orders (active and contemplative), and the increase in the number of the catechists. He insisted on establishing equality between missionary and indigenous clergy in conditions of life and culture.[202] The Pope mentioned also the missionary exhibition[203] that was held in the Vatican which displayed various specimens of Christian art from mission countries. "This is an unconscious instance of inculturation."[204]

---

[199] MI 7.

[200] MI 8.

[201] RE 21.

[202] Cf. A. SHORTER, *Toward a Theology of Inculturation,* op. cit., 182.

[203] A missionary exhibition was held in the Jubilee year 1925. "It seems almost a miracle, which gives us a new experimental proof of the vital unity and harmony of the Church of God among all nations....Indeed the exhibition was and still is like a mission encyclopaedia," says Pope Pius XII in his encyclical *Evangelii Praecones* (EP 61).

[204] A. SHORTER, *Toward a Theology of Inculturation,* op. cit., 181.

"An important landmark in the development of theology of inculturation was the address given by Pope Pius XII to the Pontifical Mission Aid Societies in 1944. It is important because it appears to be the first recorded instance in which the Church officially recognised the plurality of cultures."[205]

Yet there was reluctance from the part of the Church to accept the plurality of cultures. The Church tried to "produce a monolithic, Catholic or Christian culture."[206]

Taking into consideration the different missiological views of the Church on cultures, in 1951 Pope Pius XII wrote his encyclical letter *Evangelii Praecones*. The fall of Adam has affected human nature with original sin, yet, it has something Christian in it which should be nourished by God's grace and changed into supernatural virtue.[207] He states,

"Let not the Gospel, on being introduced into any new land, destroy or extinguish whatever its people possess that is naturally good, just or beautiful. For the Church, when she calls people to a higher culture and better way of life under the inspiration of the Christian religion, does not act like one who recklessly cuts down and uproots a thriving forest. No, she grafts a good scion up on the wild stock that may bear a crop of more delicious fruit."[208]

The Pope intends to preserve what is not bound up with error. Hence he says: "Whatever there is in the native customs that is not inseparably bound up with superstition and error will always receive kindly consideration and, when possible, will be preserved intact."[209]

Through his encyclical letter *Fidei Donum* (1957), Pope Pius XII makes an appeal to the entire Church to provide missionary priests for Africa. It did not deal with faith and culture in an explicit way, but it does speak about particular Churches which is again an implicit consciousness of inculturation. "Now the Lord said to Abram, 'Go from your country and your kindred and your father's house to the land that I will show you'" (Gen. 12:1).

Again we come across the training of the local clergy in *Princeps Pastorum* (1959), the encyclical letter of Pope John XXIII. Affirming the Church's cultural pluralism the Pope says: "The Church does not identify herself with one culture with the exclusion of the rest."[210] He points out the importance of seminary formation adapted to the locality. "Indeed it is necessary that youths not only conform to the ideal of priestly spiritual perfection in everything, but also that

---

[205] A. SHORTER, *Toward a Theology of Inculturation,* op. cit.,183.

[206] Ibid., 183.

[207] Cf. EP 57.

[208] EP 56.

[209] EP 59.

[210] PP 16.

they gradually and prudently penetrate the mentality and feelings of the people."[211] The Pope says:

"The Church, to a certain extent, consecrated native art and culture... as well as the special customs and traditional institutions of the people... Wherever artistic and philosophical values exist which are capable of enriching the culture of the human race, the Church fosters and supports these labours of the spirit."[212]

For the development of the concept of inculturation the Synod of 1974 was important.[213] "The synod asked Paul VI to embody the fruits of their discussion in a document of his own."[214] And thus his apostolic exhortation *Evangelii Nuntiandi* was promulgated. According to the Pope evangelisation means bringing the Good News to all strata of humanity, so that humanity itself becomes a new creation.[215] This leads to the evangelisation of cultures. He asserted that the very process of evangelisation is a creative process of insertion, incarnation and inculturation, even though the document does not use the word 'inculturation'. He explains "evangelisation loses much of its force and effectiveness if it does not take into consideration the actual people to whom it is addressed, if it does not use their language, their signs and symbols, if it does not have an impact on their concrete life."[216]

Pope John Paul II is prominent in the pages of the history of the Church. He has travelled far and wide in the world with special missionary interest. What stands out in the forefront in most of his addresses and pastoral letters is his real abiding interest in culture. This interest, as one understands, flows from the struggle of his own Christian Slavic culture with the "culture" of atheistic Marxism.[217] After the Synod of Bishops in 1977, in his very first apostolic exhortation, *Catechesi Tradendae*, the Pope used the term inculturation for the first time in a papal document.[218]

---

[211] PP 16.

[212] PP 19.

[213] Of course *Evangelii Nuntiandi* and *Catechesi Tradendae* are not missionary encyclicals.But these post-synodal apostolic exhortations contain ideas similar to what has been said before and so these documents can usefully supplement our study. The last and most authoritative indications up to now are found in the recent encyclical of Pope John Paul II, *Redemptoris Missio.*

[214] A. SHORTER, *Toward the Theology of Inculturation*, op. cit., 215.

[215] Cf. EN 18.

[216] EN 63.

[217] Cf. A. SHORTER, *Toward a Theology of Inculturation*, op. cit., 223.

[218] Pope Paul VI and Pope John Paul I both died in 1978, before the final document of the Synod of Bishops of 1977 could be drawn up. It was left to Pope John Paul II to sum up the thinking of the Synod in his apostolic exhortation, *Catechesi Tradendae*, issued in October 1979. As the participants at the Synod had laid considerable emphasis on cultures, we find an important section on the subject in the Pope's exhortation (cf. CT 53). (Cf. A. SHORTER, *Toward a Theology of Inculturation,* op. cit., 223).

The encyclical letter *Redemptoris Missio* of Pope John Paul II does not consider the process of the Church's insertion into people's cultures as a matter of purely external adaptation, as he explains,

"Inculturation means the intimate transformation of authentic cultural values through their integration in Christianity in the various human cultures. The process is thus a profound and all-embracing one, which involves the Christian message and also the Church's reflection and practice. ... Through inculturation the Church makes the Gospel incarnate in different cultures and at the same time introduces peoples, together with their cultures, into her own community. She transmits to them her own values, at the same time taking the good elements that already exist in them and renewing them from within. Through inculturation the Church, for her part, becomes a more intelligible sign of what she is, and a more effective instrument of mission."[219]

2.3.3. Theological Perspectives

The diversity of cultures is an important aspect for the establishment of particular Churches but also an enriching factor for the universality of the Church as well as for Catholic theology in its various forms and expressions. Theology can be understood as an earnest reflection of one's faith. Faith and culture are interrelated, so too theology and culture.[220] Thus theological understanding has also an impact on culture, but here we are mainly interested in the impact of culture on theology.

The Word of God though invisible made himself visible by his incarnation, and it is by this Word that all has been created. That is to say that the Word is present at the heart of all cultures revealing himself in various ways.[221] "Revelation is made to man who belongs to a concrete society with its concrete assemblage of values, concepts, categories of expression, worship, cultic forms, social organisation etc. which we call cultures."[222] Thus we have seen Vatican II speaking of '*semina verbi*,'[223] the seeds of the Word present not only in Christian tradition but also in all cultures and religions. This awareness and reflection of the Church leads to the acceptance of different cultures and traditions, in the process of inculturation. The self-communication of God is given to a particular person or a particular community.[224] Therefore "cultures both traditional and modern, remain the locus for God's past, present and future revelation."[225]

---

[219] RM 52. Since RM sums up all the important documents of the Church till today, we do not intend to refer to other documents such as published by the Roman Congregations, for instance "Inculturation and Faith," and "Dialogue and Inculturation" etc.

[220] Cf. P. SCHINELLER, *A Handbook on Inculturation*, op. cit., 45.

[221] Cf. A. SHORTER, *Toward the Theology of Inculturation*, op. cit., 78.

[222] S. KAROTEMPREL, "Inculturation and Missionary Formation", op. cit., 247.

[223] Cf. AG 11.

[224] Cf. P. SCHINELLER, *A Handbook on Inculturation*, op. cit., 46.

[225] Ibid., 46.

Jesus Christ is the sign and reality of God's love. Love of God in Jesus Christ is offered to all Christians as well as non-Christians. God's love is made visible to mankind in its most expressive way in the incarnation of his Son, which is the primary motivation and perfect pattern for inculturation. Jesus became man. He entered into human history. The act of God in the person of Jesus is in an eminent way unique, for in Jesus God himself became man. This is the pattern of God's actions in the Bible. Straight from creation, God intervenes in the life of man, revealing his love, manifesting and communicating his power and life, thus establishing an intimate relationship with him. He speaks to them a language that touches their lives, their history.[226] "Thus God's word always comes to man embodied in history and in human life, and man's response is not an intellectual affirmation of an abstract truth but a commitment to action."[227]

The earthly Jesus was enculturated in the culturally heterogeneous corner of Palestine known as Galilee. His mission, the proclamation of the reign of God, was addressed to all peoples rich and poor so that they be transformed by his messages. He was a threat to the Scribes and the Pharisees who did not accept this revelation of God's love. In other words Jesus while interacting with his Jewish religious and secular culture, met with hostility and finally death on a cross.[228] "Inculturation of gospel values may mean dying to one's limited cultural views and being open to the new. ... It calls for deep association with the paschal mystery of Jesus Christ, the only way to new life."[229] It can also be said that this unique word of God in Jesus can be effective and acceptable, only when it "undergoes a constant and living re-interpretation in a continuous tradition in a changing variety of historical, socio-cultural and religious forms."[230]

Inculturation is not an individualistic action. It is a communitarian act, hence the community of disciples, the Church, who are the agent of inculturation should be open to this 'kenosis' whereby they attain a newness. A living religion implies an incarnation of God's word as well as man's response to it in contemporary cultural forms. The Church is the concrete presence and manifestation of the Word in contemporary socio-cultural forms. "Church is rather like leaven, transforming every culture it encounters from the inside, expressing its deepest nature and life in the forms of that culture."[231] The Word of God touches the culture and its expressions of culture and transforms them, taking them through a death and resurrection process. The basic revelation of God calling man to share his love and

---

[226] Cf. M. AMALADOSS, "Inculturation: Theological Perspectives", in *Jeevadhara* 6 (1976), 296-297.

[227] Ibid., 297.

[228] Cf. P. SCHINELLER, *A Handbook on Inculturation,* op. cit., 48.

[229] Ibid., 49.

[230] M. AMALADOSS, "Inculturation: Theological Perspectives", op. cit., 298.

[231] M. AMALADOSS, "Inculturation: Theological Perspectives", op. cit., 300.

life, and man's response to this revelation in faith can be meaningful to him only when it is expressed in a way that is tangible, also lived and celebrated in life.[232]

2.3.4. Federation of Asian Bishops' Conferences

The Federation of Asian Bishops' Conferences (FABC) is constituted by the bishops of the various local Churches of Asia. The members of this Federation are the bishops' conferences in South and East Asia. Despite many differences the people of this region are linked together to a considerable degree by sharing quite a number of religious and moral values in their respective cultures.

In spite of the fact that Christianity was born in Asia, the vast majority of her population are non-Christians. Christians account only for about 2.8% of the total population of Asia.[233] Although the Church is appreciated for her charitable and humanitarian activities, she has not touched deeply enough the Asian spirit. Therefore the Church in Asia now gives priority to the proclamation of the Gospel "whereby living faith is awakened in non-Christians and fostered in Christians."[234] This proclamation will be effective only when the proclaiming communities live out the Gospel, identify themselves with the people, their history, their aspirations and their struggles, etc. In short, the proclaiming community needs to understand the mind of the people and groups, their deeper spirit, and help the people to transform themselves without alienating themselves from their roots, thereby letting them be fully and totally Asian in every aspect of their life. When Christ encountered persons and groups he touched their inner spirit, awakening them to respond through an internal transformation.[235] "Christ does no violence to nature, to the deeper identity of any social group. He is not an external agent imposing strange norms from without. He is an inner force stirring into life the dormant potentialities of a given society."[236] Therefore the Church

"seeks to share whatever truly belongs to the people: its meanings and its values, its aspirations, its thoughts and its language, its songs and its artistry. This comes out of the realisation that the Church should be well integrated into the larger community of peoples, something which is impossible if it doesn't share their culture and way of life."[237]

---

[232] There are many and various efforts to theologise which also lead to different approaches, as for instance: liberation theology, justice and peace theology, etc. But this study here is focused mainly on theologising about the Oraon culture as orientation for evangelisation, thus aiming at a local theology of inculturation.

[233] Cf. SECRETERIA STATUS, *Annuarium Statisticum Ecclesiae* 1993, 18.

[234] Statements of the First Plenary Assembly of the FABC, *His Gospel to Our Peoples*, op. cit., (Taipei: 1976), 49.

[235] Cf. T. MENAMPARAMPIL, "Cultures and Evangelisation", in *Evangelisation in India* (Shillong: Pastoral Centre, 1987), 10.

[236] T. MENAMPARAMPIL, "Cultures and Evangelisation", op. cit., 11.

[237] F. WILFRED, "Federation of Asian Bishops' Conferences", in *For All The Peoples of Asia*, FABC Documents from 1970 to 1991 (Quezon City: Claretian Publications, 1992), xxv.

The Church exists to offer the saving presence of the Lord. "The Church is the universal sacrament of salvation,"[238] an efficacious sign of the presence of Jesus. This sign must be made tangible, visible to all peoples, then "the sign must be incarnate, enfleshed and rooted in the concrete life of every people throughout history. Hence the law of the incarnation of the Son is continued in the law of the Catholicity of the Church and in the imperative of inculturation (indigenisation, localisation)."[239]

The FABC's first meeting held at Taipei in 1974 discussed evangelisation in Asia. The primary focus of the evangelisation in Asia is to build up a truly local Church. According to the Asian bishops "the local Church is a Church incarnate in a people, a Church indigenous and inculturated. And this means concretely a Church in continuous, humble and loving dialogue with the living traditions, the cultures, the religions.... in brief, with all the life realities of the people in whose midst it has sunk its roots deeply and whose history and life it gladly makes its own."[240]

Inculturation is not a sociological or anthropological issue. It is a theological matter. "It brings the Gospel into the heart of the people in their concrete life-situations in order to transform standards of judgement, reigning values, interests, patterns of thinking, motives and ideals, it belongs to the very core of evangelisation."[241] In imitation of Christ, the Church tries to become one with the society in whose midst she pitches her tent. Thus being incarnate in their midst as intimately as possible she offers them the Gospel values and effects in them a transformation, making them into a new creation. "Inculturation transforms the life of the community from within. It gives rise to new patterns of relationships and behaviour, a new way of worship, a new way of theologising."[242]

Incarnation of the Gospel implies not only inculturation but also purification of the culture from all that is sinful and dehumanising there by ennobling all that is good and positive in it. Such a twofold inculturation is an urgent need in Asia so that the Gospel may not appear to be an alien body. Inculturation goes far beyond mere adaptation. It is a true incarnation: "It means the intimate transformation of authentic cultural values through their integration in Christianity and in the insertion of Christianity in the various human cultures."[243]

---

[238] LG 48.

[239] Statement of the First Plenary Assembly of the FABC, *His Gospel to our Peoples,* op. cit., (Taipei: 1976), 55.

[240] Ibid., 332.

[241] FABC Papers, No. 41, 3.

[242] FABC Papers, No. 41, 5.

[243] EXTRAORDINARY ASSEMBLY OF THE SYNOD OF BISHOPS (1985, Final Report, II, D, 4., quoted in SYNOD OF BISHOPS' SPECIAL ASSEMBLY FOR ASIA, *Lineamenta* (Vatican City:1996), 50.

"This is a process that is profound, all embracing, difficult and slow. It is a true symbiosis between the culture and the Gospel. One cannot overestimate the importance of inculturation in the context of the cultures and history of Asia, since it is essential for the Church to become "an intelligible sign of what she is and a more effective instrument of mission."[244]

The Holy Spirit inspires the people to discern and to find out the good values that are present in the cultures and living traditions. Inculturation is a gift of the Holy Spirit. Therefore genuine inculturation accepts persons and communities of other living religions and traditions, also helps them to purify themselves without losing their identity.

"Inculturation touches what is most intimate and sensitive in the human heart ...It should induce a continual and ever more radical conversion, sharing the death of Christ so that day by day live in him a new life. Clearly the message of salvation needs to be transmitted in a style fully in tune with the people's life-experiences, and therefore in harmony with their cultural setting."[245]

Asian Christianity should find out what is authentically human in Asian peoples' cultures, thus promoting local Churches fully and truly incarnated in the life and culture of the people. And then the people of Asia must find their Saviour as an Asian involved and interested in "their lives, their history, their concerns and aspirations, their search for a more human, more fraternal society."[246]

2.3.5. The Indian Church

The Church of India is characterised by the particular fact that it is constituted of three distinct individual churches with their own rites: Syro-Malabar, Syro-Malankara and Latin. Each one of them and all together are responsible for the evangelisation of this sub-continent. The Church in India is also made up of very different ethnical groups, beginning from the ancient populations at the coast of Malabar to the tribal areas of the North and North East. "Perhaps nowhere in the world is such a variety of languages and of cultural and ecclesiastical traditions enshrined in one and the same local Church as in India."[247]

The Indian Church realises its responsibility to offer the Good News in such a way that it becomes relevant to her people in their concrete life situations. The Church searches for genuine Indian identity, by encouraging popular piety, by allowing para-liturgical celebrations, and by developing an indigenous theology, etc. "Therefore it is the fundamental mission of the Church in India to become

[244] SYNOD OF BISHOPS' SPECIAL ASSEMBLY FOR ASIA, *Lineamenta* (Vatican City: 1996), 50.

[245] FABC Papers, No. 41, 15.

[246] Final Statement of FABC Assembly, *His Gospel to our Peoples.*, op. cit., 223.

[247] M. TEJIDO, (ed.), The communication from C.B.C.I. to the Synod of Bishops in Rome submitted to and approved by the general assembly on January 14, 1974 (Manila: 1975), 25.

transparent to the Good News of salvation in Jesus Christ and to proclaim it by her own words, deeds and life-style."[248]

India has a mosaic of languages and cultures; it is the birth place of numerous religions. The major religious communities of the country are the Hindus, Muslims, Christians, Sikhs, Buddhists, Jains and Parsis. Of these the last two are numerically rather insignificant. Christianity in India is almost as ancient as Christianity itself. Yet Christians are only 2.43% of the total population.[249] Despite the fact that Christianity has made many praiseworthy contributions to the growth of the Country through her educational institutions, health services and social service centres, Christianity has still not really touched the Indian mind.

When we speak of the failure of evangelisation in India, we often tend to blame the missionaries, that they did not adapt themselves to the culture and customs of the country. It is true in a certain sense that they often failed in this respect. We have also instances where adaptation efforts were forbidden, e.g. in the case of Robert de Nobili and Brahmabandhu Upadhaya.[250] Many even despised the culture and customs of India and branded Hinduism as idolatry and the Hindus as devil-worshippers destined for hell. The Church cannot evangelise unless she first lives the incarnating sense of the Gospel accepting the various differences in the Church.

India is permeated with a deep religiosity of her people. Therefore to be relevant in India the Church should first and foremost become a deeply religious reality, a community rooted in God. "She must unambiguously present herself as a worshipping community in which both personal and community prayer is expressed in forms of traditional Indian spirituality."[251] This would help the Church to be a communion of believers who "worship God in a spirit of true contemplation in forms that are recognisable and dear to the Indian spirit."[252] The rich Christian contemplative and mystical tradition should be brought into dialogue with the Indian sources. "In order to be truly indigenous, contemplative communities in India must have a *Sadhana* or discipline that is rooted in Indian tradition."[253]

---

[248] M. TEJIDO, (ed.), The communication from C.B.C.I. to the Synod of Bishops in Rome submitted to and approved by the general assembly on January 14, 1974 (Manila: 1975), 25. 27.

[249] Cf. MALAYALA MANORAMA COMPANY LTD, *Manorama Year Book 1992* (Kottayam: Kerala, 1992), 427.

[250] "In 1619, the Archbishop of Goa accused Robert de Nobili of 'favouring idolatry and diabolical practices.'A hundred years ago, Brahma bandhu Upadhaya's move to found an Indian monastery was opposed by ecclesiastical authorities." (S. ANAND, "Inculturation in India: Yesterday, Today and Tomorrow, in *Indian Missiological Review*, 19 (1997), 21).

[251] M. TEJIDO, (ed.), The communication from C.B.C.I. to the Synod of Bishops in Rome, op. cit., 31.

[252] Ibid., 31.

[253] M. TEJIDO, (ed.), The communication from C.B.C.I. to the Synod of Bishops in Rome, op. cit.,40.

Considering all these factors and making serious observations about India, one may find that efforts of inculturation are done in certain areas. But Christianity has not yet attracted the Indian mind. Forgetting a partly erroneous past, the missionaries now make every possible attempt to learn the holy Scriptures of ancient India, to enter into dialogue with the different religious traditions of India, and to find doctrinal similarities to understand the culture and customs of the country, and thus to incorporate Indian cultural and religious values into Christianity. According to D. S. Amalorpavadass, the late great Indian theologian, the efforts made in the Roman Catholic Church towards inculturation are the following:

> (1) Linguistic adaptation learning and use of the Indian languages. (2) Formation of local clergy. (3) Sociological adaptation: in Kerala, Tamilnadu, Andra Pradesh and Chotanagpur- Christians have the same way of life as the non-Christians, following the same social customs in dress, food, habitation, recreation, communication. (4) Incarnation of the Gospel in the concrete life-situations. (5) The domain of art. Insufficiency or lack of adaptation: painting, decoration, sculpture, architecture, dance, music, drama.[254]

The Liturgy commission of C.B.C.I. has introduced many an adaptation in the Liturgy. For instance they introduced an Indian rite for the Eucharistic liturgy. It serves as a model of liturgical adaptation. Yet the Indian Church has a long way to go in the area of inculturation. There have been a few major initiatives: The Catholic Ashram movement is one of them which tries to enter into the Indian spiritual tradition at its very source. The efforts to develop a genuine theology is another of ongoing initiative. There are efforts to establish understanding and communion among various religious communities. The concern for the integrity of creation (mother earth) is also a step in the direction of inculturation.[255]

Today, at the threshold of the 21stcentury, the signs of the times demand of the Indian Church an enlightened approach towards the presentation of the Gospel message to the people of India. As the Word became flesh so it is necessary to assimilate, to a certain measure, the forms of life of those to whom one should carry the message of Christ, without vindicating privileges. And without maintaining the wall of an incomprehensible language, we must share common usages, put ourselves in a climate of dialogue.[256]

---

[254] D. S. AMALORPAVADASS, *Efforts Made in the Roman Catholic Church Toward Indigenisation* (Bangalore: N.B.C.L.C. 1971), 8.

[255] Cf. D. S. AMALORPAVADASS, *Official meeting of the C.B.C.I. Commission for Liturgy*, (Bangalore: National Liturgical Centre, 1978), 111-136. also cf. idem, *Towards Indigenisation in the Liturgy* (Bangalore: N.B.C.L.C. no date), 58-70.

[256] Cf. ES 87.

We cannot neglect that Christianity in India to a large extend is influenced by Hinduism, which has shaped and formed the culture of India. Therefore inculturation in India involves incarnation into a largely Hindu culture. However in the Chotanagpur context the tribal culture is the major influence and hence there is a need to assimilate its values into the Chotanagpur Church and to integrate Gospel values into the existing cultural context.

2.4. Importance of Inculturation in the Mission of Chotanagpur Church

As we have seen, the Oraons of Chotanagpur had an experience similar to that of the chosen people of the Old Testament Israel. God heard their cry and came down to liberate them from the hands of non-tribals (*zamindars*, landlords, money-lenders) through the person of Father Constant Lievens S. J., offering them the Good News - Jesus Christ. God is in Jesus Christ Emmanuel - God among His people. Also today the task of the Church is to present Christ and his message in the Oraon culture and context, as a liberating message enabling them to become a people - a chosen people. This means enabling the Oraons to become genuinely Oraon (tribal) Christians - indigenous Christians.

"It implies solidarity with men, involvement in all their problems, and entry into the dynamism and adventure of human history with all that they imply, and in all that they demand, problems of hunger and disease, ignorance and illiteracy, unemployment and frustration, struggles of men for liberation from all the forces of oppression and injustice, slavery and alienation, integral development of man, contemporary culture and its all-pervading effects, wars and world peace, religious quest and experience of God."[257]

An Oraon cannot be understood apart from his community, and his ancestors and his ancestral land and forests. "The devout tribesman is committed to God, to the tribe and to his ancestors. He also firmly believes in countless other spirits whom he is scared of offending."[258] He offers propitiatory sacrifices in order to keep them well disposed, but he is not committed to them. This will not impair his faith in *Dharmes*, the Supreme Being, in his ancestors and in the tribe. In the process of becoming a Christian, one's identity as an Oraon (tribal) should not be interrupted or destroyed. Faith in one God and the communitarian aspect of Oraon life are in line with Christian ideals. This collective dimension "plays a very important role in the communitarian life of a society. Religious rituals become central in the life of a tribal community."[259] Belonging together is the key to unity and cohesion in a tribal society. Therefore there is a fear that acceptance of Christianity or conversion to any other religion may disorganise the society. It takes time to adjust the mind to a different outlook, and to re-organise

---

[257] D. S. AMALORPAVADASS, *Main Problems in Preaching the Gospel Today,* (Bangalore: N.B.C.L.C., 1973), 10.

[258] A. VAN EXEM, "The Gospel to the Sarna Tribal", in *Bible Bhashyam,* XVII, 4 (1991), 243.

[259] C. LAKRA, "Christianity and Tribal Identity", in *Religion and Society*, Vol. 34 (1989), 36.

and to re-coordinate the old elements in the culture with the new religious outlook. It throws light unto the importance of genuine inculturation in the evangelising mission of the Chotanagpur Church. Inculturation in the context of evangelisation would also acknowledge the need for purification of every culture. "Since culture is a human creation and is therefore marked by sin, it too needs to be healed, ennobled and perfected."[260] This is applicable to Oraon culture too.

Christ became man and considered his mission as preaching the Good News of liberation and beatitude to the poor. "This implied incarnation with the people through unconditional identification, genuine solidarity with them, concrete involvement in their struggle for more human existence, and sharing their life-style in poverty and simplicity."[261] The Gospel is meant to be the Good News to its hearers. Jesus must be preached as the goal and hope of the hopeless. When the hearers can identify in him the pains of their daily life, then it makes a difference. "*Sarna* people would not analyse, systematise or vivisect the Gospel. They would savour it until it spoke for itself, and they would refrain from putting their intuition into words."[262] Inculturation will enable the *Sarna* people to worship their God in spirit and truth.

The foreign missionaries and now the natives are keenly aware of the need for preserving their tribal identity, traditional tenets, and particularly ancient values of co-operation, mutual respect, equality, brotherhood, and community life. As Oraons are a communitarian society, community gatherings and liturgy are most important. Hence the evangelisation of Chotanagpur seeks to promote in particular the inculturation of communal aspects, especially in the liturgy, as the SC says: "liturgy is the summit toward which the activity of the Church is directed."[263] No doubt liturgy is the element that unites the Oraon (tribal) Christians and promotes their community identity.

"For St. Paul, both liturgy and evangelisation were proclamations of the Gospel. Evangelisation was oriented to the liturgy in the sense that it created a community that was transformed and made capable of offering acceptable worship to the Father. Hence he calls his ministry of evangelisation a liturgical act. `He has appointed me as a priest (Leitourgon) of Jesus Christ, and I am to carry out my priestly duty by bringing the Good News (hierourgounta to euangelion) from God to the pagans, and so make them acceptable as an offering (prosphora), made holy by the Holy Spirit' (Rom. 15:16). Evangelisation here is understood in terms

---

260 RM 54a.

261 D. S. AMALORPAVADASS, "Socio-Economic Development as an Integral Part of Evangelisation in India", in *Indian Missiological Review*, 6 (1984), 217.

262 A. VAN EXEM, "The Gospel to the Sarna Tribal", in *Bible Bhashyam* XVII, 4 (1991), 243.

263 SC 10.

of total transformation and worship as an expression of the new relationship of man in Christ to God."[264]

By 'liturgy' we mean the official, public worship and prayer, the celebration and the administration of the sacraments and sacramentals. In so far as these are carried out in the language, symbols, myths and customs peculiar to the Oraons' culture, the celebration is meaningful for them. Even though the scope of inculturation in Chotanagpur is an all-embracing one, special efforts are being made in the area of worship as this has so much to do with the Oraons life.

As we have seen the liturgical renewal envisaged by Vatican II includes indigenisation of worship, in keeping with the local cultures and religious traditions based on the norms[265] of the Constitution on Sacred Liturgy. The Chotanagpur Missionaries are well aware of this fact and looking back to the past approaches of our pioneer missionaries from the period Lievens, inculturation now seems to be taken seriously. Thus some of the cultural traditions are being introduced in the celebration of the Eucharist. For instance the washing and wiping of the hands of the celebrant or celebrants as a sign of respect, love and welcome; the integration of tribal dances during the entrance procession; use of tribal dialect 'Sadri'[266] for catechesis and worship in the Churches. Native and seasonal tunes are also being adapted for Church hymns and prayers during Mass. The liturgical texts are done in vernacular and in tribal dialect. The application of tribal symbols on the Mass vestments and on the decoration of the sacrificial altar.

Considering the missionary value of evangelization attempts are being made to inculturate the local feasts into the liturgical celebrations. In this context this study is an exploration to seek out the possibilities for a meaningful evangelization through inculturation by finding out the richness of the Oraon culture in its various expressions.

Chapter Summary

The developing Church of Chotanagpur is primarily a community of tribals with a particular history as well as a particular culture. They have their aspirations, struggles, limitations and riches. And it is the task of the missionary to understand the signs of the times, to discern the Gospel message and to present it to them in a relevant way, by which a sound identity as tribal Christians is fostered to avoid unnecessary alienation. "Each local or particular Church is called in the Holy Spirit to be the sacrament which manifests Christ, crucified and risen, enfleshed in a particular culture."[267]

---

[264] P. PUTHANANGADY, "A Missionary Approach to Liturgy", in *Indian Missiological Review* 3 (July 1979), 237.

[265] Cf. SC 37-40.

[266] Eventhough *Kurukh* is the dialect of the Oraons, for liturgical celebrations *Sadri* which is the lingua franca of the tribals is being used where there is a heterogeneous language group.

[267] THE INTERNATIONAL THEOLOGICAL COMMISSION, *Faith and Inculturation*, 29.

Through these studies we have arrived at a point to understand that inculturation is an essential aspect of evangelisation of the tribals - the Oraons of the Chotanagpur Church. Since their religiosity is so much in relation with their culture, it is important to analyse the various aspects that constitute their religious and cultural heritage. Therefore in the following chapter we shall deal with the 'Basic Beliefs of Oraon Traditional Religion.'

Chapter 3

BASIC BELIEFS OF ORAON TRADITIONAL RELIGION

Introductory Remarks

After discussing the historical background of the Christian faith in Chotanagpur, and analysing the theological principles concerning inculturation in evangelising Chotanagpur, we now look at the traditional religiosity of the Oraons. In this chapter we shall investigate some 'Basic Beliefs of Oraon Traditional Religion.' The basic beliefs of Oraon traditional religion are grouped under three main categories for convenience of the present study, even though some of the written sources prefer different ways of grouping. Thus there are: the world of Supernatural Beings, Myths dealing with Creation and the Concept of Man, and the Idea of Sin and Salvation. In the traditional view, the interactions of man, always as a member of the community, with the Supernatural Beings can bring him salvation if it is according to the norms of the society. We will see how far this corresponds to Christian convictions or even may become a path for evangelisation.

3.1. Concept of *Dharmes* (Supreme Being)

Dharmes is the Supreme Being of Oraons or Kurukhar.[268] The term *Dharmes* is a *Kurukh* word which indicates to the Supreme Being. The co-existence of good and evil, the bounty of nature, the concern of sympathetic people and the cruelty of the evil-minded exploiters, form part of an everyday experience of the Oraons of Chotanagpur. Shaped by this basic dichotomy of existence, they conceive creation, birth, life, sustenance, health, happiness, prosperity, communion within the tribe as 'good'. They consider death, misfortunes, bad luck, harm, injury, crop failure, famine, sickness, moral degradation, etc. as 'evil'. While they hold the

[268] Oraons are known as *Kurukh* or *Kurukhar* in their language.

view that the supernatural agencies are responsible for both good and evil, they ascribe 'good' to their God *Dharmes*, the source and origin of all good, and 'evil' to the malicious spirits.[269]

It is not wrong if we say that the Oraons do not have a well-developed theodicy. The major portion of their religious activities are concentrated around the cult of spirits in order to placate them. In this respect E. T. Dalton writes "though acknowledged, recognised, and reverenced, he (*Dharmes*) is neglected, whilst the malignant spirits are adored."[270] E. T. Dalton is partly correct when referring to P. Ekka who says "*Dharmes* or the Supreme Being, the creator of the universe, is acknowledged as the highest divinity by the Oraons."[271] "They invoke him at every critical phase of their life. They propitiate also the minor spirits in an attempt to solve the problem of suffering."[272] Both E. T. Dalton and P. Ekka admit the fact that Oraons placate spirits and this is very much linked to their understanding of evil, also as a fulfilment of the commandment of *Dharmes* who ordered the spirits to depend on Oraons for their sustenance. However in the words of P. Dehon, "Oraons have a more perfect idea of God than any other tribes of Chotanagpur."[273]

3.1.1. Nature of *Dharmes*

"*Dharmes* is regarded as the source of light and life."[274] He is a highly beneficent being and rich in his wisdom. In his benevolent designs he created the human beings and he has preserved them in his goodness and mercy.[275] The older name used for *Dharmes* is *Biri-Belas*. It means Sun. This is not an identification of the sun with *Dharmes*. "It is rather that the Oraon sees God manifest in the sun just as the Hebrews once saw... the glory of the Lord in the fiery column and in the lightening and thunder on Mount Sinai."[276]

White, the brightness of the sun, is the appropriate colour for *Dharmes*. Therefore the sacrificial victim, a fowl or a he-goat, must be of a white colour. The Oraon must turn his face to the East in the direction of the rising sun while offering prayers or sacrifices. In support of this view, S. C. Roy, the most authoritative writer on Oraons, quotes Colonel Dalton, who writes about Oraons

---

[269] Cf. B. TIRKEY, *Oraon Symbols*, op. cit., 19.

[270] E.T. DALTON, *Descriptive Ethnology of Bengal*, op. cit., 262.

[271] P. EKKA, *The Mundas and Oraons of Chotanagpur*, Unpublished B. Litt. Thesis (Oxford: Campion Hall, 1960), 256.

[272] Idem., *Catholic Adaptation of Adivasi Customs*, A Summary of the talk given at the Missionary Meeting at Archbishop's House (Ranchi: 1967), 1.

[273] P. DEHON, "Religion and Customs of the Uraons", op. cit., 25.

[274] F. HAHN and W. CROOKE, "Oraons", in J. HASTINGS (ed.), *Encyclopaedia of Religion and Ethics*, Vol. 9 (New York: T.&T. Clark, 1917), 502.

[275] Cf. E. T. DALTON, *Descriptive Ethnology of Bengal*, op. cit., 262.

[276] P. EKKA., *The Mundas and Oraons*, op. cit., 256.

that "like Mundas,[277] they acknowledge a supreme God, adored as *Dharmi* or *Dharmesh*, the Holy one, who is manifest in the Sun."[278] As the sun is up above in the sky it sheds light on everything on earth dispelling the darkness and its terrors, bringing blessing on all the inhabitants on the earth, similarly the Oraon believes that *Dharmes* observes all that men and spirits do. Some say that he not only observes all they do but also knows all that they think.[279]

Although *Dharmes* is closely associated with the sun, S. C. Roy who has written most comprehensively on the Oraon religion is most emphatic in denying that the Oraons in any way identify God with the sun.

"But at the present day, at any rate, the idea of God or the Supreme Spirit is to all intents and purposes separated in the Oraon's mind from the great luminary of the day. And the Oraon thinks, and there appear to be good reasons to think with him, that God has been known to the tribe or revealed Himself to them from the very beginning of the creation of man, not as a *deity* but as *the Deity*. And it would appear more reasonable to hold that *Dharmes* is not the personification of an element of nature nor the personified power of society, nor the Chief of the host of spirits and ghosts that infest the world. The Oraon regards him as anterior to all, the Author and Preserver, Controller and Punisher of men, gods and spirits- of all that exists in the visible and the invisible universe."[280]

Even though the Oraon admits that *Dharmes* is very powerful and Lord of all, yet he does not have frequent recourse to *Dharmes*. Most of his time is spent in appeasing the spirits. "When everything else fails, when the spirits fail to alleviate his sufferings then he goes to him (*Dharmes*) as the last resort, as the final appeal, saying '*Akkuga Ninim ra'aday*' (Thou art my final resort)."[281] In their conversations, especially with their Hindu neighbours, they also use the term *Bhagwan*, the Hindi name for God.

3.1.2. Various Attributes of *Dharmes*

The Oraon myths and rituals give us some of the important attributes of *Dharmes*. In the creation myth *Dharmes* is presented as anterior to all. He is the maker of

---

[277] Mundas are said to be the oldest settlers of Chotanagpur, among whom Oraons live and found welcome during their settlement in Chotanagpur. Living in close contacts with each other, both tribes have shared roughly the same religious beliefs, yet differed in certain aspects. *Singbonga* is the Supreme Being of the Mundas.The term *Singbonga* means Sun God. They do believe that *Singbonga* is their creator God and the Sun is made by him. They do not worship the Sun.Worship is given only to the Supreme Being. (Cf. V. PALATTY, *The Concept of God in Sarna Religion of the Oraons and the Christian Concept of God*, Extract of doctoral dissertation (Rome: Pontificia Universitas Gregoriana, 1997), 29).

[278] E.T. DALTON, *Descriptive Ethnology of Bengal*, op. cit, 262.

[279] Cf. S. C. ROY, *Oraon Religion and Customs*, op. cit., 16.

[280] Ibid., 17.

[281] J. LAKRA, *Tribal Cultural Anthropology*, Unpublished notes (Ranchi: St. Albert's College, 1996), 23.

the world and all that lives in it. "The *Sarna* discerns an all good, transcendent and personal God,[282] creator of cosmos and man. The creator is presented anthropomorphically as an old man, with snow - white hair, a snow-white beard... and dressed in snow-white garments."[283]

Dharmes is the Creator, giver of life and protector of all that exists. He is the provider of all good. He is the giver of knowledge and wisdom. He taught the first human couple all that is needed for their life - like cultivation, procreation of children, offering of sacrifices, etc. "He is the giver of land, nature, cattle, crops, children, clans and the tribe."[284]

Though the Oraons consider *Dharmes* anthropomorphically as an old man, they are aware that "he is a 'pure spirit,' making sacrifice they tell him, 'you do not hunger for our food or thirst for our drink, yet, take and accept my offering and gift, divide and distribute it among your servants and attendants' (spirits)."[285] *Dharmes* does not have a temple or a sacred grove or any other seat specially assigned to him. There is no artistic representation in painting or sculpture. He is a transcendent God for them.

Oraons address *Dharmes* as 'Father' in their prayer. *Nin Dharme, Baba hekdae* (Thou *Dharmes* art our father). It is to him that they attribute the power to control the spirits, power to save them from the 'evil eye' and 'evil mouth' (poisonous praise).[286] Thus the immanence of a 'caring God' is expressed here.

This type of the immanence of God and his involvement in history are understood as an involvement on behalf of the tribe. He is the God of the tribe. The tribe is created and cared for by *Dharmes*. It is he who instituted, so to say, the marriage of the *Bhaiya-Bhahin* (brother-sister)[287] and taught them how to cultivate different crops.[288] It is *Dharmes* who taught the couple the religious ritual - *Dandakatta* (tooth-splitting or breaking),[289] through which they could honour their God, and seek his protection for themselves, their crops and for

---

[282] According to late A. Van Exem, the God of the *Sarna* people (Oraons) is a personal God. *Dharmes* is thought of as a wise old man.This seems to be more a theoretical concept than a practical one, because in every-day life *Dharmes* is considered a relatively distant God.

[283] A. VANEXEM, "Creation and Fall in Sarna Religion", in *Sevartham,* 9 (1984), 11.

[284] J. LAKRA, *Tribal Cultural Anthropology,* op. cit., 23.

[285] A. VAN EXEM, "Creation and Fall in Sarna Religion", op. cit., 11-12.

[286] Cf. S. C. ROY, *Oraon Religion and Customs,* op. cit., 16.

[287] Brother and sister: this must be understood as members of the same tribe; not as members of the same clan. Marriage within the same clan is not allowed whereas marriage within the same tribe is welcomed.

[288] Cf. P. KULLU, "Tribal Culture-Religion in Practice", in *Sevartham,* 19 (1994), 58.

[289] An exclusive ritual for *Dharmes.*The main purpose of the ritual is to obtain prosperity in all spheres. According to Oraons *Dharmes* is all powerful and so he eliminates the evil intentions of malicious spirits and persons who have the power to destroy or damage other people's prosperity-wealth, crops, children etc. Hence this term literally means to break down the influence of evil eye and evil words. (Cf. B. TIRKEY, *Oraon Symbols.,* op. cit., 27-29).

all their possessions. One of the main purposes of this ritual is the welfare of the tribe. Even if this ritual is performed by an individual, ultimately it is the good of the tribe that is desired. The individual is situated within the tribe, apart from which the life of the individual has no meaning for Oraons. Thus, Oraons consider *Dharmes* as 'God of the tribe' and themselves as 'God's own tribe.'[290]

The above study makes us to ask whether Oraons have a personal relationship with their Supreme God, a relationship that flowers into devotion. It is true that Oraons consider *Dharmes* to be more a 'caring' father than a 'loving' father, although the love is implied in his fatherhood. But this love is not a motive force that helps them to have a personal devotion (*bhakti*), a personal love relationship. Perhaps they need to wait for new messianic movements like the *Tana Bhagat* movement[291] to fulfil their aspirations for a personal devotion to God. The religion of the Oraons seemed to be incapable of generating in them this aspect of a personal relationship with their Supreme God. Therefore the challenge of Christianity is to help them to cultivate a deeper relationship with a God who loves each person, without diminishing their ideas of a God who cares for the whole community.

3.1.3. Uniqueness of *Dharmes*

The Oraons perform sacrificial ceremonies and make offerings to *Dharmes*, the Supreme God. The only ceremony in which *Dharmes* alone is invoked and in which sacrifice is offered to him alone is the *Dandakatta* (tooth-splitting) ceremony. This ceremony is also known by various other names, for instance "*Palkasna* - destroying evil tooth, breaking the mischief; *Danda Rengna* - dragging the twig, waving the wand; *Bhelwa phari* - Bhelwa twig-splitting; *Bhakh Khandna* - warding evil word."[292]

"The *Dandakatta* is divinely instituted, given and instructed by *Dharmes* himself."[293] Hence this ritual is performed as an act of worship to *Dharmes*. It expresses recognition of him as the Supreme Being, God and Creator. "The Oraon sacrificer offers sacrifice to *Dharmes* in his own name and in the name of the community acknowledging *Dharmes* as Creator, Father and Sustainer, who is glorious, all powerful, transcendent and immanent God."[294]

Dharmes is remembered and worshipped in every important event and phase of life. Therefore a *Dandakatta* ceremony is celebrated at birth, marriage and death,

---

290 Cf. B. TIRKEY, *Oraon Symbols*, op. cit., 30.

291 These movements flourished among the Oraons towards the beginning of twentieth century. The personal element of *bhakti* was an outstanding characteristic of them. These movements were primarily aimed at liberation from the oppression by the landlords. (Cf. P. EKKA, "Messianic Movements among the Chotanagpur Tribes", in *Sevartham*, 4 (1979), 29).

292 B. TIRKEY, *Oraon Symbols.*, op. cit., 26.

293 Ibid., 27.

294 Ibid., 26.

also at every venture of social consequences like important feasts and festivals. The blessing of *Dharmes* is sought through this ceremony at the commencement and successful completion of important tasks, such as the beginning of a new work, preparing the soil for sowing, harvesting and hunting expeditions. It is also performed for private needs and occasions.

Dharmes is the Pure Being and so he is offered a pure victim in sacrifice. White is as we have already indicated, the appropriate colour reserved for him which symbolises all his attributes. Thus they offer a white fowl, white he-goat or an egg. According to Oraons "an egg is full in itself, self contained life, serves best to symbolise pure life and is the most fitting and pre-eminent object to be offered to Dharmes, who is the source of all life."[295] Through this symbolism the Oraon offers his own life and surrenders himself to *Dharmes* his creator.

This is how *Dandakatta* is performed. "The officient at this ceremony recites the traditional Oraon genesis story, addresses prayers to God and offers him sacrifice of an egg wedged at the forked end of a split *bhelwa* (semicarpus anacardium) twig and placed over the centre of a mystic diagram of seven corners of the universe drawn in red, white and black (the Oraon rainbow) colours. The three colours are got in the form of powdered earth from the hearth, rice flour and charcoal dust. The rainbow, the biggest bow in creation, is believed to be a most potent weapon against *najar-gujar* (the evil eye) and the *bai-bhak* (evil-mouth). The egg is broken in order to symbolise and effect together with the spilt *bhelwa twig,* the bursting of the evil eye and the splitting of the evil mouth of malicious persons, wizards, witches and spirits, so that no harm may come to the Oraon's crops, but that he may be blessed with health, plenty and prosperity. The green eyes of a jealous neighbour or visitor and his curse couched in words of admiration, the Oraon holds, sure to let loose a horde of pests on his promising crops or some sickness on his now healthy family. The oil of the *bhelwa* nut is poisonous and a drop of it in the eye is sure to cause its permanent blindness, hence the use of a *bhelwa* twig to hold the sacrificial egg in order to impart it, its dreaded potency. ...To this day Oraon tradition asserts that this rite was prescribed to them by *Dharmes* himself when their crops were first attacked by beasts and pests."[296]

The *Dandakatta* ceremony is a ritual act to obtain God's blessings, i.e. healthy children, good crops and numerous heads of cattle, also protection from sickness and misfortune. It would appear to a common observer that the purpose of this ritual is confined to these pragmatic ends. But there is still another deeper dimension which we may call the 'memorial dimension.'[297]

"The memorial dimension...consists in the acknowledgement of *Dharmes* as the creator of the world and of man, in recalling the history of the (Oraon) tribe,

---

[295] B. TIRKEY, "Oraon Approaches to God and Spirits", in *Sevartham,* 7 (1982), 26.

[296] P. EKKA, *The Mundas and Oraons,* op. cit., 259-260.

[297] Cf. B. TIRKEY, "Oraon Approaches to God and Spirits", op. cit., 27.

and in professing that the ceremony is performed in obedience to the injunction of *Dharmes* himself. The words that the *Pahan* must utter while officiating at the ritual ceremony are: "Today, O *Dharmes*, I am performing the *bhelwa* twig splitting ceremony. Thou madest the twelve shades and thirteen shades (all beings)... O *Dharmes*, I, the sacrificer, have come as *Panch* (head) to perform the *Dandakatta* ceremony as commanded by Thee from Thy throne (a pair of chairs)... I am praying (saying this) as a *Panch* (for the whole community). I am speaking these words as instructed by Thee (correctly). To Thee I sacrifice now a thing without head or leg (an egg)."[298]

This ritual is an act of the highest worship to Dharmes, thus revealing his supremacy as the Supreme Being or God. It is both a specific form of worship and a ritual to obtain concrete fruits in this life. It is a complex ritual act acknowledged by the Oraons as something determined by *Dharmes* himself.

3.1.4. Convergences/Divergences and Possible Approaches for Evangelisation

In the *Dandakatta* ceremony the egg, pearl rice, and *bhelwa* twig[299] are placed at the centre of the circle with seven curves. The 'centre' stands as a "link between Heaven and Earth."[300] i.e. between Dharmes and the people. The twig is the representation of a life giving tree whose living sap eliminates the evils.[301] The egg, the twig and pearl rice, all these symbols signify the Supreme Being. And this Supreme Being can be compared to God the Father in Christianity. He is the winner over all evils, the Life and life giver. He is the new Adam who was elevated at the centre of the earth on a life giving tree-cross. "Adam was created at the centre of the earth, on the very same spot where, later on, the Cross of Jesus was to be erected,"[302] and mankind was redeemed by the blood of the Lord that he shed from the cross, the living sap.

The egg is broken and the yoke is split. The egg is self-contained life, pure and perfect life. The broken egg manifests a second birth, a supernatural birth. For Christians it can signify Christ whose body is broken in order to redeem the whole humankind from every bondage of body and spirit. The egg may symbolise again Christ in the tomb, and within the tomb the transformation takes place,

---

298 Cf. B. TIRKEY, "Oraon Approaches to God and Spirits", op. cit., 28.

299 Pearl rice: rice which is husked and cleaned after drying without par-boiled, *Bhelwa* tree is the symbol of destruction and death, it is a natural irritant to the eye. Hence it is said to destroy the evil eye and evil mouth and malicious intentions of evil minded people. (Cf. B.TIRKEY, *Oraon Symbols*, op. cit., 89).

300 M. ELIADE,. *Images and Symbols: Studies in Religious Symbolism* (New Jersey, Princeton: Princeton University Press, 1991), 41.

301 Cf. ibid., 42.

302 This text stems from a Syrian book "*The Cavern of Treasures,*" which is quoted in M. ELIADE, *Images and Symbols: Studies in Religious Symbolism,* op. cit., 43.

the resurrection. From there comes the new life.[303] "I am the resurrection and the life; he who believes in me, though he die, yet shall he live" (Jn. 11:25). Through his death Christ brings order to a disturbed world, the evil and its consequences have no power as long as a person lives in Christ and makes him the centre of his own existence. In him there is life and prosperity, there is a transforming power for all beings. He is the liberator who makes human beings free from all malicious influence. Pearl rice is also symbol of the fullness of life. It is white in colour, not touched by fire, hence full of life.

The above survey reveals that the traditional Oraon religion and Christian tradition hold, beneath the surface, similar views about God. In Christianity the Supreme Being or Absolute Reality is designated by the term 'God'. He is an absolute mystery. He reveals himself to man through his words and actions. The whole creation manifests his divine transcendence and absolute majesty. In the OT the glory of God is manifested with the metaphor of light or fire. "Yahweh both reveals and conceals his *kabod* in the cloud and in consuming fire (Ex. 16:7f; 16:10; 24: 15-17; 40:34f; 40:38; Deut. 5:24), a fire as bright and powerful as thunder and lightning, testifying to the powerful, inaccessible and terrible majesty of God."[304]

Therefore light is an element of theophany which inspires adoration and praise (cf. Ex. 15:1; Ps. 67:1, 80:3; Num. 6:25). The majesty of God has become visible in Jesus Christ. For John, God is light and this light is made seen in Jesus Christ who is the personal and tangible presence of God among men (cf. 1Jn. 1: 1-5; Jn. 1:14, 16; 3:19; 8: 12; 9:5).[305]

In Christian worship light signifies the presence of Jesus Christ, the Eternal Sun who destroys all darkness from the face of the earth. This symbol is very much familiar in Oraon religion. For Oraons the sun is the manifestation of *Dharmes*' glory and the sunlight removes darkness from the earth, then everything becomes illuminated. In other words *Dharmes*' eyes are like the sunlight. He sees everyone and everything. When Oraons offer their sacrifice to *Dharmes* they turn towards the East, the direction of the sun, thus again facing *Dharmes.*

The Bible gives a detailed account of God as the creator in Christian tradition "One of the central images of Wisdom writing is God the good creator"[306] (cf. Wis. 13:1-9). The basic thrust is the quest for order in life. God created the whole universe and humanity by his word (cf. Gen. 1-3). The parables of Jesus present God as the creator and as a watchful caretaker of the universe (cf. Mt. 6:26-30;

---

[303] Cf. R. GUENON, *Simboli delle Scienza Sacra* (Milano: Adelphi edizioni S.P.A., 1975), 197.

[304] H. BOUESSE, "Glory of God", in K. RAHNER, (ed.), *Encyclopaedia of Theology, The Concise Sacramentum Mundi,* Vol. 2 (London: Burns and Oates, 1975, reprinted 1986), 575.

[305] Cf. ibid., 575.

[306] A. FISCHER, "God", in C. STUHLMUELLER (ed.), *The Collegeville Pastoral Dictionary of Biblical Theology* (Minnesota: The Liturgical press, 1996), 386.

Mk. 4:26-29). *Dharmes* the creator is also depicted as a God who fought chaos and brought order by his well planned creation.

Christianity addresses God as father. This symbolism is used not in the context of dominating power, but of communicating life in becoming a 'father' to the people or by care for them (cf. Ex. 4:22; Deut. 32:6; Jer. 3:19; Is. 45: 9-11 64:8; Mal. 2:10).[307]

This idea of God as a father is manifested emphatically in the NT. Jesus calls God Abba-Father. And he said, "Abba, Father, all things are possible to thee; remove this cup from me; yet not what I will, but what thou wilt." (Mk. 14:36) Jesus is the only begotten Son of the Father (cf. Jn. 1:14, 18). He is the beloved Son in whom the Father is well pleased (cf. Lk. 3:22). Jesus and the Father are one (cf. Jn. 10:30). Thus Jesus is intimately related to the Father. The Gospel of Matthew depicts God as a loving and caring father (cf. Mt. 6:5-8, 26; 7:11; 10:29-31; 18:14,). He is a father of unconditional love who welcomed his prodigal son who squandered his wealth (cf. Lk. 15:11-33). Even though Oraons also call *Dharmes,* Father, this intimate filial relationship is not developed into a loving and devotional one as it is among Christians. This would be called *bhakti* in Indian tradition.

3.2. Oraon Spirit World

Besides believing in the Supreme Being Oraons also believe in the existence of numerous spirits. They recognise the seat of spiritual forces everywhere. These spiritual forces are animate and inanimate things who have the power to control human beings, their cattle, crops etc. Therefore an Oraon is preoccupied with the thought of how to please these spirits so that he may be freed from the harmful attack of the spirits. He has devised certain sacred rites, magic, spells and taboos in order to control these spirits.[308]

Spirithood is a mode of existence as it appears in the myth. In the Oraon understanding spirits are disembodied souls of *Asur* women.[309] As a punishment for their disobedience to *Dharmes*, they are forced to depend on human beings (Oraons) for their sustenance. Hence Oraons are constantly under compulsion to be on good terms with them. Therefore they offer sacrifices to these spirits in

---

[307] Cf. R. DONAHUE, "The God and Father of Our Lord Jesus Christ", in C. STUHLMUELLER (ed.), *The Collegeville Pastoral Dictionary of Biblical Theology,* op. cit., 387-388.

[308] Cf. J. LAKRA, *Tribal Cultural Anthropology,* op. cit., 25.

[309] They are the wives of the *Asur* brothers, those legendary people who smelted iron day and night. *Dharmes* punished those men for their disobedience by burning them in the furnace. Thus these women lost their husbands. Helpless as they were, they held on to *Dharmes* as he was disappearing in his glory into heavens. *Dharmes* in his kindness turned them into spirits and allowed them to depend on Oraons for their survival. (Cf. J. LAKRA, "The Genesis of Spirits: The Uraon Myth", in *Sevartham,* 11 (1986), 45-58).

order to placate them. It is not out of devotion but out of fear that they offer such sacrifices.[310]

It is also interesting to note that they have a group of spirits to guard their villages and hamlets, another group of spirits who act as guardians for young men and women, a third group of spirits for their families and kinsmen, yet another group to protect their fields, crops, and property etc. All these different spirits have different and specific jurisdictions and abodes. Besides there are spirits that are linked with hills, rivers, waterfalls and other objects like a flag, totem, emblems, weapons and musical instruments.[311]

The entire world of Supernatural Beings can be grouped further on such bases as "status," roles, functions etc. However some scholars, who speak very convincingly of monotheism with *Dharmes* as the Supreme Being or God, also refer to other divinities or deities, who are powerful and to whom the Oraons offer sacrifices. But it may seriously be questioned whether this ascription of divine qualities (except in the case of *Dharmes*) can really stand up to a more critical investigation. Perhaps one is closer to the thinking of the people themselves, to reserve for those entities, who are endowed with supernatural powers, the notion of spirits. There are ancestor spirits, village spirits, clan and class spirits, minor spirits who are ambivalent in their nature; there also appear impersonal or man made things which are believed to be animated by mysterious forces that can influence people's life. Therefore, based on the nature of spirits, we can divide them into ambivalent spirits and malevolent spirits according to their effects. (This might be the case with ancestors, nature phenomenon and man made forces). It should be added, for completeness sake, that many other categorisations are possible. Unfortunately our usual classification schemes do not always fit the phenomenological experience of many situations, and this applies also to Oraon traditions. Theoretically one could distinguish, within a scale of supernatural powers, on the one hand personal beings with *Dharmes* on the top and ancestral and the other higher spirits following, and on the other hand impersonal beings with nature phenomenon and man-made things and some undefined, anonymous forces. However, for the reasons already indicated we will remain with the criteria as mentioned above.

3.2.1. Ancestor Spirits

Oraons have a very close affinity and great regard for their *pachbalar*[312] (ancestors). They are seen as loving, good and caring relatives even after their death. The

---

[310] Cf. B. TIRKEY, "Oraon Approaches to God and spirits", op. cit., 41-42.

[311] Cf. L. P. VIDYARTHI and B. K. RAI, *The Tribal Culture of India* (Delhi: Concept Publishing Company, 1977), 251.

[312] *Pachbalar* are those Oraons who have been exalted or raised to the rank of the dead "ancestors." Only those who meet natural death (old age and sickness are considered natural) are given this honour. Those who face unnatural death (murder, suicide, dying by accident etc.) are

pachbalar or the ancestor spirits form one family or clan-group with their living descendants, whose welfare is now their special concern. "The invisible world in which the ancestors live is considered to be an extension of the visible world."[313] "The Oraons of our days believe that the spirits of their deceased fathers or grandfathers often come to attend the sick-beds of their living sons and grandsons."[314] And it is the duty of the living members to show their gratitude by offering sacrifices and making food offerings and libations, thus to ensure their repose.

Seeking assistance of the *pachbalar* (ancestor spirits) by means of a sacrifice or vow is relevant and necessary in moments of great distress, accidents or dangers and on the occasion of agricultural activities, such as sowing, paddy transplantation and harvesting. When there is a serious illness in a family, a vow is sometimes taken to offer, on recovery, a grey fowl to *pachbalar*.[315]

The soul of a deceased Oraon is believed to enter the community of the *pachbalar* (ancestor spirits) during the annual celebration of *harbora*[316] (bone burial) day. This is an annual celebration. The people collect the bones of all Oraons of a clan, who have died in the course of a year, and ceremoniously bury the bones in the clan ossuary (probably near a stream or a pond) known as *kundi*. It is believed that prior to this ceremonious admission into the community of the dead ancestors, the departed souls seek the company of the living.[317]

On the annual *harbora* day, before the bones are being deposited in the *kundi*, either a fowl or a pig is sacrificed and its blood is dropped ceremoniously into the pit dug in front of the dead persons hut. The officient of the ceremony invokes the names of the dead ancestors of that clan. A prayer is said so that the deceased may be accepted into the company of the dead ancestors.[318]

There are many other occasions the ancestors are remembered by the Oraons. When a child is given name the ancestor whose name he/she has taken is invoked and asked for his protection and blessing for the child. At the marriage of their children the two fathers-in law drink rice beer together and call on their

---

excluded from becoming *pachbalar*. Therefore the *harbora* ritual (which will be treated later) is performed only for those who had a natural death. (Cf. B. TIRKEY, *Smiling Oraon*, op. cit., 79).

[313] E. COELHO, "Ancestor Veneration Among the Hos", in *Sevartham*, 5 (1980), 98.

[314] S. C. ROY, *Oraon Religion and Customs*, op. cit., 20.

[315] Cf. P. EKKA, *The Mundas and Oraons,* op. cit., 267.

[316] "*Harbora* is the translation of the ashes of the dead to their final place of rest. As every successive cremation takes place, the half calcinated bones are picked up and piously kept in an urn, which is buried near the dead man's house. On the following January, a village pageant is organised, and the bones of all defuncts of the year are carried, amid dances, shouts and fierce drumming to the spot closer to a river." (A. GRIGNARD, *Oraon-English Dictionary* (Vienna: St. Gabriel, Administration of "Anthropos", 1924), 288.

[317] Cf. S. C. ROY, *Oraon Religion and Customs,* op. cit., 21.

[318] Cf. S. C. ROY, *Oraon Religion and Customs,* op. cit., 21.

dead ancestors' protection for the newly married couple. Similarly, when a newly built house is first occupied a sacrifice is offered and the ancestors are asked in prayer to bless the house and its inhabitants, to grant them protection from evil and prosperity in life.[319]

Thus in the life of the Oraons ancestors play a great role. They are looked upon as guardians of individuals, families and clans as well as the village community as a whole. It remains their duty to help their living members. Oraons believe that their ancestors are good people who have won the favours of the Supreme Being. Thus ancestor veneration is part of their life.

3.2.2. Convergences / Divergences and Possible Approaches for Evangelisation

Despite the fact that there is no sainthood in Oraon religion yet these ancestor spirits are like the patron saints of Christianity. Saints are persons who enjoy the beatific vision of God. "It is nothing less than full and perfect communion with God."[320] Christians venerate saints because of their participation in the life of Christ. This belief stems from the fact that even the body of the Christian is sanctified by baptism and other sacraments and is the dwelling place of the Holy Spirit. Therefore Christians show great respect to the bodies of those 'who sleep in Christ'.[321] Christians imitate saints because they are considered as heroic persons who have Christ-like virtues and qualities. Therefore it is a custom among Christians to give the names of a saint during baptism, thereby that particular saint becomes the patron saint for that person. In this respect the name day celebrations are more significant than birthdays. Christians also pray to the saints requesting them to intercede before God on behalf of their fellow Christians who are still on earth. At times special novenas are also conducted. Devotion to the saints gradually paved way to regard them as helpers in all troubles of everyday life. "The intercession of the saints depends as a concept on the idea of the Church as a family united in heaven and on earth as one body, in which all members are 'alive unto God' who is their life."[322] Together with the veneration of the bodies of the saints, there is also veneration given to other objects used by the saints (e.g. clothing, books, table etc.), also to places associated with the saints during their life (e.g. shrine of St. Antony of Padova, Saints of Assisi - St. Francis and St. Clare). These relics are tangible objects through which God may operate

[319] Cf. S. C. ROY, *Oraon Religion and Customs,* op. cit., 269.

[320] R. D. LAWLER, "Beatific vision", in R. SHAW (ed.), *Our Sunday Visitor's Encyclopedia of Catholic Doctrine* (Huntington: Our Sunday Visitor Publishing Division, 1997), 11.

[321] Cf. S LASH, "Relics, Theology of", in A. RICHARDSON AND J. BOWDEN (ed.), *The Westminster Dictionary of Christian Theology* (Philadelphia, Pennsylvania: The Westminster Press, 1983), 495.

[322] B. WARD, "Saints, Cult of the", in A. RICHARDSON AND J. BOWDEN (ed.), *The Westminster Dictionary of Christian Theology,* op. cit., 496.

in his Church and use them as channels of grace and instruments of healing.[323] Healing power was elicited by touching such things or praying in front of the image of a saint.

For Oraons ancestors are persons who link the living ones with the invisible world, through family, clan, and tribal ties. This awareness is the reflection of their family spirit and unity, one of the most important tribal values.[324] As there is no formal sainthood the above mentioned facts (veneration of the body of the saints, relics of the saints, imitation of the saints, novenas to the saints etc.) are absent in Oraon traditional religion. Yet we have seen that ancestor veneration has a positive value in their religion. Therefore the challenge of Christianity is to offer them a Christian view of such values. Proper catechesis is needed to change their belief system. They pay homage to the bones of their dead ancestors which can be considered as relics of the person. (In fact there is the transference of the remains of a saint in Christianity). The annual celebration *harbora* in itself is significant. It can be compared to All Saints day, as it signifies an incorporation into the company of *pachbalar*. Instead of an animal sacrifice, a meaningful eucharistic celebration can be offered, either on the death anniversary or on any specific day after death giving more attention to the virtues of that ancestor and thanking God for his life and the many blessings his fellow clan members received through him. This kind of sentiment may help the Oraons to get rid of their fear of the spirits (an attitude of obligation), and to stimulate love and respect which would lead to devotion.

3.2.3. Village Spirits

As already mentioned, these village spirits are ambivalent in nature, hence the Oraons propitiate them at regular intervals. There are four significant spirits, who are called general village spirits: *Chala pachcho, Darha deswali, Mahadania* and *Devimai*. They guard and protect the village from outside spirits and from sickness and calamities. The *pahan* (village priest) offers periodical sacrifices to these village spirits on behalf of the village community. "According to the tribals, guardian spirits are like police men patrolling the tribal villages and their boundaries, carrying huge axes."[325]

Besides the general village spirits, which are common to most of the Oraon villages, there are special village spirits peculiar to certain villages. These are the old *khuntbhuts* (tutelary spirit) of a clan or *manitabhuts* (family spirits) of a particular family, which on extinction of the clan or family have been promoted to the status of a village spirit. These spirits are called as *gairahi bhuts* and periodical sacrifices

---

[323] Cf. S LASH, "Relics, Theology of", in A. RICHARDSON AND J. BOWDEN (ed.), *The Westminster Dictionary of Christian Theology*, op. cit., 496.

[324] Cf. P. PONETTE, "Spirituality of Mundas", in *Sevartham*, 9 (1989), 76-77.

[325] P. KULLU, "Tribal Religion and Culture", in *Jeevadhara*, XXIV (1994), 101.

are offered to them by the local village priest lest they would cause harm to the village.[326]

Besides the spirits described above, to whom periodical sacrifices are offered on behalf of the village community, there is a whole class of undefined, indeterminate minor spirits. These are believed to reside in *ban* (woods) and *garha-dhorha* (rivers and streams) and in the nooks and corners within the *chatursima* (boundaries) of the village, and are collectively known as *ban sakti* (forest powers).[327] They are invoked on occasions of periodical sacrifices, especially on s*arhul* festival, otherwise no separate sacrifice is offered to these spirits.

3.2.4 Class and Clan Spirits

These are the guardian spirits for a particular class of people. The first to come under this class is *Chandi*, a female spirit, who is believed to bring success in hunting and war and also considered as a guardian spirit for unmarried young Oraons. Only bachelors are allowed to offer her sacrifices.[328]

Achrael is the guardian spirit of the women. The female members of an Oraon family or a group of families come together to worship this spirit. A male member officiates at this sacrifice and the female members participate in it.[329]

"The social significance of the *Achrael* cult is, then, its importance in knitting closely the women of an agnatic group after their departure from the their parental home on their marriage by occasionally gathering them together for a common worship of their patron spirit, *Achrael*."[330]

The *bhuinhars* or the descendants of the original founder or founders of an Oraon village are divided into *khunts* (clan). And these *khunts* are entrusted to make propitiation to their respective *khuntbhuts* (clan spirits) attached to the land they cultivate. The clearing of the primitive jungles for the purpose of establishing villages involved a disturbance of the spirits. Hence periodical sacrifices were made to appease them. A part of the family land is kept for these spirits by *bhuinhars* as their seats, and sacrifices are performed by a member of the family owning the land. They are believed to look after the health and crops, animals and other belongings.[331]

3.2.5. Minor Spirits

The non-*bhuinhar*[332] Oraons of a village do not have a clan or family, hence no *khuntbhut (*clan spirit). Instead they have household spirits. *Baranda pachcho*

---

[326] Cf. S. C. ROY, *Oraon Religion and Customs*, op. cit., 39-41.

[327] Cf. S. C. ROY, *Oraon Religion and Customs*, op. cit., 42.

[328] Cf. ibid., 43.

[329] Cf. ibid., 47-48.

[330] P. EKKA, *The Mundas and Oraons,* op. cit., 279.

[331] Cf. S. C. ROY, *Oraon Religion and Customs,* op. cit., 49.

[332] They are not the descendants of the original founders of the Oraon village.

(old lady *baranda*) is the guardian spirit of each separate household. This spirit is called by various names as *dangra nad* (bullock spirit) as bullocks are periodically offered to it. There is yet another name, *sakhri nad* or *chulha nad* (spirit of the hearth). When a young family separates from their parent family, setting up a new hearth (*chulha*) they need to offer a sacrifice to this spirit. It is supposed to be the guardian spirit of the threshing floor who guards the harvest in it.[333]

Since the Oraons depend very much on the help of the animals for their agricultural work, they have adopted *goensli nad* (a tutelary spirit) as the guardian spirit of the cattle shed. On the day of *Sohrai*, the feast of the cattle, they offer sacrifices to this spirit for the health and prosperity of the cattle.

Oraons offer sacrifices also to some powers mostly impersonal in nature and which are believed to be propitious or harmless. To these belong certain totem symbols, village flags and other village emblems, certain musical instruments and weapons, some bizarre fantastic-shaped natural objects or an uncanny weird-looking bit of jungle or awe inspiring hill or cascade, some particular tree or grove, a tank or a well.[334] The object itself or some part near to the object is smeared with *aruva chaval* (pearl rice) flour diluted in water and a dot of vermilion is daubed on it and occasionally a fowl is sacrificed.

3.2.6. Convergences / Divergences and Possible Approaches for Evangelisation

The disposition of the above mentioned spirits towards Oraons may be ambivalent in nature. They are venerated as guardian spirits of villages, class and clan, etc. The Oraons are eager to fulfil the obligatory rituals of these so called good (guardian) spirits. In spite of the fact that they are ambivalent in their behaviour, we can compare them to angels in Christianity. Christians practice devotion to the guardian angels. The word 'angel' designates the good spirit, envoy of the Divine, who are appointed by God for human beings in order to help, to guard (cf. Ex. 23:20; Gen. 24:7; Mt. 18:10), to lead and guide (cf. Tob. 6:2ff), to give counsel (cf. Tob. 12:6-15), and to bring the petitions of human beings before God (cf. Tob. 12:12; Rev. 8:2-4). Angels exercise a continual service by assisting the people in their daily life.[335] God could have carried out his providential and fatherly care to his children without the assistance of anybody, however he seeks his angels as his helpers and co-ordinators in order to carry out his designs. Thus an angel announced to the Blessed Virgin her election by God to become the Mother of the Saviour (cf. Lk. 1:28-38), and angels made known to the shepherds the birth of Jesus (cf. Lk. 2:9-13). In the garden of Gethsemani, Christ was consoled and strengthened by an angel (cf. Lk. 22:43), and the angels told the women

---

[333] Cf. S. C. ROY, *Oraon Religion and Customs,* op. cit., 51-55.

[334] S. C. ROY, *Oraon Religion and Customs,* op. cit., 58-59.

[335] Cf. D. HELMING, "Angels", in R. SHAW (ed.), *Our Sunday Visitor's Encyclopedia of Catholic Doctrine*, op. cit., 9.

who went to the tomb of Jesus: "He is not here, but has risen" (Lk. 24:5).[336] Today also the angels are closely associated in the Church with her members. The Church celebrates the feast of the guardian angels and archangels thus giving an opportunity for her members to imitate the virtues of angels and to seek their help.

The female figures of Oraon tradition can be replaced, at least to some extent, by the Blessed Mother Mary, who is the model of all virtues and a mother to all.

"As Virgin and Mother, Mary remains for the Church a "permanent model." It can therefore be said that especially under this aspect, namely as a model, or rather as a "figure," Mary, present in the mystery of Christ, remains constantly present also in the mystery of the Church."[337]

What is most needed in all this is the proper instruction and catechesis which would help the people to form, develop, and mature their faith.

3.2.7. Malevolent Spirits

Malevolent spirits are, as their name signifies, mal-intentioned or bad spirits, intent upon damaging human beings. These spirits are the subject of exorcism and not objects of worship. They are normally spirits of dead persons who don't form part of the ancestral spirits because of unnatural deaths. "Souls of persons dying a violent or unnatural death are thought by the Oraons to wander about restlessly and torment lonely unwary wayfarers."[338] They are also called tramp spirits and by various other names. *Churil* is the spirit of a woman who dies in pregnancy or child birth. Such women are buried, away from the village in some deserted spot. Their legs are broken and feet turned backwards, and thorns are inserted on the soles so that they are not able to chase people. There are some ways to overpower them, "that is strewing mustard seeds on their way so that they may engage themselves in picking up the seeds and people may get time to escape or call them by name and they will be put to shame."[339]

Mua is the spirit of a person dying of hunger or starvation or of strangulation or hanging or any other violence. They do not harm anyone but they can be heard in prolonged rainy nights moaning plaintively in the air.[340]*Bhaghout* spirits are spirits of persons bitten to death by tigers. These spirits are said to take the form of tigers and prowl about at night near their old homes which they seek to enter. In order to drive this spirit away, a spirit doctor is called, who drives it away by painting an outsider to the family like a tiger and by making him walk out on

---

[336] Cf. D. HELMING, "Angels", in R. SHAW (ed.), *Our Sunday Visitor's Encyclopedia of Catholic Doctrine*, op. cit., 9-10.

[337] RMa 42.

[338] P. EKKA, *The Mundas and Oraons,* op. cit., 285.

[339] J. LAKRA, *Tribal Cultural Anthropology,* op. cit., 27.

[340] Cf. S. C. ROY, *Oraon Religion and Customs,* op. cit., 70.

all fours to the village boundary. Rope is tied to his hands and feet. By means of these ropes four persons lead him away and the spirit doctor chases him out of the village reciting incantations.[341]

Pugi-Nad are private bad spirits. They are secretly adopted by some wicked people for the sake of harming others. Water spirits are known as *sat bahini* (seven sisters). They reside in water falls and attack the children who come to bathe in rivers close to water falls by inducing a fainting fit in them. To effect a cure, the services of a spirit doctor is sought.[342]

Concerning this wide-ranging spirit world, Christian faith must make itself felt as a convincing force on two fronts: battling all negative attitudes of the people by showing the weakness of many traditional aspects in this area, and proposing a positive orientation marked by absolute trust in God who reigns as sovereign Lord over all reality.

3.2.8. Occult Practices

Oraons have the experience of various kinds of misfortunes, sicknesses and death. Misfortunes are easily attributed to some anti-social elements such as *dains* (witches), *denora, mati* (sorcerers). All these derive their power from magic spells or magic objects and often seek the help of malicious spirits to injure others. Most of these people are said to be born with the 'evil eye' and 'evil mouth.'

3.2.8.1. Witches

Witches (*Dain-bishahi*) are believed to harm the people by their magic spell. The witches are supposed to acquire their art by a secret training. Popular belief has it that on very dark nights a troupe of them gathers under a tree in a secluded spot away from human habitation. By the accompaniment of very soft drumming they go on dancing dressed only in fringes of grass round their waist and faintly burning oil lamps placed on tiger skulls. While they dance they get into a trance and receive their techniques in magic. All those who take part in the dance as well as the passers-by who happen to come that way are bound to keep the strictest secrecy.[343] Witches are said to bring disease and other calamities on individuals, families and villages in a number of ways. A few details are described here.

The *nasan* or magic bundle is placed in a small earthen jar containing some varieties of grains, horns, bones, bits of fowls' legs and other things that are pleasing to the bad spirits. This magic bundle is secretly buried in the courtyard of the intended victim. A calamity is sure to happen to the victim, unless the magic bundle is detected and exposed by a witch doctor and an appropriate sacrifice is offered to the spirit.[344]

---

[341] Cf. S. C. ROY, *Oraon Religion and Customs,* op. cit., 70-71.

[342] Cf. ibid., 71-72.

[343] Cf. P. EKKA, *The Mundas and Oraons,* op. cit., 289.

[344] Cf. S. C. ROY, *Oraon Religion and Customs,* op. cit., 78-79.

The *ban* (magic arrow) of the witch can strike her victim from any distance. Any sudden and sharp pain in the body is said to be the shooting of the magic arrow. Once the cause of the pain is suspected the victim hurries to the spirit doctor to identify the witch and to take measures against her.[345] Furthermore the witches can disguise themselves into the shape of a black cat which then prowls around in the house of a sleeping victim licking saliva or biting off a bit of his/her hair. Any human or animal death without any apparent cause is attributed to this witch in the disguise of a black cat.[346]

Witchcraft is not a safe occupation. At times it causes harm to the witch herself when she looks at her cattle, crops, or even her own children with malicious intention and mutters to herself "how fine." Those words act as some malignant spirit and serious harm can happen.[347] Engaging in witchcraft is an anti-social activity. Witches do not reveal about themselves that they are witches. It is others who become victims of such horrible activities who detect the witches or accuse someone as a witch. Usually an old woman who is unable to defend herself is accused as a witch very easily. Such a woman is maltreated by the infuriated people, at times she is stoned to death without any proof.

3.2.8.2. Sorcerers

In order to counter-act the witchcraft there is another group of people who have magic powers. They are generally known as sorcerers. They practice anti-social magic for their own ends. To acquire this art, they have to undergo a long and arduous training under a *guru.* There are various ranks among them.

Sokha are witch finders or witch diviners. When any sort of misfortune happens in an Oraon family they believe that some witch has done it and so they consult a *sokha*. The *sokha* having heard their story, gets into a trance, he divines the spirits and converses with them. He then tells the client the name of the witch or the spirit that is responsible for such misfortunes.

Denora or mati is an exorcist. He depends on *sokha's* divinisation of the spirit in his work of exorcism, driving away the spirit from the house. The *denora* or *mati* gets into a trance and sees the witchcraft especially the magic bundle which is buried in or around the house. With his magic he too converses with those spirits and drives them away from the house. Psychologically people feel consoled and healthy for some time.

Mati can counter-act the witches because he is more powerful than them. Usually he is a very good medicine man too. Along with his magic he administers his medicine without being noticed by anybody while doing it, and when the person is cured he attributes it to his magic.[348]

---

[345] Cf. J. LAKRA, *Tribal Cultural Anthropology,* op. cit., 28.

[346] Cf. P. EKKA, *The Mundas and Oraons,* op. cit., 291.

[347] Cf. S. C. ROY, *Oraon Religion and Customs,* op. cit., 192.

[348] Cf. S. C. ROY, *Oraon Religion and Customs,* op. cit., 192-206.

Witchcraft and sorcery are nothing but clever manipulations of the ignorant people. They are habituated to live in the grip of fear of spirits, and this fear prompts them to believe in the power of these spirits and thus they become the victims of manipulation. Though Christianity has helped them to overcome these mal-practices, they have not yet fully been freed from their grip.

3.2.9. Convergences / Divergences and Possible Approaches for Evangelisation

The *Sarna* Oraons placate numerous spirits, because they want to be freed from the misfortunes caused by these spirits. The fear of the spirits provokes in them the need to seek any kind of occult practices. Although, occult practices are a universal phenomenon they are a crucial challenge to the Christian faith in Chotanagpur. In Christian tradition, the above mentioned mal-practices are absent. Christianity propagates the veneration of saints and angels, and devotion to these holy spirits have found place in popular piety.

It is important to understand that these occult practices have found a place in the Oraon culture. Therefore we need to have a thorough understanding of the situations which make them victims of such practices, we need to accept the slow and gradual process to deepen their Christian faith to enable them to rely on the power of Christ even in the face of difficulties and calamities. Christian revelation gives us a God who is all loving, compassionate and forgiving. He is our father, and St. John testifies "God is love" (1Jn. 4:8). The God of the Bible is essentially a God who is actively involved in his people's life. He liberated his chosen people from their slavery and brought them to the promised land (cf. Exodus). He revealed himself in a personal way in Jesus Christ who is Emmanuel "God with us," thus remaining always among his people and accompanying them through the course of their lives.[349] This sort of liberation is a lived experience for the Oraons. Christianity liberates the people from fear. Jesus Christ the liberator by his victory over sin and the devil has freed us from such enslavement. "I am with you always, to the close of the age" (Mt. 28:20). He is the one and only saviour of all humankind. "And there is salvation in no one else, for there is no other name under heaven given among men by which we must be saved" (Acts 4:12).

These mysteries should become part of the Oraons' life, and thus faith in a loving God should be infused and deepened through adequate catechesis and instruction, para-liturgical services, prayer, use of sacramentals, popular piety, etc. The stages through which a person is prepared for the reception of the various sacraments should be considered seriously and be given proper catechesis that will help the candidate to accept Christ as his/her personal Saviour. Ongoing catechesis

---

[349] Cf. M. SCHMAUS, *God and Creation: The Foundations of Christology*, Dogma, Vol. 2 (Kansas City: Sheed & Ward, 1969), 17, 28.

for adults should be regarded important for the maturation of faith.[350] As the Oraons have various symbols for their traditional sacrifices, among the Christians the use of sacramentals like medals, crosses, rosaries, holy water, holy pictures, blessed palm leaves, blessed oil, etc. should be propagated and encouraged. In order to be authentic, Christianity must attend to the needs of the people, their hopes and their anxieties, their problems and their uncertainties. Thus it should help them to change their belief system from the fear of spirits to the love of God. This is what we see in the evangelising activities of the early missionaries like Fr. Constant Lievens. Through education and the use of various symbols and signs they led the people to a new faith. These methods are relevant even today in order to deepen their faith.

As the Oraon traditional religion does not have any sacred books, the use and reading of the Holy Bible is another way of faith formation. The Bible offers in a privileged way the Word of God, which inspires and strengthens the human soul. For illiterate people the recitation of the rosary would be of great value as it presents and explains the paschal mysteries. Thus devotion to the Blessed Virgin becomes a way to be a faithful follower of Christ.[351]

"While all God's creation is good, human life has a special dignity and sanctity."[352] It is the duty of every human being to respect life, for we are made in the image and likeness of God (cf. Gen. 1:26-7). Therefore attention should be paid to the well-being, particularly to the healing of the body of the humans. "Healing is a process that takes place throughout life and which culminates in the new life of the resurrection."[353] Important is constant guidance and adequate education regarding health and hygiene which would help the Oraons to become aware of the causes of death, sicknesses, and thus they will abandon their undue anxiety about sickness and death. Ministry to the sick has held a significant place in the life of Christ and the Church. Praying over the sick and the dying (cf. Jas. 5:13-16), bringing the Eucharist to the sick, visiting the sick should be encouraged.[354] Such pious practices would help the people to seek the assistance and guidance of a priest in times of difficulties like sickness and death or even other calamities instead of a witch doctor or *mati*. Exhortations can be given concerning the salvific value of suffering and the cross in the life of a Christian when he faces various sorts of difficulties, that he too participates in Christ's suffering.

---

[350] Cf. F. ARINZE, "The Present-Day Challenge of Bringing Christ to People of Traditional Religions", in *Indian Missiological Review* (September 1993), 32.

[351] Cf. F. ARINZE, "The Present-Day Challenge of Bringing Christ to People of Traditional Religions", op. cit., 34.

[352] R. DOERFLINGER, "Human Life, Dignity and Sanctity of", in R. SHAW (ed.), *Our Sunday Visitor's Encyclopedia of Catholic Doctrine*, op. cit., 303.

[353] R. RYAN, "Healing", in STUHLMUELLER (ed.), *The Collegeville Pastoral Dictionary of Biblical Theology*, op. cit., 421.

[354] Cf. ibid., 420.

"The Redeemer suffered in place of man and for man. Every man has his own share in the Redemption. Each one is also called to share in that suffering through which the Redemption was accomplished. He is called to share in that suffering through which all human suffering has also been redeemed. In bringing about the Redemption through suffering, Christ has also raised human suffering to the level of the Redemption. Thus each man, in his suffering, can also become a sharer in the redemptive suffering of Christ."[355]

As the human person is a unity of body and spirit, physical as well as spiritual healing is necessary. Therefore many needs have to be respected: prayers for both physical and interior healing, repentance before God and with fellow human beings, but also the assistance of doctor and the means of medical science.[356]

As the Oraons are farmers, it is important for a pastor to show interest in their agricultural activities. Thus knowledge about the climatic conditions, modern irrigation facilities, use of fertilisers and pesticides would give them clearer ideas about good and bad crops. This can lead them to the path of a healthy secularisation giving preference to rational thinking over magical attitudes, thus liberating themselves from the grip of an irrational thinking and fear-inspired activities. Therefore the Church in Chotanagpur should take into account all these factors and be patient and compassionate with the failings of her people without any legalist rigidity, following Christ who hated sin but not the sinner. "Those who are well, have no need of a physician" says Our Lord, "but those who are sick.... For I came not to call the righteous, but sinners" (Mt. 9:12-13). The Second Vatican Council recalls very clearly:

"The good news of Christ continually renews the life and culture of fallen man; it combats and removes the error and evil which flows from the ever-present attraction of sin. It never ceases to purify and elevate the morality of peoples. It takes the spiritual qualities and endowments of every age and nation, and with supernatural riches it causes them to blossom, as it were, from within; it fortifies, completes and restores them in Christ."[357]

3.3. Idea of Creation

Like most peoples of the world, Oraons too have their own creation story that expresses their spiritual aspirations and their religious convictions. The creation myths[358] reveal *Dharmes* as creator of the cosmos and of all that is in the world.

---

[355] SD 19.

[356] Cf. F. ARINZE, "The Present-Day Challenge of Bringing Christ to people of Traditional Religions", op. cit., 34.

[357] GS 58.

[358] While dealing with Oraon creation myths we are faced with the difficulty of not having a written tradition. Myths have been handed down to posterity through oral tradition. As a result no definite version of their creation story is available for our study except for a few recent efforts. Fr. J. Lakra has published the creation myth in two parts. (1) "Genesis of Man: The Uraon Myth,"

He is the source of life and his actions have a lasting effect. The Oraon creation story can be divided into two parts - creation of the world of man and creation of the spirits.

3.3.1. Creation of Man

The focal point of creation was man. Man with his unique place in creation is the object of special respect. Before the creation of man, *Dharmes* made the earth. Now *Jammudeep*[359] in *Sat-pati-raji*[360] was in flood. In creation *Dharmes* takes counsel from the heavenly court.[361] At the request of the old mother,[362] *Dharmes* made a bird, *klkilia* (king fisher), and gave life to it. The bird brought to *Dharmes* the seed of the earth from *Patalpur* (subterranean world) and *Dharmes* made the earth: *Sat-pati-raji.*

Dharmes found that the earth was dry and appeared like extensive fields. Taking advice from *Sita,*[363] *Dharmes* moulded human beings from clay. But before he could infuse life into the clay model, Dharmes' horse *Hansraj* trampled them down out of fear of being ridden by man. Dharmes, again at the counsel of Sita, made dogs in order to chase away the horse. He then made human beings and soon the earth was filled with human beings.

Dharmes made many other creatures too. In the beginning *Dharmes* provided food for human beings and all other creatures, "even for tiny worms, beetles and flies."[364] When the human beings increased in number and filled the earth they began to find food for themselves.

The latter part of the genesis of man talks of God who destroys his creation. One day *Dharmes* went out hunting. He was so nauseated with the stench of

---

in *Sevartham*, 9 (1984), 33-55. (2) "The Genesis of Spirits: The Uraon Myth", in *Sevartham*, 11 (1986), 45-58. However what is said of one tribe is mostly valid for other tribes as the Oraons have roughly the same religious system as the Mundas and Kherias of Chotanagpur.

[359] It is supposed to be the island of Jammu, inhabited by men, obviously Chotanagpur. For all practical purposes *Sat-pati-raji* and the *Jammudeep* seem to be the same thing. (J. LAKRA,"The Genesis of Man: the Uraon Myth", in *Sevartham*, 9 (1984), 35).

[360] Seven strips of land. The country of the seven strips of land symbolises the totality of land, i.e. the whole world. (J. LAKRA, "The Genesis of Man: the Uraon Myth", op. cit., 35).

[361] *Dharmes,* old mother, *Sita, Mahado* etc. (J. LAKRA, "The Genesis of Man: The Uraon Myth", op. cit., 35).

[362] Old mother - according to the creation myth old mother is the sister of *Dharmes.* (Cf. J. LAKRA, " The Genesis of Man: The Uraon Myth", op. cit., 41).

[363] According to J. Lakra, *Sita* is the image of *Dharmes* himself in his attribute of all wise God. In the biblical *Book of Wisdom,* Wisdom is the personification of God's active power and goodness (Wis. 7:26), so also *Sita* with her counsels seems to be the personification of God's own wisdom. (J. LAKRA, "The Genesis of Man: The Uraon Myth", op. cit., 39).

[364] V. ROSNER, "Myths from Chota Nagpur as Retold by V. Rosner, S.J.", in *Sevartham*, 17 (1992), 125.

human excreta[365] all over the earth that he could not put his foot on the earth. So he decided to destroy the world he had created. He showered down a rain of fire and *Sat-pati-raji* was ablaze for seven days and seven nights. Thus everything was consumed except two infants, *Bhaiya-Bahin*[366] (brother-sister) whom *Sita* had hid first in the knot of her hair and later in a crab-hole. *Dharmes* poured down rain in order to clean the earth from the ashes. He went for hunting and he could find nothing on the earth. There was no human being to offer him rice and eggs. So, *Dharmes* relented of having destroyed man. He came to *Sita* for wisdom, who told him about the *Bhaiya-Bahin* (brother-sister) in the crab-hole. *Dharmes* went to the field and brought them home and took care of them.[367]

"Oraons believe in a Creator-God who creates, provides, destroys and recreates. It is clearly expressed in their prayer: "Here do thou accept; it is thou who art called the little Sun-Moon. Thou art called too the great Sun-Moon. It is thou who spoil our crops and harm children and our eyes and ears. And it is thou who succour us; O God, O Lord, have mercy on us; have pity on us."[368]

The creation myth presents *Dharmes* as a God who is like a father to the humans. He was totally interested in the welfare of *Bhaiya-Bahin.* He taught the grown-up youth to clear the forest and cultivate the land. *Dharmes* made day and night for man so that man could work during the day and rest at night. When the crop was infested by pests he taught him the ceremony of *Dandakatta* (tooth breaking) against the 'evil eye' and the 'evil mouth.' *Dharmes* taught the first humans to make rice beer. When they reached marriageable age he made them husband and wife. They multiplied and filled the earth.

Dharmes divided mankind into twelve professional clans and assigned each a profession. Oraons are one of the twelve clans of Dharmes. Thus the creation myth ends with origin of the Oraon tribe.[369]

"The simplicity of the *Sarna* creation myths is striking. They stand in sharp contrast with complex emanations, theogonies and stories of nature deities found in more 'advanced' civilisations. They have this serenity in common with Genesis. It is distinctive of strict monotheism."[370]

---

[365] "Human excreta is one of the most disgusting, despicable, dirtiest, stinking thing an Uraon can imagine. Its unbearable stench can cause in him a vomiting sensation. It can also be interpreted as the stench of man's sin." (J. LAKRA, "The Genesis of Man: The Uraon Myth", op. cit., 43).

[366] These two infants represent the first ancestors who survived the world-wide conflagration and eventually became the first parents of the mankind. (Cf. J. LAKRA, "The Genesis of Man: The Uraon Myth", op. cit., 43).

[367] Cf. J. LAKRA, "The Genesis of Man: The Uraon Myth", op. cit., 42-47.

[368] A. PARAPULLIL, "Tribal Theology", op. cit., 35.

[369] Cf. J. LAKRA, "The Genesis of Man: The Uraon Myth", op. cit., 48-55.

[370] A. VAN EXEM, "Creation and Fall in Sarna Religion", op. cit., 15.

3.3.2. Convergences / Divergences and Possible Approaches for Evangelisation

The Creation myth of the Oraons seems to be very similar to that of the biblical creation story. Both stories visualise a 'nothingness' prior to creation. "The earth was without form and void, and darkness was upon the face of the deep, and the Spirit of God was moving over the face of the waters" (Gen: 1:2). And in the Oraon creation myth "In the beginning *Jammudeep* in *Sat-pati-raji* was deluged with water. There was no trace of the earth." This nothingness is visualised as watery chaos. Therefore to bring harmony and order into this chaos can be understood as one of the purposes of creation in both cases.[371]

Creation is not a static process. It has dynamic purposes, it aims at creating living things. The Biblical creation story uses two different verbs: 'to make or to create' to display the creative activity of God. God made the earth, the sea, the beasts, the creeping things etc., and He created man in his own image. In the Oraon myth too there are two different verbs for the creative activity of *Dharmes*. The verb *kamna* means to 'make' and it is used for the creation of animals and other things whereas the verb *sirjana* means to 'create' and it is used only for the creation of human beings. Thus the creative activity of God is differentiated. In fact the gift of life is more important than the harmony and order which God brought out through the creation of the earth. It reveals that man is the finest of all creation.[372] "And God blessed them and God said to them, 'Be fruitful and multiply, and fill the earth and subdue it; and have dominion over the birds of the air and over every living thing that moves upon the earth'" (Gen. 1:28). In the Oraon creation myth there are no explicit words to depict the blessing of *Dharmes* for the increase in number, but the myth says that the human beings increased and filled the earth.

In the Oraon creation myth *Dharmes* takes counsel from *Sita* for his creative activity. *Sita* is a female principle in *Dharmes,* similar to the wisdom in the OT which also appears feminine. "Wisdom has been called a 'kindly spirit' (1:6) the mother of all good things (7:11-12) who provides 'friendship with God' (7:14; cf. 7:27) and who 'loves good'" (7:22).[373]*Dharmes* in his divine wisdom creates human beings. When his anthropomorphic principle (human wisdom) destroys humans, his divine goodness saves the human pair. In other words these are two sides of *Dharmes,* who in reality appears as a father-mother God. Therefore when a disciplined father chastises his children, the unfathomable love of a mother saves them from the fury of their father. Thus the female principles[374] in this myth are the representation of *Dharmes* himself in his wisdom.

---

[371] Cf. A. VAN EXEM, "Genesis 1-11 as Living Tradition", in *Sevartham*, 21(1996), 4-5.

[372] Cf. A. VAN EXEM, "Creation and fall in Sarna Religion", op. cit., 12-13.

[373] AAVV, *The New Interpreter's Bible* Vol. 5 (Nashville, Abingdon Press, 1994), 504.

[374] *Sita*, old mother who is *Dharmes'* sister.

And in Genesis we come across "Let us make… "(Gen. 1:26). These words show that there must be someone other than God himself. Exegetes now generally hold that God's words are addressed to the celestial beings who form his court.[375] Moreover the OT refers to them in a number of passages (cf. Is. 6:2, 1Kg. 22:19, Ps. 82:1). It can be taken that God, who dominates creation up to this point, now recedes into the background asking advice from his council. Thus he manifests himself not as an authoritarian controller of events but as a generous delegator of his power.[376]

Creation was an act of Dharmes. It reached its perfection when he filled the dry earth with living creatures. He "puts blood into them."[377] Blood is the sign of life. "The gift of life is of a higher order than the organisation of the cosmos. God is life in absolute dimension: he communicated life to creatures."[378] And in Christianity we know that creation is the beginning of divine revelation. Finally, God created human beings and endowed them with life-force. "Then the Lord God formed man of dust from the ground, and breathed into his nostrils the breath of life; and man became a living being" (Gen. 2:7). This "breath of life" is God's own breath which he shares with human beings, thus raising them to the level of sharers in his divine life. This is an infusion of God's own spirit.[379]

The Bible says that "God created man in his own image" (Gen. 1:27). Image makes man God's representative on earth. "The image is a capacity to relate to God."[380] Therefore God has given to man those qualities by which he can converse with God, accept God as his friend and companion and also enter into a covenantal relationship with God.[381] God in his designs creates woman out of already existing material (cf. Gen. 2:21 23). This can be compared to that of the potter who both designs and fashions an object. Unlike the dust, by which man was created, the rib is a living material. The theological force of this creation is expressed in Gen. 1:26-27, which depicts the equality of man and woman created in the image of God. Certainly the relationship of the woman to the 'rib' of the man entails no subordination to man but equality.[382] Thus the 'rib' brilliantly displays the relationship between man and his wife. "Just as the rib is found at the side of the man and is attached to him, even so the good wife, the rib of her husband, stands at his side as helper-counterpart, and her soul is bound up with

---

[375] J. BISWAS, "Man in Genesis Chapters 1-11", in *Jeevadhara*, 26 (1975), 115.

[376] Cf. AAVV., *The New Interpreter's Bible* Vol. 1 (Nashville, Abingdon Press, 1994), 352.

[377] J LAKRA, "Genesis of Man: The Uraon Myth", op. cit., 41.

[378] A. VANEXEM, "Creation and Fall in Sarna Religion", op. cit., 13.

[379] Cf. AAVV., *The New Interpreter's Bible*, Vol. 1, op. cit., 350.

[380] G. J. WENHAM, *Word Biblical Commentary*, Vol 1 (Waco, Texas: Word Books Publisher, 1987), 31.

[381] Cf. ibid., 31.

[382] Cf. AAVV., *The New Interpreter's Bible*, Vol 1, op. cit., 53.

his."[383] This equality and importance of man and woman can be expressed in other words. The woman was "not made out of his (man's) head to top him , nor out of his feet to be trampled upon by him, but out of his side to be equal with him, under his arm to be protected, and near his heart to be beloved."[384] This is a relationship that is characterised by harmony and intimacy between man and woman, which is established by God himself. God placed them in the garden of Eden, which is again a sign of complete communion with God.

An Oraon myth seems to symbolise this idea, says Van Exem. "*Dharmes* gave life to man by putting part of his right lower rib in the mouth of one of two clay-models, and part of his left lower rib in the mouth of the other: the former became a living man, the latter a woman."[385] In the Oraon creation myth man and woman are created out of clay and given life at the same time. Here *Dharmes* uses part of his ribs to give life to the clay models which he had made. Thus *Dharmes* shares his divine life with man and woman and calls them to enter into an intimate relationship with him and with each other. Despite the fact that the creator *Dharmes* is a loving and a caring God, Oraons' relationship with this all good God is rather superficial. Although, it is so inspiring to know that he shares his own life with humans, they have not developed a filial relationship with their Creator. Therefore it is the prime duty of Christianity to inculcate in them a sense of relationship which comes out of their deep love and confidence in a loving and caring God.

3.3.3. Genesis of Spirits

Dharmes divided the whole mankind into various clans and to each he assigned a job. But there was a group *agrialohar*[386] which was left out by *Dharmes*. He assigned to them the work of smelting the iron ore. They are the twelve *Asur* brothers and the thirteen *Lohar*[387] brothers.

They smelted iron ore and polluted the entire cosmos and thus they disturbed all living beings by their action. Therefore God sent his bird messengers with his message that they should stop working at least during midnight. They did not heed to anyone instead they maltreated the messengers. They said that they are gods and they need not obey anyone. Finally *Dharmes* in the guise of a

---

383 G. J. WENHAM, *Word Biblical Commentary*, op. cit., 69.

384 Ibid.,69.

385 A.VANEXEM, "Creation and Fall in Sarna Religion", op. cit., 13.

386 *Agria* is derived from the *Sadri* word *agral* which means: left out. Thus the *agria lohar* gets his name from the fact that he was left out, he remained 'extra' in the process of the distribution of professions by *Dharmes,* rather than from the fact that he was busy with *aag* (Hindi word for fire) (Cf. J. LAKRA, "Genesis of Spirits: The Uraon Myth", in *Sevartham,* 11 (1986), 56.

387 The descendants of the *agria Lohar* are supposed to be the twelve brothers of *Asurs* and thirteen brothers *Lodhar.* They co-operated in the iron melting work.The numbers 12 and 13 stand for the totality of the people working on the furnace. (Cf. J. LAKRA, "Genesis of Spirits: The Uraon Myth", op. cit., 56).

boy who is suffering from itching sores went to them. They did not recognise him and they also treated him badly.

In the course of time their furnaces began to fail. They were anxious and went in search of a spirit diviner. They could not find anybody other than this boy. They asked the boy to help. The boy asked them to offer a human sacrifice in order to cast away the evil. The *Asur* brothers desperately searched for a human being to be sacrificed. But no one was willing to help them. Finally the boy agreed to be sacrificed. The boy asked them to put him inside the furnace and to blow it for three days and three nights. They did so. On the third day when they opened the furnace the boy came out gloriously all covered with silver and gold. The *Asur* brothers were happy to get more gold. Therefore they were ready to get inside the furnace to search for more gold. When they went inside the furnace, *Dharmes* asked their wives to blow the bellows as soon as they entered. But when they opened the furnace after three days they found that their husbands were burned to ashes.

At that moment *Dharmes* revealed his identity and told them about the harm they have done to other living things. He then mounted on his horse. But the wives stopped him and asked him to show them the way of living. He then instructed them to go to different parts of the cosmos as spirits and to live on the sacrifices offered by the Oraons.[388]

The myth gives us valuable information about Oraon's relationship with *Dharmes* and the spirits. By the sacrifice of *Dharmes* the condemnation of the *Asurs* is effected, and their wives became evil spirits. The self sacrifice of *Dharmes* resulted in a transformation. The greedy *Asurs* could not recognise *Dharmes* even in his transformed body "adorned with gold and silver in glory and honour."[389] Having fixed their attention in acquiring more gold and silver, they entered into the furnace. The fire reduced them to charred bones and ashes. Hearing from *Dharmes* that this was the consequence of their stubbornness to his words and he commands the wives of the *Asurs* who readily promise obedience to him. But it was too late. Yet *Dharmes* allowed them to obtain their sustenance as spirits of nature.[390]

3.3.4. Convergences / Divergences and Possible Approaches for Evangelisation

The central event in this myth can be taken as the sacrifice of *Dharmes* and his glorification. Dharmes adapted a human form and appears in the guise of a boy, a suffering person. The divine made himself visible to his creatures in a human form as one among them but they could not recognise him, and they rejected

[388] Cf. J. LAKRA, "Genesis of Spirits: The Uraon Myth", in *Sevartham,* 11 (1986), 46-55.

[389] J. LAKRA, "Genesis of Spirits: The Uraon Myth", op. cit., 53.

[390] Cf. A. VAN EXEM, "The New Dispensation in Sarna Religion", in *Sevartham,* 10 (1985), 75-77.

him. Analysing the dispositions of *Asurs*, one can understand that their action was not a religious act. In their misery and sinfulness their eyes were blind to accept *Dharmes* as their God. It was *Dharmes* who suggested the sacrifice and it is he who offered it. Therefore he himself was the sacrificer and the victim and as the same time it is he to whom the sacrifice was offered.[391]

Through this sacrifice *Dharmes* the creator became a saviour. In his divine self he has always been a saviour. The compassionate love of the creator culminated in his saving actions. In other words creation reached its climax in salvation. *Dharmes* saved the world form destruction, from the wickedness of evil people.

The primordial event of the Oraon myth is very much similar to the paschal mystery of Jesus Christ. Christ, the innocent one of the father, took the form of a human and lived among them. He is the self-communication of God the creator. Yet his own people did not recognise him (cf. Jn. 1:11) and finally they hanged him on a cross. The innocent one, the suffering servant (cf. Is. 53) was crucified, in order to restore the brokenness of humans, to put an end to every form of injustice, sin and death.

"He, though innocent, takes upon Himself the sufferings of all people, because He takes upon Himself the sins of all. "The Lord has laid on him the iniquity of us all:" all human sin in its breadth and depth becomes the true cause of the Redeemer's suffering." In His suffering, sins are cancelled out precisely because He alone as the only-begotten Son could take them upon Himself, accept them with that love for the Father which overcomes the evil of every sin; in a certain sense He annihilates this evil in the spiritual space of the relationship between God and humanity, and fills this space with good."[392]

He willingly accepted obedience to the creator, God. He is the sacrificer and victim who immolated himself on the cross, and thus saved the world from sin and its consequences. He is the saviour too. God exalted him and transformed him to glory (cf. Phil. 2:6-11).

For the grace of God has appeared for the salvation of all men, training us to renounce irreligion and worldly passions, and to live sober, upright, and godly lives in this world, awaiting our blessed hope the appearing of the glory of our great God and Saviour Jesus Christ who gave himself for us to redeem us from all iniquity and to purify for himself a people of his own who are zealous for good deeds (Tit. 2:11-14).

The conception of creation and the fall which we found in the Oraon traditional religion is similar to that of the biblical creation story. The rejection of God's designs bring destruction into the order of the creator God, which needs to be remedied. Thus there is the need for salvation. It is the unfailing love of *Dharmes* for mankind that he appears in the form of a boy (Son), even a suffering servant. "The power and wisdom with which God both generates the Son and exalts him

[391] Cf. A. VAN EXEM, "The New Dispensation in Sarna Religion", op. cit., 77.

[392] SD 17.

high above could be ascribed to the Spirit."[393] Therefore raising *Dharmes* to glory can be attributed to the Spirit of the creator God. Thus we can display some similarities between the traditional Oraon religion and Christianity. In reality, the working of the Spirit may be reflected in their community life.

3.4. Oraon Concept of Man

Man experiences himself as a rational and social being. He is constituted with a body, mind and will and lives in a socio-historical context. The importance of his personality is determined by his relationship with his fellow beings, also with the Other.

Oraons understand their empirical self as a unity of body and life (or vital principle) and believe that their deeper self transcends the empiric and extends into the world of spirits which we might have to identify with supernatural beings. In this case their understanding of man appears more theological than philosophical.[394]

3.4.1. Man as the Purpose of Creation

According to the Oraon creation myth *Dharmes* created human beings in his own image and likeness (cf. Gen. 1:27). *Dharmes* made clay figures of human beings and infused life into them by putting part of his right and left ribs in them. Since there were no other beings apart from *Dharmes* he made those clay figures in his own likeness. Thus human beings received life from him and he wanted that they would remain in intimate relationship with each other and with him.[395]

Oraons understand themselves as creatures of *Dharmes* who has endowed them with vital power, i.e. life. "The whole creation had a single purpose: man."[396] In fact the whole creation gains meaning and attains beauty only with the presence of man on the earth. The myth manifests the importance of man in the whole of creation. The narrator of the myth explains the creation activity of *Dharmes* with great care and attention. The horse destroys the clay model of human beings. Then *Dharmes* makes dogs to chase the horse. This is not to play down the power and wisdom of the creator but to emphasise the uniqueness of man in creation. The horse can be considered as the embodiment of evil. *Dharmes* who is all good wins over evil in his creation by destroying the evil. Man becomes the climax of creation and all other creatures stand at the service of man.[397]

---

[393] S. K. KUJUR, "Tribal Concept of the Divine: A Trinitarian Perspective", in *Sevartham*, 21 (1996), 119.

[394] Cf. A. VAN EXEM, "The Self understanding of the Sarna Man", in *Sevartham*, 11 (1986), 59.

[395] Cf. P. KULLU, "Tribal Religion and Culture", in *Jeevadhara*, XXIV (1994), 100.

[396] A. VAN EXEM, "Creation and Fall in Sarna Religion", in *Sevartham*, 9 (1984), 13.

[397] Cf. C. DAS, "The Santal Creation Myth", in *Sevartham*, 11(1986), 120-121.

3.4.2. Man as Co-creator and Co-operating Being

The plan of *Dharmes* did not stop with the creation of man. Man is the pride of creation and so he should co-operate with the creator in his creative activity. The second part of the creation myth reveals man's responsibility in this work of creation. *Dharmes* in his providence and wisdom took care of *Bhayia-Bahin* (brother-sister), a human pair, who were saved by his divine wisdom (*Sita*) from the rain of fire and whom he wanted as the progenitors of the tribe. This was possible only by revealing to them his designs and entrusting them with responsibility. In his wisdom he brought them together to fructify and multiply. "Procreation is the first sign of man's co-operation in the life giving act of creation."[398] By the institution of marriage he arranged that this human pair should continue the work of creation of the human race. Thus man is entrusted with the mission of multiplying and filling the earth according to the plans of the creator.

Earth is for man. Man should till it and produce his own food, and this is another dimension of creation. Finally in all these activities man should maintain his harmony with nature. Man is the custodian of nature.[399] All that is on earth is for the well-being of man and everything on earth is under him. He is above all creatures.

Oraons have a deep sense of belonging to a family and living within a community - tribe. The understanding that man is a co-operative being exists from the very fact that the tribe was established by *Dharmes* who brought up the human pair (who were set aside from the rain of fire) and led them to function as the progenitors of the tribe. An Oraon finds his fulfilment in being a member of the tribe. He has no significance apart from the tribe. "The nature of human existence is typically corporate: the tribe is created and cared for by *Dharmes*, life means communality (equality and harmony)."[400] There is almost no individualism in the Oraon community. "The family, the extended family and the larger community of village or clan celebrate together their joys and their sorrows. They plan and work together."[401]

3.4.3. Convergences / Divergences and Possible Approaches for Evangelisation

On analysing we realise that the Oraon concept of man is similar to that of the Christians. Christianity believes that man is created in the image of God. "Let us make man in our image, after our likeness" (Gen. 1: 26). God created man in his own image. In Col. 1:15 Christ is presented as the image of the invisible God,

[398] C. DAS, "The Santal Creation Myth", op. cit., 123.

[399] Cf. A. VAN EXEM, "Creation and Fall in Sarna Religion", op. cit., 13-16.

[400] B. TIRKEY, "Oraon Ethical Values", in *Sevartham*, 9 (1984), 67.

[401] F. ARINZE, "Present Day Challenge of Bringing Christ to People of Traditional Religions", op. cit., 34.

and all of us are incorporated into that body through the sacrament of Baptism. Created in God's likeness man is privileged to attain his companionship and blessings. The whole world is made subject to him. All these instances manifest man as the object of the creator's benevolence. God fashioned man from dust and breathed into him the principle of life. Thus in every aspect man is the finest of all creation, created in the very image of God.[402]

Humans are created for life in a community. God created them in the companionship of man and woman so that they could establish communion among themselves and with other persons. Male and female he created them (Gen. 1: 27). The communitarian nature of man is his vocation and corresponds to the will of God.[403] "In his fatherly care for all of us, God desired that all men should form one family and deal with each other in a spirit of brotherhood."[404] This union and co-operation as members of the same family can be a foretaste of the union that exists among the divine persons: Father, Son and Holy Spirit. This consciousness is an important value for Christian faith. The Church is the family of the people of God redeemed by Christ. In the Church we are all brothers and sisters. "All baptised in Christ, you have all clothed yourselves in Christ, and there are no more distinctions between Jew and Greek, slave and free, male and female, but all of you are in Christ Jesus" (Gal. 3:27-28).

"Indeed, the oneness and indivisibility of the Eucharistic body of the Lord implies the oneness of his mystical body, which is the one and indivisible Church. From the Eucharistic centre arises the necessary openness of every celebrating community, of every particular Church. By allowing itself to be drawn into the open arms of the Lord, it achieves insertion into his one and undivided body."[405]

The Oraon community is ethnocentric, consists of persons of the same culture, customs etc. This community is limited to this particular region, whereas the Church is universal, it has members belonging to many cultures. "...The universal Church" is seen to be "a people brought into unity from the unity of the Father, the Son and the Holy Spirit."[406] For Christian Oraons, the community concept must, therefore gradually open also to others and finally acquire worldwide dimensions. Such realisations should help the Christian Oraons to shed off the sentiments of discontentment in front of outsiders (non-tribals).

---

[402] Cf. J. BISWAS, "Man in Genesis Chapters 1-11", op. cit., 117-119.

[403] Cf. GS 12 and 24.

[404] GS 24.

[405] CONGREGATION FOR THE DOCTRINE OF THE FAITH, Letter to the Bishops of the Catholic Church, *On Some Aspects Understood as Communion* (Rome: May 28. 1992), 11.

[406] LG 4.

3.5. Idea of Sin and Reconciliation

"Tribal religious ideas are not expressed in logical sentences, but hidden in myths and ancient stories."[407] Struck by the universality of sin that coexists with the universal aspiration to goodness, the Oraons too have expressed this human experience of sin in a mythic form, describing it as primal sin. An analysis of this myth will provide us with an understanding on the Oraons' concept and experience of sin.

3.5.1. Sin as Expressed in the Myths

In the Oraon creation myth the sinful condition of man is expressed in a rather crude metaphor. *Dharmes* on his hunting expedition to the earth finds it dirty with human excrement.[408] Here sin is presented as the worst impurity an Oraon can imagine, i.e. human excreta. Man has desecrated *Dharmes'* creation. That is man became more and more independent in his behaviour and attitude towards the creator. He began to destroy the creation, both animals (by killing and eating) and plants (by cutting down the fruit trees). Certainly man was the crown of creation: but it did not mean that he should act against the will of God, and rely on his own strength. Earth was entrusted to man. But man did not co-operate with his creator's designs, instead he lived in a most disgusting way, and thus rejected his creator in every possible way. These actions were like human excreta, the most detestable thing; man did not remain in communion with *Dharmes*, and with his fellow beings.[409]

In the myth on the genesis of spirits, which is also known as '*the Asur Legend*' we find a better expression of the human experience of both the personal and social aspects of sin. Here "evil is typified in the *Asurs*."[410] These legendary people (*Asurs*) were iron smelters. They smelted iron day and night and so the whole universe was disturbed. "The *Asurs* neither helped nature in its task of providing man's food, nor did they regulate their life according to the setting of the sun."[411] As a result the whole universe suffered. There was no food and water for man, plants, and other living beings on earth and, anthropomorphically speaking, even for *Dharmes* himself.

Asurs are the image of evil, sinners. They are blacksmiths, working with iron, i.e. belonging to another culture, not to Dharmes' own people. In the Bible we have Cain as an image for evil. Tubal-cain from the lineage of Cain, probably

---

[407] S. FUCHS, "Concept of Salvation in Tribal Religions", in *Indian Missiological Review*, 14 (1982), 362.

[408] Cf. A. VAN EXEM, "Creation and Fall in Sarna Religion", op. cit., 18.

[409] Cf. J. LAKRA, "The Genesis of Man: The Uraon Myth", op. cit., 43., Cf. P. KULLU, "Tribal Culture-Religion on Practice", in *Sevartham*, 18 (1993), 22.

[410] A. VAN EXEM, "Creation and Fall in Sarna Religion", op. cit., 19.

[411] A. VAN EXEM, "Creation and Fall in Sarna Religion", op. cit., 19.

means 'smith' who works iron and metals.[412] Cains' lineage shows that they do not till the land, they are wanderers, they forge bronze and iron, they build cities and are given to vengeance. Thus there are some images for having rejected their roots in God, images of sin and evil.[413] The simplicity of the myth does not detract from the deep truth it contains. Sin is presented "as the rejection of God's cosmic plan; which would be tantamount to the sinner's rejection of his own being."[414]

A threefold dimension of sin is alluded to in this myth. The social dimension of sin is seen from the effect that it has on other human beings. This is evidently in keeping with the Oraons concept of man 'as a member of the community,' the tribe. "The smoke has reached up to heaven."[415] Sin has a theological dimension. "Man was made to give meaning to creation and therefore to the creative act; instead, he harms it, the cry of creation naturally rises up to God. The Creator is offended in his handiwork."[416] Finally sin has an ecological dimension. Nature is in distress. Man is entrusted with the duty of caring for nature. He depends on nature for his very survival. A 'mindless' exploitation of nature will necessarily lead to its destruction. In other words sin may be understood as a rejection of God which is expressed through the rejection of one's status as creature, including even others and nature. That means having dethroned God, self, others and nature, the ego is enthroned in their place. This rejection manifests itself in various ways, of which the following are important for the Oraon concept of sin.

3.5.2. Nature and Classification of Sins.

The Oraons have not got any written moral codes. Yet they hold certain values which are as good as written moral codes of so-called developed people. There are certain negative attitudes which they try to detest in themselves and in others. Among them the most significant ones are greed, pride and envy. These can be seen as the cardinal sins of the Oraons. "For the tribals greed and pride are the capital or original sins, because according to their creation myth, these were the sins which caused death and destruction."[417] Therefore the Oraons think it is a commandment of *Dharmes* to be content with what they have and to live in fraternal charity. Because *Dharmes* is a providing God, men need to be submissive to the designs of this supreme God.

---

[412] Cf. L. BARTOLI, *La Chiave per la Comprensione del Simbolismo e dei Segni nel Sacro*, (Trieste: Edizioni Lint Trieste, 1982), 147.

[413] Cf. A. VAN EXEM, "Genesis 1-11 as a Living Tradition", in *Sevartham*, 21 (1996), 22.

[414] Ibid., 19.

[415] J. LAKRA, "The Genesis of Spirits: The Uraon Myth", op. cit., 49.

[416] A. VAN EXEM, "Creation and Fall in Sarna Religion", op. cit., 20.

[417] P. KULLU, "Tribal Religion and Culture", in *Jeevadhara*, XXIV (1994), 92.

3.5.2.1. Greed, Pride and Envy

Asurs were greedy for more wealth. So they smelted iron day and night, thus transgressing the natural order. Such a greedy intention of depending on oneself, hoarding for the future, rather than relying on God's providence, is against the Oraon mind.

The *Asurs*' greed led them to pride. They were proud of their numbers, of their unity and their achievements. They obviously despised others. When *Dharmes* sent the bird messengers to forbid the *Asurs* from working the furnace day and night, the *Asurs* retorted in their pride that they themselves are gods and kings and that there is no one greater than they.[418] "Out of greed and pride they make up their mind to obey no orders: they turn their material disobedience into a formal one."[419]

Oraons believe envy to be the root cause of most of the physical evils. The myth about the genesis of man tells us that the *Dandakatta* (tooth-splitting) ceremony was taught to the *Bhaiya-Bahin* (brother-sister) as a counter measure to the evil caused by the 'evil eye' and 'evil mouth' (poisonous praise). Whenever any evil takes place, the Oraons suspect that it is caused by the envy of someone. Envy manifests itself as the rejection of God, because God's universal will for the happiness and prosperity of mankind is not accepted. It also shows lack of faith in a God who provides and who wants the good of everyone.[420]

The seriousness with which the Oraons consider these sins is shown by the fact that these sins are most abhorred, both in themselves and in others. The Oraons are particularly careful in trying to avoid greed and pride in their own lives. They are aware that envy is a cancerous evil that often cripples their tribe.

Therefore Oraons make every effort to avoid these negative attitudes. Instead they try to cultivate anti-greed and anti-pride values in their lives. "Their religion and morality was such that they have rightly been called *animae naturaliter Christianae*, i.e. people with an inborn propensity towards things Christian."[421] Significantly these values occupy an important place in the teachings of Jesus. Jesus stands out as a challenge to the Israelites both old and new and calling them for a religious and social renewal. Jesus reaches out to all humankind.

"Israel's anti-greed and anti-pride was expressed in legislation and social protest which sought to control the accumulation of private property (Dt. 15, Is. 5, Mic. 2) and to prevent the setting up of a rigid hierarchy of status. Jesus

---

[418] Cf. J. LAKRA, "The Genesis of Spirits: The Uraon Myth", op. cit., 47-49.

[419] A. VAN EXEM, "Creation and Fall in Sarna Religion", op. cit., 20.

[420] Cf. V. PALATTY, "The Religious World-View of the Oraons", in *Sevartham*, 19 (1994), 110.

[421] A. VAN EXEM, *Evangelisation Today, A Local Church Reflects* (Ranchi: Ranchi Jesuit Society, 1975), 1.

called for a radical dispossession of goods (Mk. 1:16-20; 10:17-23) and for a radical attitude of service (Mk. 10:42-45)."[422]

Thus, these values are brought to new levels of radicality in the teachings of Jesus. He teaches us to forego all sorts of negative attitudes and to bind one another with bonds of agapeic love. Today when Indian society faces so much social oppression and economic exploitation which are caused by the pride of the caste and the greed of consumerism, Chotanagpur Oraons would stand as a challenge and a witness.[423]

3.5.2.2. Sin and Tribe

Besides greed, pride and envy, which may be seen as cardinal sins, there are other failings too. These can be classified into those that go against the tribe, their customs and traditions and those that go against social taboos. "In the eyes of the tribals any offence against tribal laws and traditions is a sin, which thus has a more ritualistic than moral character."[424]

The Oraon understanding of sin is closely linked with their concept of man. They consider man as a 'corporate being.' The existence of the individual has little significance apart from the tribe. The tribe is God's elected people. "The ultimate good of the Oraon is the well-being of the community; plenty to eat and drink, cattle, crops, land and children. Whatever is done against this is sin. Hence theft, adultery, murder, incest, false testimony, calumny, neglect of parents when they are old, insulting or striking them and any violation of social customs are sins."[425]

The good of the tribe is the most important thing they long for in this life. Their ultimate goal is to be incorporated into the community of their ancestors in the next life. Thus the tribe, visible as well as invisible, is the focus of their religious living. Hence, sin has a definite relationship to the tribe.

The violation of the social customs and taboos which surround marriage goes directly against the enhancement and propagation of tribal life. Tribe endogamy, clan exogamy and avoidance of commensality are very sacred practices for them. Violations of these can never be condoned. All these violations are believed to go directly against tribal life, and God, the author of life. Hence, for such sins reconciliation must be effected both with God and with the community.[426]

Oraons give great importance to the communitarian or social dimension of sin. Sin is understood as a transgression of God's law, and the seriousness of sin derives from the fact that this transgression has serious repercussions on the community, the tribe.

---

[422] G. M. SOARES PRABHU, "Anti-Greed and Anti-Pride", in *Jeevadhara,* XXIV (1994), 137.

[423] Ibid., 133.

[424] S. FUCHS, "The Concept of Salvation in Tribal Religions", op. cit., 362.

[425] A. PARAPULLIL, "Tribal Theology", op. cit., 37.

[426] Cf. V. PALATTY, "The Religious World View of the Oraons", op. cit., 111-112.

There is a positive element in what we find in this 'social consciousness.' This is where some non-tribal people still have to arrive at. Many modern societies need to become aware of this aspect of sin that is bound up with social consciousness so that every injustice towards fellow human beings can be understood as an offence against God. All the same, the Oraons need to be educated with regard to the individual dimension of sin whereby they may find it easy to accept their personal responsibility for sin.

3.5.3. Convergences / Divergences and Possible Approaches for Evangelisation

The above discussions have portrayed that the Oraon traditional religion, even though it understands sin as a rejection of God's law, it gives more importance to the social than to the personal dimension of sin. Even if the offender has no awareness of his offence, he is punishable because the community has judged him as a sinner. Thus a wrong becomes a sin only when it is discovered by the community. In this sense there is no personal dimension, sin is communitarian.

Sin can be defined in Christian terms as "an offence against reason, truth, and right conscience, it is failure in genuine love for God and neighbour caused by a perverse attachment to certain goods. It wounds the nature of man and injures human solidarity. It has been defined as "an utterance, a deed, or a desire contrary to the eternal law."[427]

"Sin, in the proper sense, is always a personal act, since it is an act of freedom on the part of an individual person and not properly of a group or community."[428] The human person is free to accept or reject God's ways for him/her. However this personal responsibility cannot be transferred to external factors such as structures, systems or other people. Thus as a personal act, sin has its first and foremost consequences in the sinner, that is in his/her relationship with God who is the very foundation of human life.[429]

By virtue of human solidarity, each individual's sin in some way affects others. Therefore every sin has repercussions on the entire ecclesial body and in the whole human family. This is the social dimension of sin. Thus sin is a personal act and it has theological, personal, and social dimensions and the arbiter of sin is the individual himself/herself. The acknowledgement comes from the part of the sinner. "For I know my transgressions, and my sin is ever before me. Against thee, thee only, have I sinned and done that which is evil in thy sight" (Ps. 50:3-4). This should be the attitude of a sinner and this is what the Oraons need to pay attention to in a much more explicit way where personal responsibility plays a central role.

[427] CATECHISM OF THE CATHOLIC CHURCH, para. 1849.

[428] RP. 16.

[429] Cf. RP 16.

3.5.4. Reconciliation

Sin is a transgression of God's law with its serious effect on the community, the tribe. Hence, reconciliation must be effected both with God and with the community. The act of reconciliation varies according to the gravity of the offence. It is not the *pahan* (village priest) whose function as the minister or officient, but as a representative of the community is usually an elderly person. "If the offence is an intra-clan relationship, the whole family of the clan is in some way affected and the officient must be of another clan."[430]

"Every sinner is primarily answerable to the community."[431] "For the tribal, community is the final arbiter and deals out punishment to the offender."[432] Among the Oraons the *panchayat*[433] is the sole authority for punishing and reconciling a sinner. The offender is publicly convicted and visible sanctions are imposed. A member who betrays the unity of the community is excommunicated from the tribe. He is considered as an outcast until he is reconciled with the community by paying a heavy fine.[434]

Every reconciliation, even that of an individual sinner, is a communal event. It is effected through the sacrifice of a white animal as victim to *Dharmes*, a purificatory ritual[435] and finally a community meal. *Dharmes* is represented by the community, or as it is commonly said, by the *panches*. "The reconciliation with God symbolised by this ritual must be confirmed and completed by a community meal. Reconciliation with the tribe cannot but express reconciliation with God."[436] The *panchayat* which represents the community is given the food offered by the offender, "signifying his absolution and fellowship with the community and moralisation of affairs."[437]

Even though the Oraon reconciliation rite is not a sacrament, yet it has some close similarity to Christian practices. In Christianity, the climax of brotherhood and reconciliation is the Eucharistic Meal.

"With every good reason his (Jesus') passion and death, sacramentally renewed in the Eucharist, are called by the liturgy the "sacrifice of reconciliation:"

---

430 A. VAN EXEM, "The Tribe: God's Own People A Theological Perspective", in *Sevartham*, 12 (1987), 58.

431 A. PARAPULLIL, "Tribal Theology", op. cit., 38.

432 S. FUCHS, "The Concept of Salvation in Tribal Religions", op. cit., 363.

433 A group of five elderly persons.

434 Cf. A. PARAPULLIL, "Tribal Theology", op. cit., 39.

435 All the furniture has to be changed, clothes and vessels washed, and the house cleaned. The offender is shaven the head, and he is given to drink the blood of the sacrificial victim, either a fowl or a goat.Then there is a ritual bath after which the head of the *panchayat* receives water from the hand of the culprit and drinks, which signifies that he takes the burden up on himself and re-admits the culprit to the community. (Cf. A. PARAPULLIL, "Tribal Theology", op. cit., 40).

436 A. VAN EXEM, "The Tribe: God's Own People", op. cit., 58.

437 A. PARAPULLIL, "Tribal Theology", op. cit., 40.

reconciliation with God and with the brethren, since Jesus teaches that fraternal reconciliation must take place before the sacrifice is offered (cf. Mt. 5:23)."[438]

Therefore, in order to participate fully in this celebration, the participant needs to admit his/her failings and shortcomings before the God of mercy and the community present. Participation in the Eucharistic meal is considered as sign of reconciliation and communion with the rest of the people. "The Eucharist is indeed the Sacrament of transformation of the world. …It proclaims and brings about the transformation of every fragmented kingdom into the one kingdom of God."[439] It is on their sharing of the Eucharistic bread that St. Paul bases the union of all faithful. "Because there is one loaf, we who are many are one body, for we all partake of the same loaf" (1Cor. 10:17). By the sacrament of penance man is incorporated in Christ and united with his members.

"Those who approach the sacrament of penance obtain pardon from God's mercy for the offences committed against him, and are, at the same time, reconciled with the church which they have wounded by their sins and which by charity, by example and by prayer works for their conversion."[440]

Similarly by sharing the reconciliation meal the offender is re-incorporated into the life of the community and its members.

3.6. Idea of Salvation

Oraon soteriology is essentially linked with their understanding of reconciliation. Salvation is a central issue in man's relation with God. They understand that "salvation or reconciliation is a restoration of order and life, a re-creation."[441] It is sin that destroyed the harmony that existed in creation. Sin is destruction or absence of life, a return to chaos, whereas salvation is the removal of chaos and death, thus restoring the creation to life, to harmony.

Oraons believe in salvation in relation to nature and creation. Their religion shows the goodness of God's creation as an eschatological hope. "To him (Oraon) the order of the world according to fixed laws is not a prison in which he would feel incarcerated. The world is good because God made it for man's well-being."[442] And it is in this world that he would attain his salvation.

The creation myth also throws some light on Oraon's understanding of salvation. The creator God, *Dharmes,* is at the same time the God who saves. He saved *Bhaiya-Bahin* (brother-sister) from the rain of fire and made them the progenitors of the tribe. This myth reveals a reality. Human beings were destroyed because of their wrongdoing. They were incapable of redeeming themselves as a

[438] RP 7.

[439] E. LaVERDIERE, "The Eucharist, Sacrament of the Transformation of the World", in *Omnis Terra* (English edition, May 1994), 382.

[440] LG 11.

[441] A. VAN EXEM, "Sin and Salvation in Sarna Religion", in *Vidyajyoti,* 47 (1983), 298.

[442] A. VAN EXEM, "Tribal for Ever. The Eschatology of Sarna", in *Sevartham,* 13 (1988), 28.

consequence of sin. *Dharmes'* intervention was absolutely necessary and *Dharmes* in his goodness restored creation by saving those two infants through whom he founded the tribe. Thus we come across the sacredness of their tradition and their firm belief that a tribe is a God-given means for salvation.[443] And it is in and through the tribe that one attains salvation, and the individual's salvation is aimed at the salvation of the tribe, - obviously a communitarian understanding of salvation.

Of course, the tribe is to be understood in its vertical dimension, as "the link of the individual with his ancestors as well as with his descendants,"[444] and not merely in its horizontal dimension as the unity of all the members of the present generation. Therefore one who has been faithful to one's duty to the tribe, one who has fulfilled his duty as a parent of the family, one who has been faithful in his sacrifices to Dharmes and offerings to spirits and ancestors, can be accorded the full rites of obsequies and is thus considered to have attained salvation. If one has failed in any of these matters, he/she is not accorded the full and proper obsequies and so considered not to have achieved salvation.[445]

Accordingly what counts for salvation is whether one has breathed his last within the tribe or outside of it. Thus a mother dying at child birth and a person dying in an accident are judged to have failed the tribe; to them salvation is denied for no fault of theirs.[446] Thus it is the tribe that has the power to judge whether the person deserves the full and proper obsequies that would incorporate one into the community of ancestors, and thus include or exclude one from salvation.

"Oraons consider that *Dharmes* is too good to punish them, and that they are not answerable to Him for their conduct in any way. All of them will go to '*Merkha*' (heaven) which is a replica of a good and happy earthly life. Therefore there is no room for a hell or any such 'place' of punishment."[447]

In the light of the Oraon understanding of salvation the above statement is true only for those who die in the tribe. The unfortunate ones, who die outside the tribe are considered to be spirits in the 'wild' and excluded from the ancestors. The loneliness of this separation can be seen as hell. The fortunate majority who die in the tribe become ancestors and their incorporation into the ancestral community is understood as the attainment of heaven.

"Heaven is portrayed as the happy ploughing grounds, where everybody will have plenty of land, bullocks to plough and rice-beer to drink after labour."[448] It conveys their belief in an existence after life, a state of happiness or fullness of

---

443 Cf. A. VAN EXEM, "The Tribe: God's Own People", op. cit., 47-48.

444 A. VAN EXEM, "Man and His Imperceptible Self: The Munda Philosophy of Man", in *Sevartham,* 5 (1980), 88.

445 Cf. B. TIRKEY, *Oraon Symbols*, op. cit., 73.

446 Cf. ibid., 73.

447 A. PARAPULLIL, "Tribal Theology", op. cit., 43.

448 A. PARAPULLIL, "Tribal Theology", op. cit., 43.

life. As sin is a social reality, so too is salvation. They understand salvation as a gift entrusted to the tribe by *Dharmes*. This communitarian nature of salvation brings the tribe into focus. Understanding oneself as a link in the tribe, an Oraonworks out his/her salvation by fulfilling his/her duties within the framework of the tribal order.

3.7. Convergences / Divergences and Possible Approaches for Evangelisation

In the Oraon traditional religion, even though the original harmony was destroyed by the wrongdoings of men, there was no promise of a saviour. As in the Christian tradition, the creator God in his goodness endowed man with freedom by which man is able to accept or reject God. However in the Oraon traditional or *sarna* religion, salvation is attained in and through the tribe; it is even determined by the tribe. One finds one's salvation within the frame work of one's tribe by fulfilling the duties as a corporate being. In other words salvation is an incorporation into the company of ancestors. Therefore it is a human judgement which has a ritualistic meaning rather than a spiritual value. In fact, the tribe is *Dharmes*' election, yet he is seen as a far away God who has nothing to do directly with salvation.

In Christian tradition salvation means life in Christ, who is the promised saviour of the world, through whom the destroyed original harmony is re-established. "God desires all men to be saved and to come to the knowledge of the truth"(1Tim. 2: 4). Salvation is an act of love, an act of God's self-communication. "Salvation in Christ, as witnessed and proclaimed by the Church, is God's self-communication."[449] "It is love which not only creates the good, but also grants participation in the very life of God: Father, Son and Holy Spirit. For he who loves desires to give himself."[450] Jesus Christ is the personification of God's love. Those who accept Jesus Christ and surrender to him by an act of faith attain salvation. He is saved into the company of the divine Trinity.[451] "Therefore, if anyone is in Christ, he is a new creation, the old has gone, the new has come! All this is from God, who reconciled us to himself through Christ and gave us the ministry of reconciliation" (2 Cor. 5:17-18). St. Paul in his letters refers to salvation as a future event in which God is the judge giving the reward to the good people and destroying the wicked, then establishing his kingdom on earth (cf. Phil. 3:18ff).[452] "Judgement is the deepest personal awareness of what one has

---

[449] RM 7.

[450] DM 7.

[451] Cf. X. LEON-DUFOUR (ed.), *Dictionary of Biblical Theology* (London: Geoffrey Chapman, 1969), 460.

[452] Cf. J. C. FENTON, "Salvation", in A. RICHRDSON and J BOWDEN (ed.), *The Westminster Dictionary of Christian Theology* (Philadelphia, Pennsylvania: The Westminster Press, 1983), 519.

become in one's personal relation with God. It is not merely a future reality but an element of the present experience as well."[453] Thus for a Christian salvation is an everyday experience, i.e. being liberated from the oppressive forces of evil. This is actualised in him by Christ for "Jesus Christ ...is the centre of God's plan of salvation."[454]

"The Church is the sign and instrument of salvation."[455] The Church is the mystical body of Christ and he operates on the Church through the sacraments. "Sacraments are "powers that come forth" from the Body of Christ, which is ever-living and life-giving. They are actions of the Holy Spirit at work in his Body, the Church."[456] Therefore sacraments are means to obtain salvation. In other words sacraments are channels that lead to Christ who is the author of salvation. "Salvation which always remains a gift of the Spirit, requires man's co-operation, both to save himself and to save others."[457] In this sense in the Oraon traditional religion there are no sacraments and no sacramentals that would lead and guide the people to liberate them from their personal bondages from evil as the Church understands them. But they do have the community reconciliation, as explained above. Therefore it is important to integrate these two practices of sacramental life to establish communion with God and fellow beings.

3.8. Idea of Priesthood

Oraons have their own religious leader, a village priest whom they call *pahan* or *baiga*. He is ordinarily a descendant of the original settlers of the village, through the first born son or his nearest male agnates.[458] He is entitled to possess a certain amount of rent-free land for his sustenance and for religious ceremonies. Nowadays people also give some help so as to facilitate his priestly task.[459]

"He is highly respected in the village. His role is purely cultic. He has no training or any sort of formation for his office. His only requirement is familiarity with the rites and formulae."[460] Only married men are entitled to be priests. The propitiation of the village spirits is the prerogative of the *pahan* (village priest). He offers in the presence of the village community the periodical sacrifices at the *Sarna* or the sacred village-grove. Generally at least one assistant called *panbhara* or *pujar* helps the village priest in these sacrifices by supplying the water required for

---

453 Z. HAYES, "Judgement", in C. STUHLMUELLER (ed.), *The Collegeville Pastoral Dictionary of Biblical Theology*, op. cit., 509.

454 RM 6.

455 RM 9.

456 CATECHISM OF THE CATHOLIC CHURCH, para. 1116.

457 RM 9.

458 Cf. V. ROSNER, "Pahan, Cult-Priest of the Munda", in *Sevartham*, 4 (1979), 57.

459 Cf. S. C. ROY, *Oraon Religion and Customs*, op. cit., 7.

460 V. A. BHAT, "Priestly Functions among the Hos", in *Sevartham*, 5 (1980), 90.

the cooking of the sacrificial meat.[461] "They (*pahan* and *pujar*)are representatives or mouth-pieces of the community."[462]

In spite of the fact that the office of the *pahan* is hereditary, there are occasions which may demand the selection of a new *pahan*. "This may happen when an epidemic has struck a village community or their cattle; some virulent blight attacked the crops, and despite sacrifices of the *pahan*, there is no respite over the years."[463]

In such a case all the adult male members of the village assemble at the *sarna* on a special day either in January-February or in December-January, bringing with them the *sarna-soop*, a winnowing basket.[464] They also bring along with them a *sal* (shorea robusta) pole split into two at one end and attached in the manner of a fork to this winnowing basket. The outgoing *pahan* brings along with him a new winnowing basket with *aruachaval* (pearl rice)[465] in it.

A young bachelor who is known to be susceptible to psychic and supernatural forces acts as a medium in the process of the election of the *pahan*. The old *sarna soop* is placed in his hands. Each one present throws a few grains of pearl rice into the old *sarna soop* saying: "do enter O *Chala pachcho*, into the house of the man with whom thou art well pleased." Now this blind folded young bachelor, believed to be led by the *sarna* spirit, walks to the village holding the *sal* pole with the *sarna-soop* (winnowing basket). The outgoing *pahan* follows behind scattering intermittently a few grains of rice from the new *soop* and dropping water from a brass jug. A few men may accompany them. Others wait in the *sarna*.

On arriving at the house of a person whom the lady of the grove wants to be the new *pahan*, the blind folded man places the winnowing basket at the threshold of the house of that man. He is recognised as the new *pahan*. They then return to the *sarna* with the newly elected *pahan* who carries the new winnowing basket and the blind folded man the old winnowing fan. The same method is done for the election of the assistants of the *pahan*.[466] The *Pahan* is responsible for the whole community in spiritual matters as he is the public sacrificer. "Apart from the village priest and other ministers, the head of the family also plays the role of a priest in offering family sacrifices."[467]

---

[461] Cf. S. C. ROY, *Oraon Religion and Customs*, op. cit., 5.

[462] Ibid., 5.

[463] V. ROSNER, "Pahan, Cult-Priest of the Munda", op. cit., 58-59.

[464] It is believed that the lady of he grove *Chala pachcho* sits on this winnowing basket, and so this is the emblem of the *pahan's* office.This has been used at every *puja* (sacrifice) at *Sarna*. It is placed carefully and religiously on a beam of compartment in *pahan's* house known as *chalakutti* or compartment sacred to the *sarna* spirit. (Cf. S. C. ROY, *Oraon Religion and Customs*, op. cit., 6).

[465] Paddy that is dried and husked, not par-boiled.

[466] Cf. S. C. ROY, *Oraon Religion and Customs*, op. cit., 6-7, cf. P. EKKA, *The Mundas and Oraons*, op. cit., 296-297.

[467] A. PARAPULLIL, "Tribal Theology", op. cit., 47.

3.9. Convergences / Divergences and Possible Approaches for Evangelisation

In Oraon traditional religion there is a sort of hierarchical priesthood order: *pahan* (the village priest), his helpers and the head of the family. A *pahan* holds his office by virtue of his birth or selection and his role is purely cultic and honorary. He is elected by the people and so it is a people's call. He offers sacrifices in the name of the tribe hence he is the mediator between *Dharmes* and man, a vertical relationship exercised only during the cultic activities. He has no leading and guiding authority. The cultic aspect of the Oraon tribal priesthood stands out much more than the shepherding and prophetic role in Christianity.[468] Priesthood in Oraon traditional religion is hereditary and marriage is a prerequisite.

In Christianity the priest is a person who has received a special election or call from God, and who responds to this call by establishing a covenantal relationship with God. Therefore it is God's election, not man's. Priesthood is a special grace which is linked to Christ Jesus the unique "high priest after the order of Melchizedek" (Heb. 5:10), "holy, blameless, unstained" (Heb. 7:26). The person who is selected by God receives the authority to exercise his office through the sacrament of Holy Orders. Therefore this office which the Lord entrusts to his chosen one is 'service,' which is called diakonia in the Sacred Scripture (cf. Acts 1:17, Rom. 11:13).[469]

"It (priesthood) is entirely related to Christ and to men. It depends entirely on Christ and on his unique priesthood; it has been instituted for the good of men and the communion of the Church. The sacrament of Holy Orders communicates a "sacred power" which is none other than that of Christ. The exercise of this authority must therefore be measured against the model of Christ, who by love made himself the least and the servant of all. The Lord said clearly that concern for his flock was proof of love for him."[470]

The priest in Christianity is one from the people and for the people. He is the guide and shepherd for his people leading them to Christ the eternal priest, thus bringing communion between God and his people and between people and people. "The Priest was above all the one commissioned to act in *persona christi*, mediating divine grace through the offering of the Sacrifice of Christ's Body and Blood and the absolution from sins."[471]

---

[468] Cf. A. PARAPULLIL, "Tribal Theology", op. cit., 47.

[469] Cf. LG 24.

[470] CATECHISM OF THE CATHOLIC CHURCH, para. 1551.

[471] R. K. SEASOLTZ, "Priest Pastoral-Liturgical Tradition", in C. STUHLMUELLER (ed.), *The Collegeville Pastoral Dictionary of Biblical Theology*, op. cit., 779.

Chapter Summary

The above study, shows that the religion of the Oraons is a complex system of beliefs and practices which is part of their everyday life. They worship *Dharmes* whom they consider the creator of the universe, also the maker of their tribe. It is to him that they turn in their difficulties when all other means fail them. Their belief in spirits - both benevolent (ambivalent) and malevolent is an obvious reality. To live in harmony with these spirits, the Oraons offer them timely offerings, but what is predominant in these offerings is their fear, their anxiety to escape from the harm these spirits can cause in their life. Moreover such beliefs make them victims of many occult practices.

They believe that man is the crown of creation. He is entrusted with a mission to be a co-creator with *Dharmes*. He is called to stay in communion with his fellow beings and with nature by adhering to the tribal ethos. The Oraons' main concern is to live according to the designs of *Dharmes* which are expressed in unwritten moral codes and values of the tribe.

Through this analysis we have found that the Oraon traditional religion (or *sarna* religion of Oraons) has many praiseworthy elements that can be purified and transformed, and thus play an important role within a Christian frame work. In this way ancient religiosity becomes a path for the new faith. Oraons can be considered a people who are relatively close to the good news of Jesus Christ. The Gospel message is dynamic, transforming and productive. It meets man in his actual life situations, challenging him to die to himself, to his "limited vision, inadequate attitudes and imperfect cultural values, and constantly strive towards a closer fidelity to the Gospel."[472] As the Oraons have some particular festivals connected with their traditional religion it is important to analyse these aspects of their culture too. Therefore in the next chapter we shall deal with "Various Festivals and Rites with Religious Connotations."

[472] A. R. CROLLIUS (ed.), "Inculturation", Working papers on Living Faith and Cultures, Vol. VII (1986), 9.

Chapter 4

VARIOUS FESTIVALS AND RITES WITH RELIGIOUS CONNOTATIONS

Introductory Remarks

We have seen in the preceding chapter the 'Basic Beliefs of the Traditional Oraon religion.' In order to express their basic beliefs they have various means. There are celebrations that speak in the language of symbols, are narrated in myths and performed in rituals. Although on the surface many of these events may appear as purely cultural folklore or as socially interesting entertainment, at a deeper level such occasions reveal also important religious dimensions. These are ways to deepen the Oraons' relationship with the Sacred. Of course there are also other possibilities to express and to foster their communion with God. Here much attention should be paid to the question of prayer in its private as well as a communitarian expression of religiosity, in the manner it is presented in spontaneous invocations or in a highly formulized recitation in simple words or in structured songs. One would have to analyse its content as well as its intention: petitions or thanksgiving or praise and adoration. But as important as all this is a deeply lived personal or communitarian religiosity. In the present chapter we consciously omit the entire field of prayer and concentrate uniquely on the precise area of concern on this study - the various festivals and rites with religious connotations.

4.1. Cyclical Feasts of the Community

In the history of mankind every people has set aside certain days or periods of time to commemorate, to celebrate or to re-enact social events or natural seasons of importance which are connected with their life. These celebrations give meaning and cohesion to their religious, political, socio-economic life in the community.

Such commemorative celebrations usually include sacred community meals and are called feasts or festivals.[473]

Celebrations of festivals and the performance of rituals reveal the spiritual and material aspects of human nature, and implicitly establish a link between these two realms of reality. At the basis of such a link lies religion with its functions and meanings.[474] According to Mircea Eliade, a Romanian-American historian of religion, festival time is sacred. That is to say a festival helps man to participate in the transcendent (or supernatural) realm in which the patterns of man's religious, social, or cultural institutions and activities were or are established. Through ritualistic re-enactment of the events that inform man about his origin, identity, and destiny, a participant in a festival identifies himself with the sacred time.[475]

Therefore festivals with their obvious collective character are the best expressions of the religious life of human groups. No one celebrates a festival all alone. Thus festivals have an essential community dimension and even religious depth. For the Oraons of Chotanagpur too festivals are important sacred actions. Yet, these festivals are not commemorations of definite historical events, but cultural-religious activities intimately connected with nature and their day-to-day life. That is to say their socio-economic experience is fashioned according to the sequence of the seasons; hence, these festivals are seasonal and closely linked to the corresponding activities.

The Oraons celebrate feasts and festivals with great rejoicing. Normally this takes place at the beginning or at the end of a season. It is a public occasion with elaborate rites, sometimes protracted over several days. Its high point is the public sacrifice or a series of sacrifices, made to the Supreme Being, to the ancestor spirits and to those various other spirits. It is inauspicious if the Oraons do not celebrate a festival.[476]

There is a cycle of festivals for the Oraons of Chotanagpur. They call it *Parab* (feast), a sacred action which aligns the life of the tribe with nature and the supernatural. "These are days of intense communion between the visible and invisible world."[477] Any festival is a manifestation of their success in their economic

[473] A feast, as the term indicates, consists of feasting (eating and drinking) in connection with passage rites, commemorative celebrations, seasonal observances, etc. Festivals, besides feasting often include dramatic dancing and athletic events, as well as revelries and carnivals. (Cf. L. FREDERICKSEN, "Feast and Festival," in *The New Encyclopaedia Britannica*, Macropaedia, Vol. 7 (1974), 197-198.

[474] Cf. M. AMALADOSS, "Man and Feast", in *Jeevadhara*, 6 (1976), 405.

[475] M. ELIADE, *The Sacred and the Profane: The Nature of Religion*. Translated from the French by W. R. Trask (New York: A Harvest Book, Brace & World, Inc. 1959), 78-79.

[476] Cf. A. VAN EXEM, "Munda Sacrifice and Festival", in *Sevartham*, 7 (1982), 88-91.

[477] P. PONETTE, "Spirituality of the Mundas", in *Sevartham*, 9 (1984), 76.

activities and an expression of the blessings from God. "The feasting with food and drink, with song and dance belongs to the essence of the festival."[478]

Here we shall examine the various festivals of the Oraons by studying the basic aspects of their celebration of feasts and discover some important religious implications. We shall deal with the most significant celebrations. These festivals can be divided into two different categories: forest festivals, *Phagua* and *Sarhul,* and agricultural festivals, *Karam, Dhanbuni, Hariari, Kadleta, Khalihani, Nayakhani, Maghe* and *Soharai.*

4.1.1. Forest Festivals

Even though the Oraons are farmers, they supplement the produce of their fields with edible flowers, fruits, tubers which they collect from their forests, but also with meat from occasional hunting activity. In this sense, forest festivals are two in number. They are *Phagua* and *Sarhul,* referring to the animal world and to the plant world respectively and thus recalling the Oraons' original socio-economic system as hunters and gatherers.[479]

4.1.1.1. Phagua

The life of the Oraons is very closely connected with nature. Hence many of their feasts coincide with the agricultural cycle and time itself appears as cyclical, and in this even repetitious. *Phagua* occurs in February-March. This is an important feast because it marks the beginning of a new year. The Oraons think that it is their duty to join nature's newness and freshness and they do it in a festive way. They want to throw away the evils of the past year and have a fresh start. Unless this feast is celebrated no one collects the fruits of his labour and jungle products. Only after this feast the fields are prepared for fresh crops. Thus this is putting an end to the old and welcoming the new.[480]

During the celebration of *Phagua,* the Oraons organise hunting in order to commemorate their old tradition of hunting which is also an activity for gathering food. This hunting festival is called *Phagua Sendra* which means spring hunt. In this festival the celebrant of the *Dandakatta* prays to *Dharmes* to protect the hunters from all evil and danger and to send plenty of game for the hunt. All other rituals are the same as in the case of *Phagua.*[481]

4.1.1.1.1. Celebration

The day before the festival young men of the village bring a branch or a young plant of the *erendi* or castor oil (palma christi) plant and one or two branches of the *semar* (bombax malabaricum) tree. These are planted in an open place where

[478] A. VANEXEM, "Munda Sacrifice and Festival", op. cit., 89.

[479] Cf. A. A. KUJUR, *The Oraon Habitat,* op. cit., 171.

[480] Cf. J. LAKRA, *Adivasi Missa Samgrah* (Ranchi: Catholic Press, 1982), 7.

[481] Cf. J. LAKRA *Tribal Cultural Anthropology,* op. cit., 44-45.

the Oraons celebrate their feast so that they can serve as a tripod. These branches are then covered with straw. With the whole village assembled the *pahan* (village priest*)* makes an offering of bread, incense and a black fowl to all the spirits, also venerating the ancestor spirits and seeking their blessing for their tasks. A *Dandakatta* ritual is performed in individual families.[482]

The afore-mentioned branches are set on fire amid loud shouts of rejoicing. A living fowl is thrown into this fire. As the fire blazes the *pahan* chops off the burning branches with a stroke. Children take these branches and throw them at the trees shouting 'bring forth good and plenty of fruits'. When the last sticks of the tripod are burned off, people apply the ashes on their forehead. Finally all the families join together to celebrate by drinking and dancing.[483]

4.1.1.1.2. Symbolism-Interpretation of Meaning

The main symbols used in the *Phagua* feast are: branches of *semar* (bombax malabaricum), fire, fowl, ashes and things directly connected with the Oraons' daily life, to which they ascribe some meaning. *Semar* (bombax malabaricum) is a tree which stands for death and destruction in the Oraon culture. Therefore burning these branches signifies their desire to be freed from all sorts of evils that harm their life - sickness, death, bad crops, other calamities, etc. In other words it symbolises a total destruction of the past so that nothing of it remains in the new year.[484]

Fire has several functions: to illumine, to warm but also to destroy. The Oraons use fire to cook, to warm themselves especially during the winter season and to clean the forests. Before the monsoons in the hot summer when the forest is covered with dry leaves they set fire there. During the rains, the water washes away the ashes to the fields whereby the forest is cleansed and the fields are fertilised. Ashes are used as a manure, as a pesticide for plants, as a means to clean the vessels. Ashes dissolved in water serve as a detergent to clean Oraons' clothes, hence as a purificatory agent. Children throw torches of fire on the fruit trees. This manifests the Oraons' desire to have good products, abundance in everything. Fruitfulness and prosperity are essential to their concept of life.

Many religions of the world have used 'fire' as a symbol in their acts of worship. It is in fact one of those items which can be found almost in all cultures of the world. (These are elements closely related to archetypical forms as they are known in psychology.) This seems to apply also to different societies on the Indian sub-continent. Thus it does not appear to be far-fetched to mention also the case of a typical Hindu feature which seems to be tightly linked to what we see in the Oraon culture too.

---

[482] Cf. S. C. ROY, *Oraon Religion and Customs*, op. cit., 40-141.

[483] Cf. M. KUJUR, *Oraon Sanskriti* (Ranchi: Catholic Press, 1993), 81-82; cf. J. LAKRA, *Adivasi Missa Samgrah*, op. cit., 7.

[484] Cf. B. TIRKEY, *Oraon Symbols*, op. cit., 32.

"In the Indian tradition fire is the first element that came into existence. It had its origin from God. The most important offerings were placed in the fire and were consummated in it. This was an action of *Agni*, god of the fire who acted as mediator between worshipper and the divinity."[485]

In the OT fire is one of the symbols used to manifest the presence of God as well as his actions. God revealed his designs to Moses in the midst of a burning bush (cf. Ex. 3:2). The Chosen People were led through the desert from Egypt to the promised land by God, "present" in a pillar of fire (cf. Ex. 13:21). On Mount Sinai God appeared to his people in the form of fire and thus the Israelites experienced God concretely (cf. Ex. 19:18, 24:17). The anger of God is also expressed by using the image of fire (cf. Ps. 18:8, Jer. 21:12, Is. 66:15). Fire which consumes everything is also a symbol of purification (cf. Sir. 2:5, Mal. 3:2-3).[486]

In the NT fire is used as a metaphor for God who consumes everything (cf. Heb. 12:29). Speaking about Jesus, John the Baptist says "he will baptise you with the Holy Spirit and fire" (Mt. 3:11). And Jesus himself says, "I came to cast fire upon the earth and would that it were already kindled" (Lk. 12:49). St. Peter in his second letter writes about the new heavens and the new earth which would be formed by a consuming fire that purifies all impurities, thus prepares a place for the righteous (2 Pt. 3:12).

The use of fire throws light to the primordial. *Dharmes* used fire to clean the world from its impurities that it might bring forth new life. We have a similar action of God in the book of Genesis. God used fire in order to destroy the city of Sodom and Gomorra because of its evils (cf. Gen. 19:22, 24). A living fowl is thrown into the fire and fire is the symbolic representation of *Dharmes* himself. This ritual re-enacts the primordial. The fire of *Dharmes*, consumes everything that is evil; the *Asurs*, are burned to ashes like the living fowl which is thrown into the fire. In order to put an end to those demoniac actions of the *Asurs, Dharmes* had to enter into the furnace, and on the third day he came out of it in glory. This furnace can be compared to hell where there is disharmony-chaos. On the third day there was a transformation, evil is eliminated, and harmony is restored. There was victory over death and disorder.

Fire destroys and paves the way for newness, new life, a new generation. Fire is a gift from God, as also our Christian tradition confirms. On the day of Pentecost the Holy Spirit descended upon the apostles in the form of tongues of fire and filled them with the life of his Spirit, a renewed life (cf. Acts 2:2).[487] Fire is used to symbolise the creative and redemptive presence of God in the world. The Church begins the liturgical celebration of the Easter vigil with the blessing of

---

[485] P. PUTHANANGADY, "Symbolism of Fire in Indian Worship", in *Word and Worship*, X (1997), 312.

[486] Cf. M. LURKER, *Dizionario delle Immagini e dei Simboli Biblici* (Milano: Edizioni Paoline, 1990), 89-90.

[487] Cf. P. EKKA, "Adivasi Riti Rivaj", in *Sevartham*, 1 (1979), 87.

fire. The darkness which symbolises the original chaos (cf. Gen. 1:1ff) is dispelled by the paschal candle, the symbol of the Risen Christ who is the saving presence of God in the midst of his people.[488]

Ashes are symbolic of the destruction of past evils and misfortunes. They are also a sign of penance, of humility. They symbolise the fragility of human life (cf. Gen. 18:27, Job 39:19). Therefore the application of ashes helps the Oraons to recall that evil is destroyed, and this is possible only through the help of the Supreme Being. One is reminded of the Ash Wednesday practice in Christianity, which contains aspects of penitence and conversion and thus also indicates the end of the old and the beginning of a new life. This ritual represents a primordial event that eliminated everything that is impure.[489]

4.1.1.1.3. Phagua in the Light of Christian Faith

The celebration of *Phagua* includes many praiseworthy values, but we shall discuss only the following dominant values among them.

- There is an earnest desire to be freed from the various bondages that oppress life.
- Divine assistance is sought by offering sacrifices.
- Acknowledgement of creatureliness before the Supreme Being.
- Transition from death to life.

The *Phagua* feast expresses a longing to be freed from all forces of evil that harm the Oraons' life. It is worthwhile to give importance to this festival for its thrust is on a new beginning. This new start means to get rid of all evils and thus be liberated from the various bondages. The rites have a purificatory effect. Symbols of fire, ashes, immolation are apt to convey meaningful messages to open-minded people. By the symbolic manifestations of the rituals, the Oraons reveal their unworthiness before the Supreme Being and seek his assistance as he is the author of everything they possess.

In our Christian tradition some of these symbols are used with the same meaning. For instance the *Phagua* feast cleanses the tribe and all rejoice in the new life they receive. It can be compared to the celebration of the Easter vigil where the old is burned and new fire is lit. Christ the eternal Sun destroys the darkness by his death on the cross. He thus won over all evils. In Christianity we recite in the Apostles' Creed, He (Christ) descended into hell and on the third day he rose again. "Jesus did not descend into hell to deliver the damned, nor to destroy the hell of damnation, but to free the just who had gone before him."[490] This action

---

[488] Cf. P. PUTHANANGADY, "Symbolism of Fire in Indian Worship", op. cit., 313.

[489] Cf. B. TIRKEY, *Oraon Symbols,* op. cit., 33.

[490] CATECHISM OF THE CATHOLIC CHURCH, para. 633.

of Jesus reveals that Jesus by his death has conquered all evil and its influences in the world and thus he has won the victory.

In Oraon traditional religion the celebration of the *Phagua* feast manifests a new beginning. It denotes a transition, a passage into a 'cycle' which happens each year marking the end of 'old' disorders and the beginning of a 'new' order and harmony. For the Oraons it is a repeated nature phenomenon full of meaning and they join with nature to celebrate this feast, hopeful to be renewed in their life.

In Christianity there are no cyclical feast celebrations in the same sense as in traditional religion which simply follows the course of nature where everything repeats itself in a non-ending cycle. The Christian understanding conceives of time as lineal; history goes ahead to the future leaving the past behind. Christ the Paschal lamb was crucified and died on the cross 'once and forever'. It is a unique historical event. Yet in the liturgy this event is re-actualised; thus every year we are renewed in life. Yet, this does not mean a repetitious sequence, but a moving ahead, so to speak, in a spiral form, focused on the central and definite event of salvation history: the Paschal Mystery.

For a meaningful celebration of the *phagua,* it is important to recall to mind the significance of this feast. This feast can be inserted into Christian worship especially in the Holy Eucharist. "For the liturgy, 'through which the work of our redemption is accomplished,' most of all in the divine sacrifice of the Eucharist, is the outstanding means whereby the faithful may express in their lives, and manifest to others, the mystery of Christ and the real nature of the true Church."[491]

The Eucharist can be offered in an 'Adivasi rite.'[492] The faithful are asked to bring certain symbolic objects: a dry branch, dry leaves, dry grass, dry flower, an old and used broom, etc. which would display their 'disorders' (envy, hatred, calumny, indifference, etc.) in life. As in the Easter vigil let there be the fire burning. After the introductory greeting, the priest can bless the fire, for it symbolises Christ who destroys all disorders and brings order into life. In this context let the catechist or one of the elders of the village, who is very much

---

[491] SC 2.

[492] In 1979 during the biennial general body meeting of the CBCI which was held at Ranchi, it was decided to leave the matter of liturgical inculturation to Regional Bishops' Councils. (Cf. F. MATTIHIJS, "The Contribution of the Chotanagpur Church and its Impact", in *Indian Missiological Review*, 7 (1985), 60. The implementation of this decision is explained by Archbishop P. Ekka. "Bearing in mind the norms laid down by *Sacrosanctum Concilium* the Vatican II Constitution on the Sacred Liturgy, especially the hierarchic and communitarian character of the sacred liturgy (Nos. 26-32), its didactic and pastoral importance (Nos. 33-36) and the need to adapt it to the cultures and traditions of peoples, (Nos. 37-40) the Church everywhere has procceded with the process of vernacularisation and inculturation of the sacred liturgy.Imbued with the same spirit, the bishops, clergy, religious and faithful of the "Lievens' Mission" have also tried to vernaculrise and to inculturate it....The Adivasi Missa Sangrah (Adivasi rite) has the approval for use in their region by the Bishops of the tribal areas in Chotanagpur." (P. EKKA, "Tribals and Inculturated Liturgy", in *Indian Missiological Review*, 7 (1985), 145-147.

in touch with the peoples' life explain to them what is the significance of such symbols. He can exhort the participants in the words of St. Paul who speaks of the purification. "Cleanse out the old leaven that you may be a new lump, as you really are unleavened. For Christ, our paschal lamb, has been sacrificed. Let us, therefore, celebrate the festival, not with the old leaven, the leaven of malice and evil, but with the unleavened bread of sincerity and truth" (1Cor. 5:7-8). "Before men come to the liturgy they must be called to faith and to conversion."[493]

In an opportune moment with a contrite heart the faithful come forward one by one and throw their symbolic objects into the fire. They may or may not call out their disorders of life in a louder voice. When this symbolic action of purification is over the assembly can be further strengthened by the words of Jesus. "I am the light of the world; he who follows me will not walk in darkness, but will have the light of life" (Jn. 8:12). At the end of the catechetical instruction the priest can light the candles with the 'blessed fire' and distribute to the faithful. Also he distributes to them green branches, green leaves, green grass, a new flower, a new broom, etc. as the symbolic representation of the graces from the Lord. The participants with a renewed and determined heart receive these symbols, but they offer the lighted candles at the foot of the cross as a sign of their renewed life in and through Christ. The mass can be continued.

When the fire is dead the ashes can be taken home which reminds them that they are on the path of conversion and renewal and this new life can be obtained only through Christ who is the winner over all evil, darkness and untruth.[494] Christ the fire has consumed the malicious things and nothing of the old remains, for he is the light of the world, in him there is the new beginning.

4.1.1.2. Sarhul

Sarhul is the main festival of the Oraons. Since *sal* blossoms form the main element in this celebration it is called *Sarhul.*[495] *Sarhul* is celebrated in the month of March-April. During the spring season the earth is green and multicoloured with rich vegetation. The trees are adorned with colourful flowers. These *sal* blossoms form the most striking feature of blossoming nature in Chotanagpur. This feast is also known as 'flower feast'. In Oraon language they call it *khaddi* also *khekel-benja* or the marriage of the earth. During this festival the Oraons perform the marriage of 'mother earth' with the sky which is symbolically represented by the marriage of the *pahan*, the village priest and his wife. This is done to ensure the fertility of the earth. Until this feast takes place no Oraon will eat or use the

---

[493] SC 3.

[494] Cf. M. SODI, "Benedizione", in *NUOVO DIZIONARIO DI LITURGIA*, a cura di D. SARTORE e A. M. TRIACCA (Roma: Edizione Paoline, 1984), 171.

[495] *Sarhul* is formed of two sadri words: *sar* and *hul. Sar* means year and *hul* means beginning (literarly), but as this feast is celebrated in view of prosperity in every aspect it denotes blessings of generation. (Cf. M. KUJUR, *Oraon Sanskriti*, (Ranchi: Catholic Press, 1993), 222.

new flowers, fruits, and edible leaves of the season. It is celebrated in order to obtain a good harvest, good rain and thus prosperity in every aspect.[496] There is no fixed date for the celebration of this feast. Every village fixes its own day of celebration.

4.1.1.2.1. Celebration

The *sarhul* festival consists of the performance of many complex, partly overlapping rituals that cannot easily be isolated from each other, for instance, cleaning the *sarnadanri* (village spring) bringing augural water, catching chicks, crabs, fish, and performing the ceremonial bath of the *pahan* and his wife. This is followed by the solemn procession of the menfolk to the sarna, by the preparation for the *puja* (sacrifice) and by offering sacrifices to *Dharmes* and to the spirits.[497] Already on the eve of the feast, every family offers a sacrifice to their ancestors.

Around midday the *pahan* and *pujar* (*pahan's* assistant) go for a ceremonial bath. They are accompanied by musicians just like in a marriage procession. After the bath they and their wives are made to sit side by side as if they are getting married. They go through various rites of marriage like applying oil on the head and *sindur* (vermilion) on their foreheads. Many pots of water are poured on them saying *bariso* which means 'rain down'. This is done to symbolise the marriage of the earth and sky.[498] After these ceremonies the men go to the *sarna* accompanied by the marriage band.

After reaching *sarna* the *pahan* cleans a small part in the *sarna* and smears it with cow dung diluted in water. He then takes an un-bleached thread and winds it round the trunk of the main tree three to five times. He anoints it with oil and *sindhur* (vermilion). He anoints himself from the forehead to the chest and sits down - cross legged, facing east in front of the altar. Before the chickens are sacrificed, a handful of pearl rice is placed on a clean spot before them. The *pujar* selects chickens of appropriate colour for each spirit, washes their feet anoints their head with *sindur,* hands them over to the priest. The priest makes the victims to peck at the rice. While these chickens are busy feeding on the grains the *panches* throw some rice on the victims uttering some prayers of petition.[499]

The priest, after finishing the offering to the spirits, washes his hands and knife, then offers the sacrifice of a white fowl or an egg to *Dharmes*, in a specially prepared place for him. A special place of sacrifice shows the superiority of *Dharmes.* The Oraons believe that *Dharmes* controls all spirits who are evil.

A sacrificial meal is prepared out of pearl rice and meat of the fowls offered and with the help of augural water from the new pot of the *pujar.* This meal is shared by all the participants. When all the rituals are completed the people return

---

[496] Cf. S. C. ROY, *Oraon Religion and Customs*, op. cit., 142.

[497] Cf. B. TIRKEY, *Oraon Symbols*, op. cit., 34.

[498] Cf. P. EKKA, "Adivasi Riti Rivaj", op. cit., 88-89.

[499] Cf. S. C. ROY, *Oraon Religion and Customs*, op. cit, 151-153.

to their homes with great rejoicing, singing, dancing, and carrying *sal* flowers with them. Now the priest has become the representative of God. Hence he is carried by the villagers so that his legs do not touch the ground. When he reaches back home his wife washes his feet as a sign of welcome. She is given consecrated rice and augural water. She sprinkles this sacred water in all parts of her house, especially in the cattle shed and on the roof, also on the paddy seeds to be sown.[500]

The next day the priest goes to each family in order to distribute the *sal* flowers and sacred water. The housewife of each family receives the sacred water in a jar and other things in a *soop* (winnowing basket). She sprinkles the augural water in all the parts of her house. The Oraons receive it with much respect, for it is the blessing of God. As the priest and his assistant go around in this distribution ritual people pour water on them with loud cries "bariso, bariso" (rain down, rain down). The housewives give them pearl rice in return for the blessings. The priest receives it and returns a part of it to the giver which signifies communion and blessing.[501] When all the sacrificial rituals are completed the Oraons say: "Now the spirits have been seated in their respective places, and the earth got married; therefore plough, dig and sow seeds."[502]

4.1.1.2.2. Symbolism-Interpretation of Meaning

Sarhul is, as already said, the principal religious festival of the Oraons. Here not only the symbols that are used but also the rituals themselves are rich in meaning. In this ritual the symbolism is multiform. But all centre at the same idea "the progenitors are, and the tribe is, a tree of life."[503] Three parts can be distinguished in the ritual: the sacrificial rites, the water rites and the flower rites.

Sacrifices are offered to the Old Lady of the *sarna,* to all the ancestor spirits and other tutelary spirits and to *Dharmes.* The symbolism of the sacrifice is complex. The blood of the victim is sprinkled on the rice heaps. During the sacrifice the sacrificer identifies himself with the victim. It is an act of offering of one self, for blood stands for life. This can be understood as a sign of self-surrender. Yet no Oraons will agree to this interpretation as they sprinkle blood of the victim even when they offer sacrifices to evil spirits. What is prominent in their mind is that they surrender their total life to *Dharmes* who is the author of life.

"Spirit sacrifice is not pure, no virgin-colour victim is ever assigned to any spirit. The stipulated colours of the victim reveal something to the nature of the spirits-they are a class by themselves, and different from Dharmes. The victims are symbols of life, or something of life. They lack purity and wholeness. Diversity

---

[500] Cf. S. C. ROY, *Oraon Religion and Customs*, op. cit., 153.

[501] Cf. J. LAKRA, *Tribal Cultural Anthropology*, op. cit., 48; cf. P. EKKA, "Adivasi Riti Rivaj", op. cit., 89-90.

[502] J. LAKRA, *Tribal Cultural Anthropology,* op. cit., 48.

[503] A. VAN EXEM, *The Religious System of the Munda Tribe*, op. cit., 152.

in the victims offered signifies absence of totality, and signifies keeping back, as it were, of something of life from the spirits. Life in its purity and totality, symbolised by the sacrificial victim, serves as substitute for human life, which belongs fully to Dharmes alone."[504]

Sacrifice is a means to be in communion with *Dharmes* the Supreme Being. The victim which they offer to *Dharmes* (usually an egg, or a white fowl or a white goat) is a concrete embodiment of life in its simple and total sense, and they offer it to *Dharmes* so that he may transform the people's life and, keep them away from all evils.[505] All these sacrifices, except one to the ancestors are done in the *sarna*.

In a careful analogy, we can compare this *sarna* sacrifice to the sacrifice of Christ. In this ritual there is the immolation of the victim, total life is given. Christ, in his sacrifice, offered his life to the Father on the cross so that he (and with him the character of the world) would be transformed according to the designs of his Father. Here Christ is the victim, and the sacrificer; he shared his body with the community during the last supper in which he anticipated his self immolation. Its liturgical re-enactment is the Holy Eucharist.[506]

"*Sarhul* sacrifice and Eucharist are meant to bring God's deeds to the here and now so that they may overcome the consequences of primordial sin and restore the community into the harmony of God's designs. They differ because Eucharist recalls a historical and not a primordial or mythological event, and because it has no victim but the One who offered himself once for all. Christ is the Father's mighty deed. He is made present to be consumed."[507]

There is sharing of the sacrificial meal in the *Sarhul* sacrifice The meat of the fowls as well as rice beer have a prominent place in the meals of the Oraons. They offer these things to their close friends and relatives and these are the best things they have which they can offer to anybody in order to establish or deepen a relationship. Sharing a meal signifies reconciliation and harmony among themselves, with God and with their ancestors in the other life (in Christian terminology this comes close to the communion of saints at the heavenly banquet).[508] "Since all the faithful form one body, the good of each is communicated to the others. We must therefore believe that there exists a communion of goods in the Church. Therefore, the riches of Christ are communicated to all the members, through the sacraments."[509]

Human beings are created to live, to multiply and to take care of the earth. Water brings life, fertility. The sprinkling of water, the symbolic of rain, signifies the fecundity of nature and the tribe. If the monsoon is good then the harvest is

[504] B. TIRKEY, "Oraon Approaches to God and Spirits", in *Sevartham*, 7 (1982), 31.

[505] Cf. A. VAN EXEM, "The Sacrifice and Meal", in *Vidyajyoti,* LII (1988), 130-131.

[506] Cf. A. VAN EXEM, "The Sacrifice and Meal", op. cit., 133-134.

[507] Ibid., 135.

[508] Cf. P. KULLU, "Tribal Culture-Religion in Practice", in *Sevartham*, 18 (1993), 25.

[509] CATECHISM OF THE CATHOLIC CHURCH, para. 947.

likely to be good and the well-being of the tribe is ensured. Thus the level of water in the pitchers foreshadows good crops and an increase in the tribe.[510]

The symbolic marriage of the earth with the sky is expressed in the re-enacting marriage ritual of the *pahan*. It is a fertility rite. In order to produce good crops the earth needs to be prepared well, should get enough rain and sunlight. In this ritual the main thrust is on a good yield of crops. It also aims at the fecundity of the tribe.[511] Anointing of the *Sarna* (*sal*) tree is done in order to welcome the "lady of the grove" *Chala Paccho*. The anointed tree is believed to be her throne.

According to the Oraons young chickens represent innocent children. Hence innocent victims are offered to the spirits and the different colours signify the difference in the spirits. Always a white victim is offered to *Dharmes*, because the sacrifice offered to *Dharmes* should be perfect, pure and total. This ultimately signifies an offering of self, hence it involves the whole life of the sacrificer and the people.[512]

The distribution of *sal* flowers and augural water signifies the blessings of God. It also shows the Oraons' participation in the festival. It announces the beginning of a new vegetation and expresses the hope for prosperity and fecundity. However, in our Christian tradition, one could consider these *sal* flowers and augural water as sacramentals. Of course sacramentals are sacred signs instituted by Church and signify spiritual graces which are imparted through her intercession, thus sanctifying every event of people's life with the divine grace that flows from the Paschal Mystery of Christ.[513] Sacramentals bring blessings from God.

"Among sacramentals blessings (of persons, meals, objects, and places) come first. Every blessing praises God and prays for his gifts. In Christ, Christians are blessed by God the Father "with every spiritual blessing." This is why the Church imparts blessings by invoking the name of Jesus, usually while making the holy sign of the cross of Christ."[514]

4.1.1.2.3. Sarhul in the Light of Christian Faith

The celebration of *Sarhul* contains many values yet we shall discuss only some prominent features among them:

- A unique worship is given to *Dharmes,* the Supreme Being.
- Prayer is said to obtain good rains and fertility for the land.
- Sacrifices are offered to the ancestor spirits and all the other spirits.
- Sharing of the sacrificial meal.
- Distribution of the *sal* flowers and water as a sign of God's blessing.

---

[510] Cf. A. VAN EXEM, *The Religious System of the Munda Tribe*, op. cit., 151-152.

[511] Cf. B. TIRKEY, *Oraon Symbols*, op. cit., 35.

[512] B. TIRKEY, *Oraon Symbols*, op. cit., 36-37.

[513] Cf. SC 60-61.

[514] CATECHISM OF THE CATHOLIC CHURCH, para. 1671.

The attitude of the Oraons toward God is clearly expressed in this sacrifice to Dharmes. The insistence on the purity of the victim, the sacrificer and the participants is quite noteworthy. Sacrifice to *Dharmes* is offered on a special altar, exquisitely prepared. Acknowledging his supremacy over the spirit world, the Oraons plead with him to keep away all spirits who may harm their health and wealth. Believing in his power to provide for their needs (good rains and good crops, prosperity in everything), they make their prayers.[515]

Dependence on and trust in a God who provides for their needs is a leading principle in the life of the Oraons. Land, rain, good crops and many children are gifts of God. Therefore with confidence they ask him for these blessings. Their prayers are simple but cover all spheres of life. They do not have any written formulas, but they speak out their every day experiences, every day needs. As they express their desire to have plenty of fruit, prosperity and good health, they also acknowledge their total dependence on the Supreme Being.[516]

The Oraons remember all their ancestral spirits by offering sacrifices to them. Their desire to be in communion with the deceased ancestors is expressed in these sacrifices. They believe that ancestor spirits are persons who have won the favour of God (which is tied to their forms of life in the tribe), and they keep guard over their relatives. It is certainly a very praiseworthy attitude to remember those dead ancestors. They have loved their descendants in this life and seek their welfare even after death. This is especially true with persons who lived a just life. They are "mediators saints". Therefore it is reasonable for the Oraons to remember their ancestors together with all other clan and household spirits.[517] When there is an army of such guardian spirits no evil can harm them. Hence they should not be frightened by evil spirits, yet still they are!

Sharing the sacrificial meal is another important aspect. It shows communion with the divine and community, and communion among humans. It is a sign of reconciliation and friendship. In Christianity the Eucharistic meal is shared to show our union with the Lord. In order to partake in this meal reconciliation is needed. "So if you are offering your gift at the altar, and there remember that your brother has something against you, leave your gift before the alter and go; first be reconciled to your brother, and then come and offer your gift" (Mt. 5:23-24).

Water is an essential element in man's life. It has many functions: to wash away the impurities, to quench the thirst, to destroy the fire, to make the plants grow. "Water in the Bible, as in the Indian and other traditions, is a symbol of God's life-giving, thirst-slaking, sanctifying activity."[518] In this context water is the

---

515 Cf. B. TIRKEY, *Oraon Symbols*, op. cit., 35.

516 Cf. B. TIRKEY, "Oraon Approaches to God and Spirits", in *Sevartham*, 7 (1982), 33.

517 Cf. A. BRUGGEMAN, "Worship: Sarna and Christian Theological Reflections on the Munda Ba-Parab", in *Sevartham*, 7 (1982), 48-49.

518 VANDANA, "Water Symbolism in the Gospel of St. John in the Light of Indian Spirituality", in R. S. SUGIRTHARAJAH and C. HARGREAVES, *Readings in Indian Christian Theology*, Vol. 1

symbol of life for the Oraons. When there is water there is abundance in every sphere of life.

In Christian tradition the waters of baptism bring eternal life, to those who search for it. Baptism cleanses and heals the human being from all impurities, thus bringing forth in them a new life, "to be born of water and the Spirit" (cf. Jn. 3:5). The water that Jesus gives quenches the thirst of everyone giving them eternal life as was the case with the Samaritan woman (cf. Jn. 4:7-14). Jesus the Good Shepherd will lead his sheep to "the springs of living water" (Rev. 7:17). And all who want this life and thirst for it would have the water of life and have it free (cf. Rev. 22:17). The festival with its sacrifice is an attempt to rectify the fallen conditions of man. Life is a gift from God and life needs to be shared: giving life to one another, bringing everyone to the fullness of life.[519]

The *pahan* stands as a mediator between God and men. He intercedes for his people before God. He distributes the blessings in a tangible way to them. We have Christ who is the visible dispenser of divine life to humanity and the visible expression of God the Father, the source of all life. Today in the Church Christ continues his work through his ministers. Seeking the blessings of the elders, ministers, priests, and of our parents, etc., is an attitude compatible with the tenets of traditional religion as well as with genuine Christian convictions.

In order to celebrate *sarhul* in a Christian way let the faithful bring *sal* flowers and water in a container and be assembled in a convenient place outside the village church. After the preliminary introductory services the people go in procession singing and dancing into the church. At the entrance of the church the people are allowed to wash their legs, and be further purified by the sprinkling of the holy water by the priest. In order to express the unity of minds let the people greet each other and exchange their flowers. Then they go in silence up to the altar and place their flowers and water containers around the altar, to be blessed by the priest. At this moment the priest can offer his catechetical instruction by taking a suitable passage from the Bible, for example Sir. 39. 22-27 or Mat. 6. 24-33. After a stage of assimilation, prayers should be offered to God and to our ancestors in faith (saints in heaven) that they may bless the faithful with success in their efforts. Then the priest blesses the *sal* flowers and water by sprinkling holy water and by incensing. When all the celebrations are over the people can take the *sal* flowers and water home. These can be kept as a sign of God's protection and which will remind them of their commitment to God.[520]

These para-liturgical services are means to infuse and deepen the faith in which the Oraons may find their cultural traits. The Constitution on the Sacred

---

(London: SPCK Holy Trinity Church, 1993), 200.

[519] Cf. A. VAN EXEM, *The Religious System of the Munda Tribe*, op. cit., 155.

[520] Cf. J. CASTELLANO, "Religiosita Popolare e Liturgia", in *NUOVO DIZIONARIO DI LITURGIA*, a cura di D. SARTORE e A. M. TRIACCA (Roma: Edizione Paoline, 1984), 1170-1176.

Liturgy (cf. SC 37-39) clearly explains the attitude of the Church towards such adaptations.

"The Church does not wish to impose a rigid uniformity in matters which do not involve the faith or the good of the whole community. Rather does she respect and foster the qualities and talents of the various races and nations. Anything in these peoples' way of life which is not indissolubly bound up with superstition and error she studies with sympathy and, if possible, preserves intact. She sometimes even admits such things into the liturgy itself, provided they harmonise with its true and authentic spirit."[521*]

4.1.2. Agricultural Feasts

The principal agricultural festivals are *Dhanbuni, Kadleta, Hariari, Khalihani, Nayakhani, Maghe, Soharai and Karam*. The Oraon's wealth and agricultural life depends on cattle, and so it is apt to categorise the feast *soharai* along with the agricultural feasts. In the Oraon society the cultivation of the paddy is evidently of immense value. Therefore the people take great care to protect the standing crops by worshipping the *karam raja.* In this sense the *karam* feast is grouped under agricultural celebrations, even though it is a socially relevant feast of and for the unmarried girls and boys. Therefore before we investigate the other agricultural feasts let us study the *karam* feast.

4.1.2.1. Karam

The *karam*[522] festival is adapted by the Oraons from their non-tribal Hindu neighbours. This feast is centred around productivity and fertility. It is celebrated to get good and abundant crops, healthy children, etc. In fact the *karam* feast has particular importance for women, above all for the young unmarried maidens preparing themselves for marriage. Therefore the married daughters come back to their parents' house to celebrate this feast. Young unmarried ladies observe a fast and say prayers in order to obtain their hearts' desire from the *karam raja,*[523] i.e. a good husband, many healthy children and wealth.[524] At the same time this feast is also meant for the standing and maturing of crops. Thus the main thrust of these celebrations aims at having everything in abundance.[525]

---

[521] SC 37.

* As this study is a scientific research, we do not intend to articulate a project of inculturation. Therefore we limit such process here with the forementioned examples.

[522] The name of a tree (*nauclea parvifolia)*, found in Chotanagpur to which the Oraons assign the power to give good fortune.

[523] A deity like the spirit to whom the *karam* tree is dedicated.

[524] Cf. J. LAKRA, *Adivasi Missa Samgrah*, op. cit., 67; cf. M. KUJUR, *Oraon Sanskriti,* op. cit., 230.

[525] The young maidens offer barely shoots to young men and all keep these barely shoots in their hair. S. C. Roy writes: "It may not appear unreasonable to infer that these barley shoots that have been ceremonially nurtured by the maidens and, after consecration, presented by them to the

4.1.2.1.1. Celebration

Young unmarried ladies collect different types of flowers, especially white flowers and leaves, for about seven days and fill their *karam* baskets (baskets used for the *karam* festival). Towards evening young unmarried men and ladies accompanied by the *pahan* go to the jungle singing and dancing to cut the *karam* branches. On reaching the spot the *pahan* puts vermilion on the tree three times, also an unbleached thread. They select and cut those branches which are full of healthy leaves, and bring them in procession amidst singing and dancing to the courtyard of the *pahan*.[526]

The wife of the *pahan* puts *sindhur* (vermilion) on these branches, then they are planted on the *akhra* (village dancing place). The young women have in their *karam* baskets some *aruvachaval* (pearl rice), *chiuda* (beaten rice) and a tender cucumber wrapped in a coloured cloth, an earthen lamp, new shoots of various plants and fruits. They pay special reverence to the *karam* branches by placing their ornaments on them. The *pahan* ties these branches with an unbleached thread and offers incense to them.[527]

Those women who are newly betrothed are led around the *karam* branches three times while sacred water is sprinkled on those branches. Then the earthen lamps in the baskets are lit. All sit around the bunch of branches in order to listen to the *karam* story[528] narrated by an elderly person.[529] While the narration is in progress the young maidens throw pearl rice and flowers on the *karam* branches at regular intervals. Young men and women offer milk pearl rice and other grains to the *karam raja*.

The narration of the story ends with a prayer. "O *karam raja*, I ask your blessings upon all, give your gifts to all: those who do not have wealth give them wealth. Those who do not have children, give them children. Give your blessings upon granaries, courtyards and streets of the village. Give your blessings upon our households, fields and flowers abundantly. May you be praised, O *karam raja* again and again."[530]

---

young men, may be intended to stimulate, by a process of sympathetic magic, the fecundity of the young people or perhaps to stimulate the growth of the standing crops on the fields, or perhaps to serve both ends which are indeed in the Oraon's estimation parts of the same process."(S. C. ROY, Oraon Religion and Customs, op. cit., 179-180).

[526] Cf. P. EKKA, "Adivasi Riti-Rivaj", op. cit., 90-91.

[527] Cucumber covered in coloured cloth symbolizes a new born child. Cf. P. EKKA, "Adivasi Riti Rivaj," op. cit., 92.

[528] A story which speaks about the origin of this cult. Cf. A. TIRKEY, "Karam festival Myth", in *Sevartham* (1982), 19.

[529] Cf. S. C. ROY, *Oraon religion and Customs,* op. cit., 178-180. cf. J. LAKRA, *Tribal Cultural Anthropology,* op. cit., 52.

[530] A. TIRKEY, "Karam festival Myth", op. cit., 19.

After this, all those who are present there, prostrate themselves or bow down before the *karam* branches. Then they sing and dance around the *karam* branches. This may continue even for the next day. In the afternoon the *karam* branches are uprooted. Amidst singing and dancing they are taken to each family where the mistress of each house puts vermilion on the branches and offers *karam* bread to the party. Finally, the branches are taken to a river or a tank and immersed in water, while they sing farewell songs to *karam raja*.[531] During this festival brothers give new clothes to their sisters and sisters offer new shoots of barley plants to their brothers.

4.1.2.1.2. Symbolism-Interpretation of Meaning

"Symbols ...link physical things with mental concepts."[532] The symbols used in this feast are *karam* tree, *karam* basket, fruits and flowers, unbleached thread, *sindhur* (vermilion) and pearl rice, etc. They denote important ideas. "But the power of the symbol, analysed or not, clearly rests on its comprehensiveness, on its fruitfulness in ordering experiences."[533]

"In ancient past, a tree was considered as the symbol of fertility and in a general way the mysterious source of life in itself."[534] A tree with lots of green foliage, which produces fruits according to the season, is a manifestation of life and hope. The tree which grows like the palm tree straight upward in the sky is a sign of unity between heaven and earth. The shade of the tree is considered a sacred place where offerings can be made. Thus the tree is a symbol of divinity.[535] The *karam* tree symbolises the *karam raja* who has the qualities of a divinity from whom the Oraons receive many blessings. It is also symbolic of life and fertility, life of the cosmos, of growth, of generative and regenerative processes. Thus it stands for inexhaustible life and immortality. *Karam raja* is seen as the bridegroom par excellence.[536] In many cultures a tree stands for the symbol of life. As this is true with the Oraons, it also plays a role in biblical tradition.

In the OT the tree is pictured as a symbol of life (cf. Gen. 3:22, Is. 65:22) and at times as an image of arrogance (cf. Is. 2:13). In the garden of Eden life was sustained by the fruits of the trees (Gen. 1:29). The tree of knowledge is linked to the story of how original sin came into the world (cf. Gen. 2:16-17). The prophet

---

[531] Cf. J. LAKRA, *Tribal Cultural Anthropology,* op. cit.,53.

[532] P. G. HIEBERT, *Cultural Anthropology* (Grand Rapids, Michigan: Baker Book House, 1983), 375.

[533] C. GEERTZ, *The Interpretation of Cultures* (New York, N.Y.: Basic Books, A Division of Harper Collins Publishers, 1973), 128.

[534] E. URECH, *Dizionario dei Simboli Cristiani* (Roma: Edizioni Arkeioes, 1995), 22. The original text is in Italian, translation is mine.

[535] Cf. M. LURKER, *Dizionario delle Immagini e dei Simboli Biblici* (Milano: Edizione Paoline, 1990), 8.

[536] Cf. B. TIRKEY, *Oraon Symbols*, op. cit., 40.

Ezekiel writes about a branch of a tree that was planted on a high mountain which grew into a big forest; here it represents the people of Israel (cf. Ez. 17:22).[537]

In the NT the image of a tree is used allegorically to explain the growth of the Kingdom of God (cf. Mt. 13:31-33), but also to describe the good and bad people in the world (cf. Mt. 3:10). Jesus had used this image in the case of the sterile fig tree (Lk. 13:6-9). Christ encountered Nathanael under the fig tree, thus the fig tree becomes a tree that provides divine experience and so Nathanael confesses Christ as the King of Israel (cf. Jn. 1:48-50). The branches of the palm tree stand for Christ's triumphant entry into Jerusalem on Palm Sunday.[538] "They took branches of palm trees and went out to meet him, crying Hosanna ...." (Jn. 12:13). The tree of life is pictured in the book of Revelation as a reward for those who have lived on this earth in accordance to the will of God (cf. Rev. 2:7, 22:2,14,19).[539]

Mankind obtained the remission of its original sin through the tree of life, the Cross on which Jesus died. The Cross, made of the wood of the tree of good and evil appears as a life giving tree, which rises from the earth to the heavens.[540] The Byzantine liturgy sings on the feast of the exaltation of the Holy Cross, "of 'the tree of life planted on Calvary, the tree on which the King of ages wrought our salvation,'...sanctifies the Universe unto its limits."[541] Christ, the new Adam, in his own person is the tree of life, author of all blessings and graces: "I am the vine, you are the branches. He who abides in me, and I in him, he it is that bears much fruit, for apart from me you can do nothing" (Jn. 15:5). He is the *raja* (king) of the universe.

The *karam* basket is meant for collecting and keeping the offerings for *karam raja*. Objects like tender shoots of many crops, flowers, fruits, tender cucumbers wrapped in coloured cloth, are symbols of life and fruitfulness. All this expresses a desire to have good and healthy crops and children (the cucumber symbolises a baby.)[542]

Flowers are signs of larger realities, and individual species have been used metaphorically as symbols. Flowers make us hopeful of fruits, they indicate beauty and abundance. Flowers are expressions of reverence and love. In the Bible flowers are referred to man's life blossoming and withering within the swift passage of

---

537 Cf. E. URECH, *Dizionario dei Simboli Cristiani*, op. cit., 22.

538 Cf. P. R. FRESE and S.J.M. GRAY, "Trees", in M. ELIADE (editor in chief), *The Encyclopedia of Religion*, Vol. 15 (New York: Macmillan Publishing Company, 1987), 26.

539 Cf. M. LURKER, *Dizionario delle Immagini e dei Simboli Biblici*, op. cit., 9.

540 Cf. M. ELIADE, *Images and Symbols Studies in Religious Symbolism*, translated by P. MAIRET (London: Harvill Press, 1961), 161.

541 H. De LUBAC, *Aspects du Boudhisme* (Paris: 1951) quoted in M. ELIADE, *Images and Symbols: Studies in Religious Symbolism*, op. cit., 162.

542 Cf. B. TIRKEY, *Oraon Symbols*, op. cit., 40.

time. (cf. Jb. 14:1; Ps. 103:15-16; Jas. 1:10; Mt. 6:28).[543] In the *karam* ritual flowers stand for future fruits which these young maidens hope for, also as a sign of their love towards the *karam raja*, who is the bridegroom par excellence. They offer to him white flowers, and white stands for purity, and virginity. By offering these flowers which is a symbolic action they surrender their lives to *karam raja* and seek his blessing for life.[544] The traditional offering of flowers can be compared to the Christian self offering to Christ, and even to the union with him who is the king of the universe. One attains this life in Christ through baptism, which is conferred in the name of Jesus (cf. Acts. 8:16, 10:48, 19:5), and accepts the claims of Jesus and unites himself to Jesus and other fellow followers of Christ.[545]

The unbleached thread, *sindhur* (vermilion), pearl rice, etc. stand for new life or fecundity. The future of the tribe depends on these young maidens. They stand for the good of the tribe. They are the future mothers of healthy Oraon children through whom the continuity of the tribe is secured.[546] Thus "the force of a religion in supporting social values rests on the ability of its symbols to formulate a world in which those values, as well as the forces opposing their realisation, are fundamental ingredients."[547]

4.1.2.1.3. Karam in the Light of Christian Faith

As the *karam* festival is significant for fertility and productivity the celebration reveals a number of good and meaningful elements. But we shall consider only a few among them.

- Worship is rendered to the divine.
- Ascetical Practices.
- The awareness that the divine is the cause of their life.

The tree represents the *karam raja* who gives them a good fortune. To people who are close to nature this type of worship and celebration is an enrichment to their life. Though this festival is particularly significant for the young maidens, the whole village participates in it. All of them venerate the *karam raja* with due respect, imploring his blessings upon them and their families. The *karam* story reveals that the *karam* tree stands for a redeemer who saved a family or a village through a repentant worshipper. Where there is true repentance, wrongs are forgiven and the penitent receives abundant blessings.[548] The *karam* tree branches

---

543 Cf. M. LURKER, *Dizionario delle Immagini e dei Simboli Biblici*, op. cit., 9.

544 Cf. X. IRUDAYARAJ, "Flowers as Religious Symbols", in *Word and Worship*, X (1977), 330.

545 Cf. J. L. McKENZIE, *The Dictionary of the Bible*, op. cit., 79.

546 Cf. B. TIRKEY, *Oraon Symbols*, op. cit., 41.

547 C. GEERTZ, *The Interpretation of Cultures*, op. cit., 131.

548 Cf. A. TIRKEY, "Karam Festival Myth", op. cit., 7-17.

receive great honour by being anointed with vermilion. They are brought in procession for the common worship and then are taken again in procession to each family. It can perhaps be compared to Eucharistic procession in our Christian tradition. We do offer our worship by spreading flowers, by sprinkling holy water, also by offering incense, etc.

Purity of mind and heart is a welcome even necessary attitude to approach the divine. The ascetical practices (fasting and praying) of the maidens are indeed noteworthy. These young women consider themselves as spouses to *karam raja*, thus prepare themselves to meet him. They have their little offerings which they bring in their baskets. Those are symbols of their eager longings to have a happy and healthy life with their bridegroom, to have everything in abundance - children, good crops, plenty of cattle, etc.[549] These maidens might be compared to those well-known Gospel figures, the wise virgins who waited for the bridegroom with lamps lit (cf. Mt. 25:1-13). Jesus is the bridegroom par excellence, the redeemer who gives life. "I came that they may have life, and have it abundantly" (Jn. 10:10).

From the various rituals of the *karam* festival it can be deduced that the Oraons are very religious people. Their dependence on God and their search for communion and friendship with God is present in all their celebrations. In this perspective *sarna* religion is rather close to Christianity. In Christianity there is a redeemer, who brought salvation to all of mankind, by transforming the death bringing wood into a tree of eternal life. The cross is our sign of salvation.

Most of these traditional values also make sense in Christianity and should be inserted in a meaningful inculturation process. For instance let there be a cross made of the branches of *karam* tree, and homage can be given to it in each village church, by offering flowers, incense and lighted lamps. Care should be taken to display maximum veneration of the cross. Such dispositions can be expressed by being carried by one of the important personalities of the village.[550] When we venerate the *karam* cross we worship *karam raja* (our redeemer) who blesses us with the fullness of divine life. But this cross cannot be drowned in the river of time. Instead it must be kept erect in every village chapel as sign of our never-ending life in Christ. The *karam* festival teaches us to put our trust in God and not in worldly things which are perishable, but it also shows that earthly realities may become valid channels for heavenly grace (sacraments and sacramentals in Christian terminology).[551]

"The religious sense of the Christian people has always found expression in various forms of piety surrounding the Church's sacramental life, such as the

---

[549] Cf. B. TIRKEY, *Oraon Symbols*, op. cit., 40-41.

[550] Cf. A. MISTRORIGO, *Dizionario Liturgico-Pastorale: Dai Documenti del Concilio Vaticano II e dagli altri documenti Ufficiali fino al 1977* (Paduva: Edizioni Messaggero, 1977), 534.

[551] Cf. P. EKKA, "Adivasi Riti Rivaj", op. cit., 90.

veneration of relics, visits to sanctuaries, pilgrimages, processions, the stations of the cross, religious dances, the rosary, medals, etc."[552]

When the people are allowed to express the Christian faith in their cultural garb, they may feel more at home with it and find it easy to understand the mysteries of Christian faith.[553]

4.1.2.2. Dhanbuni, Hariari, Kadleta and Khalihani

These are feasts which mark various important moments of agricultural activities. Though they are celebrated in different months we have grouped them together for the convenience of study. *Dhanbuni*[554] is celebrated when the Oraons sow the paddy seeds, *Hariari*, when the paddy is ready to be transplanted, *Kadleta*, when the paddy plants are full with grains, and *Khalihani* before the threshing operation of the paddy. Since these festivals have the same rituals we shall discuss in detail just one among them.

4.1.2.2.1. Celebration

The village elders in consultation with the villagers select a day for the celebration of *hariari* festival. About noon the *pahan* and his assistant accompanied by the villagers go to the open upland where the festival is annually held. The site for sacrifice is cleaned with cow-dung and water. The materials for the sacrifice such as *soop* (winnowing basket), knife and pearl rice are kept on the ground. A handful of pearl rice is placed on *sal* leaf plates in the name of the different spirits. This is known as *kuri*.[555] The *pujar* reverently washes the feet of the fowls to be sacrificed and hands them over to *pahan*. The *pahan* holds each victim in his hands and addresses it as if it were the spirit itself.

"Look I am doing *hariari* to thee. See that no sickness or other trouble enter the village or visit its houses, affect its people, its children, its cattle and its luck. Thou art the *malik* (owner) of the village, should any disease or calamity seek entrance into the village, do not thou admit them, but do thou make them deviate their course. May all in the village remain in peace and happiness. Do thou bring us sufficient rain, may we have a bumper crop."[556]

The sacrificial animal is identified with the spirit to which it is to be sacrificed. Each fowl is made to feed on the *kuri* (the handful of pearl rice in a leaf plate). When the victim has fed on the *kuri* the *pahan* holds the victim in

---

[552] CATECHISM OF THE CATHOLIC CHURCH, para. 1674.

[553] Cf. J. CASTELLANO, "Religiosita Popolare e Liturgia," in *NUOVO DIZIONARIO DI LITURGIA*, a cura di D. SARTORE e A. M. TRIACCA (Roma: Edizione Paoline, 1984), 1176.

[554] *Dhanbuni* means to sow the paddy; *Hariari* means green, the colour of the paddy seedlings that are ready for transplantion; *Kadleta* the meaning is unknown; and *Khalihani* means threshing operation. Cf. A. A. KUJUR, *The Oraon Habitat*, op. cit., 165.

[555] Cf. J. LAKRA, *Tribal Cultural Anthropology*, op. cit., 50.

[556] S. C. ROY, *Oraon Religionand Customs*, op. cit., 174.

his hands and repeats similar prayers for health, good rains, good crops, etc. He then cuts off the head of the sacrificial victim and drops a little of its blood on the ground where the *kuri* is kept. The meat of the animal is cooked as *tahri*[557] and it is shared by all Then the *pahan* bows down in front of the *kuris*.[558] All eat and drink. When the sacrifice is over the *pahan* plants a few seedlings in his field. After this the villagers begin to transplant their paddy. Before leaving the place of *puja,* all the utensils and vessels that were used for the sacrifice are buried underground.

The sacrifice offered at *kadleta* and its rituals are similar to that of the *hariari* feast except that the *Dandakatta* ritual is also performed on this feast. The Oraons celebrate this festival in order to ward off the evil eye and evil mouth. Branches of *bhelwa* (semicarpus anacardium) and *keond* (drospyros melanoxylon) are brought from the jungle. These are planted in the fields to avert an evil eye and all other evils.[559]

Khalihani is the festival of the 'threshing floor'. It is celebrated in the month of November when the winter crops are ready to be threshed. The rituals are the same as for *hariari* and *kadleta.*

4.1.2.2.2. Symbolism-Integration of Meaning

In the above mentioned festivals there are no outstanding symbols except the use of *bhelwa* (semicarpus anacardium) and *keond* (drospyros melanoxylon) tree branches. These trees are believed to provide spiritual protection against wicked spells, evil eye and evil mouth. Therefore the Oraons plant these tree branches in their paddy fields whereby they hope to be liberated from all evil forces, and obtain abundant crops. Thus a tree may represent protection from evil.

Similar convictions can be found in the Bible. The oil of the olive tree was traditionally used to soothe pain, and so the olive tree has become a symbol of Christ's graces and blessings to a person who is sick.[560] Through the anointing of the person with this holy oil (olive) he/she is freed from sin and its consequences. Trees are a form of nature that represent life and sacred powers. Through association with a particular religious or historical event, an individual tree or an entire species of trees acquire symbolic significance and meaning. Joshua set up a pillar at Shechem under an oak tree in order to commemorate his covenant with God (cf. Jos. 24: 26). Abraham had an experience of God by the oaks of Mamre (cf. Gen. 18:1). The tree trunk is commonly used to make coffins, that is to say

---

557 Meat of the sacrificial victim cooked along with pearl rice.

558 Cf. S. C. ROY, *Oraon Religion and Customs*, op. cit., 176-177.

559 Cf. B. TIRKEY, *Oraon Symbols*, op. cit., 38; cf. J. LAKRA, *Tribal Cultural Anthropology*, op. cit., 51.

560 Cf. P. R. FRESE and S. J. M. GRAY, "Trees", in M. ELIADE (editor in chief), *The Encyclopedia of Religion*, op. cit., 27.

that in a tree trunk, symbol of life, a person is buried. In Hindu tradition, for the funeral pyre a mango tree is important.[561]

As we have already seen, it is through the Cross, the tree of life, which is erected at the centre of the earth, that communication with heaven is opened and that by the same token the entire universe is saved from the clutches of evil. Therefore it is Christ who liberates human beings from the dominion of demonic forces and offers life in its fullness.

4.1.2.2.3. Dhanbuni in the Light of Christian Faith

In *dhanbuni, hariari, kadleta and khalihani* too there are some positive elements which attract our attention. Among them the following are worth discussing.

- An earnest dependence on God.
- Sentiments of community and solidarity.
- Participation in the sacrificial meal.

The Supreme being and the ancestor spirits are remembered with sentiments of gratitude. In all the festivals there is an element of dependence on God. Prior to any agricultural activities the assistance of the Supreme Being is sought by prayers and sacrifices which are offered by the *pahan* in the name of the village community.

Another very positive element in these celebrations is the community feeling and solidarity. The whole village considers themselves as one single community and this community celebrates the important moments of their life. Unless the *pahan* as the representative of God initiates the paddy transplantation, no one will begin it in his field by himself. This is an acceptance of the visible representatives of God and submission to them. By fulfilling the regulations of the tribe, and the respective community, they live as a people pleasing to God.

Participation in the sacrificial meal is important. In today's world when people are so busy and find very little time for religious activities, the Oraons can be an example. Their sacrifices are not accidental happenings. They prepare themselves and they partake in them wholeheartedly, thus keeping up their communion with *Dharmes* and with one another. It is a natural desire to have a good and comfortable life, being protected from sickness and misfortune. People are happy when they attain the fruits of their labour. The Oraons plant branches of *bhelwa* and *keond* in order to be freed from evils and to attain a good harvest.

In Christianity the Cross stands as the symbol of our redemption, a sign of life. When the Israelites were bitten by poisonous snakes, which was the consequence of their own wrong doing, God told Moses to make a bronze serpent and set it on a pole. All those who gazed at it were saved (cf. Num. 21:8-10). This pole stands for the Cross on which Jesus Christ won victory over evil. "And as

---

[561] Cf. P. R. FRESE and S. J. M. GRAY, "Trees", op. cit., 26-31.

Moses lifted up the serpent in the wilderness, so must the son of man be lifted up, that whoever believes in him may have eternal life" (Jn. 3:14-15). Therefore in a Christian context it may be suggested that branches of *bhelwa* and *keond* be erected in the fields in the form of a cross. This would be a simple expression of faith but rich in meaning, tangible and efficacious.[562]

God and ancestors are remembered and thanked for being so good to the people by enabling them to plant, to grow and to harvest the paddy and thresh it. It is certainly praiseworthy that the Oraons remember God and worship him in every important moment of their life. As farmers they seek God's assistance in a special way for all the major agricultural activities.

Such values can be easily integrated in our Christian celebrations with practical consequences for everyday attitudes and behaviours. Instead of an animal sacrifice, a Eucharistic sacrifice may be offered in order to give thanks to God and to ask for his blessings. Even though the simple blessing of rice grains and paddy seedlings are being practised, it would be meaningful if there were a more elaborate Eucharistic celebration (in Adivasi rite). In this Eucharist, *aruva chaval* (pearl rice), which stands for life in its fullness, and rice-beer can be offered to God. In the NT Christ, during his last supper offered bread and wine, 'works of the human hands and fruit of the earth and of the vine,' to God (cf. Lk. 22:17-21). Jesus used bread and wine, earthly necessities of humans in order to reveal to them the need for nourishment of the spirit. It should never be forgotten that last the supper was celebrated with bread and wine. St. Paul in his letters confirms of course the use of these species in the liturgical meetings (cf. 1Cor. 11; Heb. 10:10ff). Such NT perspectives could be accompanied by preceding OT parallels, like "When any one brings a cereal offering as an offering to the Lord, his offering shall be of fine flour; he shall pour oil upon it, and put frankincense on it" (Lev. 2:1). A part of the offerings can be brought back home and be buried in the fields of paddy or of other crops. The offering is done to the Lamb of God who transforms all impurities by taking them upon himself thus enriching everyone with his blessings and graces (cf. Is. 53:4-12).

4.1.2.3. Nayakhani

It is the festival of eating the first fruits of the field. This feast is celebrated when the upland paddy is ready. From the paddy *chiuda* (beaten rice) is prepared and offered to *Chala Paccho,* the lady of the grove. It is to thank the Supreme Being for the new harvest. At the same time thanks are also expressed to the ancestors who were the cause of their land, life and wealth. In this feast the ancestor spirits are remembered and special veneration is given to them in sentiments of gratitude for their heritage, life, land, wealth, etc. Sacrifices are offered to the Supreme Being individually.[563]

---

[562] Cf. P. EKKA, "Adivasi Riti Rivaj", op. cit., 90.

[563] Cf. S. C. ROY, *The Oraons of Chotanagpur*, op. cit., 88.

4.1.2.3.1. Celebration

As with other agricultural feasts, this too is initiated by the village priest. On the appointed day early in the morning the *pahan* and his assistant go to collect some ripe paddy from the neighbouring village. The *pahan* brings the harvested paddy home. His wife prepares beaten rice out of it. The priest purifies himself with cold water ablutions. He then takes the beaten rice to the room in his house where the *sarna soop* (winnowing basket which is believed to be the seat of the *sarna* lady) is kept. He offers the beaten rice to the *sarna* lady in the presence of the assembled villagers. The beaten rice thus offered and sanctified is then distributed among the people present.[564]

After this celebration *Nayakhani* is celebrated in each house. Special remembrance is made of the ancestor spirits by offering them the best food and drink available. Prayers are addressed to them seeking their protection and guidance.[565]

4.1.2.3.2 Symbolism-Interpretation of Meaning

There are no special symbolic things used except the sheaves of paddy from which the beaten rice is prepared. These sheaves are from grain that has undergone a transformation in the womb of the earth. They are the fruit of hard work and serve as the sign of new life and fertility.[566]

On this point again, the Oraons show striking similarities to the mentality of ancient Israelites who considered the first fruits as sacred to Yahweh. They offered them to God in order to thank him for his benefits. This was the wish of God. Only after such an offering they were free to eat the fruit of their labour (cf. Lev. 23:9-14). Among the Oraons too, the first grains are offered to God in order to thank him and to implore his blessings.[567]

Sheaves of grain are a sign of fecundity and fertility. The book of Genesis recounts the dream of Pharaoh, in which the seven ears growing on one stalk, full and good, denote fertility and plentyfulness (cf. Gen. 41:5-27). The words of Ruth the Moabitess are another example with a similar significance. Ruth finds favour in the eyes of God and her life becomes fruitful (cf. Rt. 2:1-12).[568]

The grain that has fallen on the ground and has undergone a transformation in the heart of the earth, that is to say that it accepts a renunciation of its original shape and size, thus attains a new life. A good harvest is obtained only through the co-operation of many factors: good seeds, fertile land, plenty of rain, human

---

564 Cf. S. C. ROY, *The Oraons of Chotanagpur*, op. cit., 89.

565 Cf. J. LAKRA, *Tribal Cultural Anthropology*, op. cit., 53.

566 Cf. M. LURKER, *Dizionario delle Immagini e dei Simboli Biblici*, op. cit., 99.

567 Cf. J. L. McKENZIE, *Dictionary of the Bible* (Bangalore: Asian Trading Corporation 1984), 278.

568 Cf. M. LURKER, *Dizionario delle Immagini e dei Simboli Biblici*, op. cit., 99.

effort, and above all God's blessings. The seed when it accepts a certain amount of change in its self, it becomes a new creation, no more a seed. It has a different destiny and produces a good crop. In other words 'through death to life' (cf. Rom. 5:10, 21). A Christian is called to participate in the life of Christ and be configured in an image of him.

"The eloquence of the cross and death is, however, completed by the eloquence of the resurrection. Man finds in the resurrection a completely new light, which helps him to go forward through the thick darkness of humiliations, doubts, hopelessness and persecution."[569]

"Very truly, I tell you, unless a grain of wheat falls into the earth and dies, it remains just a single grain; but if it dies, it bears much fruit" (Jn. 12:24). This transformation throws light on the death and resurrection of Christ. Through his passion and death he obtained new life in fullness and glory. It is in him and through him that a person has life, a life that is abundant. A person nourishes his life in accordance with his designs. Jesus says, "I am the bread of life, ...if anyone eats of this bread, he will live for ever,..." (Jn. 6: 48,51).

4.1.2.3.3. Nayakhani in the light of Christian Faith

As *Nayakhani* feast is mainly focused on ancestors, let us discuss the enriching values of this feast.

- Sentiments of gratitude to the Supreme Being and ancestors.
- Seeking of blessings upon the new rice.

Nayakhani is the celebration with which the Oraons start eating the new rice of the year. The rituals reveal their indebtedness to their Supreme Being and to their ancestors. A special sacrifice is offered to the Supreme Being with thanksgiving and prayers "Oh sun-moon (God) you have been generous towards me, I offer you this sacrifice and I worship you."[570] They acknowledge that their wealth is due to their ancestors and it is their duty to venerate them also with sacrifices. It is surely a notable attitude full of profound value. The Supreme Being is addressed as sun-moon, which is a symbolic expression of his qualities. It can be interpreted as the providential care of a father and the life giving love of the mother. God is a reality on whom they depend for their life.

We know that the Israelites offered the first fruits to Yahweh (cf. Dt. 26:1-10). Hence this is an old custom with ever new sentiments. It would be very meaningful if these values could be lived out in everyday life; gratefully acknowledging God is an important element of our well-being, and the consciousness to walk in the steps of our predecessors in faith is part of our Christian heritage. The grain of

---

[569] SD 20.

[570] J. LAKRA, *Adivasi Missa Samgrah,* op. cit., 46 The original text is in Hindi. Translation is mine.

rice stands for the staple food of the Oraons, which satisfies their hunger and gives them physical strength and life. This food is the fruit of their labour and work of human hands. Food and drink (water) are the bare necessities of life; to satisfy the hunger and to quench the thirst.

Christ instituted the Eucharist by blessing the bread and wine and gave it a new meaning. The Eucharistic bread is made out of wheat and is the actual food for the soul, and wine the drink. In the Eucharist not only the bread and wine are offered, but it is eaten together after rendering thanks to the author of these gifts. Thus it signifies unity, sharing, and friendship as a result of this spiritual nourishment.[571] "The miracles of the multiplication of the loaves, when the Lord says the blessing, breaks and distributes the loaves through his disciples to feed the multitude, prefigures the superabundance of this unique bread of his Eucharist."[572] Therefore on the *nayakhani* feast a special celebration of the Holy Eucharist could be performed (in Adivasi rite), recalling the importance of the day and the significance of the symbol. The Holy Eucharist is the "source and summit of the Christian life."[573] It is an action of thanksgiving to God, and it recalls the jewish blessings; i.e. rendering thanks during a meal for God's works: creation, redemption, and sanctification.[574] "Do not labour for the food which perishes, but for the food which endures to eternal life, which the Son of man will give to you; for on him has God the Father set his seal. ... For the bread of God is that which comes down from heaven, and gives life to the world" (Jn. 6:27,33).

It is significant to understand that the presence of the risen Christ to his disciples for the last time is also manifested under the sign of food (cf. Jn. 21:9-13). Peter affirms that the apostles are witnesses of Christ's resurrection because they have eaten with him after his resurrection (Acts 10:40ff).[575] Proper instruction should be given to the people so that they may find meaning in their celebration.

4.1.2.4. Maghe

Maghe[576] marks the end of the festival cycle. It is celebrated in January-February. By this time the agricultural activities of the year come to an end. Therefore this feast has a two fold aim: first to thank God and the ancestors for all the blessings received, and secondly to terminate or to renew the contract with the servants.

---

[571] Cf. S. ROSSO, "Elementi Naturali", in *NUOVO DIZIONARIO DI LITURGIA*, a cura di D. SARTORE e A. M. TRIACCA (Roma: Edizione Paoline, 1984), 441-442.

[572] CATECHISM OF THE CATHOLIC CHURCH, para. 1335.

[573] LG 11.

[574] Cf. CATECHISM OF THE CATHOLIC CHURCH, para. 1328.

[575] Cf. S. ROSSO, "Elementi Naturali", in *NUOVO DIZIONARIO DI LITURGIA*, a cura di D. SARTORE e A. M. TRIACCA (Roma: Edizione Paoline, 1984), 443.

[576] *Maghe* is the name of the month in which this feast is celebrated, hence it is called *maghe*. Cf. M. KUJUR, *Oraon Sanskriti,* op.cit, 262.

4.1.2.4.1. Celebration

No special sacrifice marks *maghe*. But the servants are given great respect and honour as a token of their service rendered to their masters. For the Oraons the duration of service is one year. The servant considers it as his duty to complete this term.[577] On this day the mistress of the house washes the feet of the servant, oils his hair and combs it. Then he is given rice beer to drink. The servant who wishes to continue his service, after tasting the rice beer, says 'it is good'. If he does not want to continue his service he remains silent. The master for his part renews or terminates the service of the servants.[578] This feast signifies the end of the agricultural activities. It is a feast which helps to evaluate the hectic days of labour and to rejoice over the result. Hence it is a thanksgiving day.[579]

4.1.2.4.2. Symbolism-Interpretation of Meaning

The *maghe* feast has no special symbols, except some symbolic actions which are common among the Oraons. The washing of the feet, anointing with oil, offering of rice beer to drink, etc. are ordinary features of hospitality. The Oraons wash and wipe the feet of their guest, and if the guest is a rare visitor (for example a bishop, a priest, a religious) then they anoint the hair with oil. These are signs of acceptance, welcome, respect, and joy. Rice-beer is one of the best things that they offer to someone.

In the NT Jesus washes the feet of his disciples before his passion and death. In the Jewish tradition the washing of the feet was done by servants. But Jesus by his own actions gave mankind an example of love and service, thus translated his love into actions. "So if I, your Lord and Teacher, have washed your feet, you also ought to wash one another's feet. For I have set you an example, that you also should do as I have done to you" (Jn. 13:14-15). Thus Jesus transforms the humble actions of a servant to the noble actions of a master.

Anointing with oil as a refreshing or consecrating action was common in the ancient world. Kings were anointed (cf. 1Sam. 10:1; 16:13). The anointing of Saul and David were done by a prophet and that of Solomon by a priest, which probably points to the sacred character of this ceremony. Anointing marks the person as sacred, set apart for a special mission (cf. Is. 61:1), and this obviously refers to Christ too who is the anointed one of the Father who announces the good news to the poor (cf. Lk. 4:18-21).[580] Anointing has a significance in burial. Jesus was anointed at Bethany by Mary and Jesus approves her action as something out of devotional love which would be done after his death before burial (cf. Jn.

---

[577] Cf. M. KUJUR, *Oraon Sanskriti*, op. cit., 266.

[578] Cf. B. TIRKEY, *Oraon Symbols*, op. cit., 43.

[579] Cf. M. KUJUR, *Oraon Sanskriti*, op. cit., 266-267.

[580] Cf. J. L. McKENZIE, *Dictionary of the Bible*, op. cit., 34.

12:1-09). Joseph of Arimathea anointed the body of Jesus according to the jewish custom before he buried Jesus in the tomb (cf. Jn. 19:39-41).

In this respect, anointing with oil can be interpreted as a recognition of the service rendered by the employees to their masters, also entrusting them with further responsibilities. Man by himself is not self-sufficient. For the smooth functioning of human society, men need to co-operate with one another. In this sense the words of St. Paul are important: "For in the one Spirit we were all baptised into one body-Jews or Greeks, slaves or free-and we were all made to drink of one Spirit" (1Cor. 12:13).

4.1.2.4.3. Maghe in the light of Christian Faith

From a closer examination we may learn some of the significant values that are present in this agricultural feast which has a special reference to the employees.

- Gratitude to the employees for their services rendered.
- Acknowledgement of the blessings received from God throughout the agricultural year.
- Loving acceptance of employees as human beings.

Often the household employees and daily wage earners are exploited and hardly any recognition is shown to them for their services. In this context, the Oraons give us, generally speaking, a good example. Normally they treat their employees as family members. But on this feast they publicly acknowledge the service rendered by the servant and honour him.

This noble practice can be adopted by all, irrespective of religion and class. On this day, for instance the Catholics should offer a thanksgiving mass by recalling the blessings the house members received through the servants. The employees could be honoured in the traditional way by washing their feet and wiping them, also anointing with oil. Besides, this will not only promote the dignity of human labour, but above all, the dignity of the human person. It will be a help for the servants too to be happy with the work they do, to accept their own role and to see its real sense in the service they render.

"The Christian finds in human work a small part of the Cross of Christ and accepts it in the same spirit of redemption in which Christ accepted His Cross for us. In work, thanks to the light that penetrates us from the Resurrection of Christ, we always find a glimmer of new life, of the new good, as if it were an announcement of "the new heavens and the new earth"(cf. 2Pt. 3:13; Rev. 21:1) in which man and the world participate precisely through the toil that goes with work. Through toil-and never without it. On the one hand this confirms the indispensability of the Cross in the spirituality of human work; on the other hand the Cross which this toil constitutes reveals a new good springing from work itself, from work understood in depth and in all its aspects and never apart from work."[581]

All work whether manual or intellectual is linked with toil. A Christian through his work not only contributes to human comforts but also for the growth of the Kingdom of God, enhancing human dignity brotherhood and freedom. A person is more precious for what he is than for what he has.[582] Whatever may the type of work, it is a sharing in the activity of the creator. Jesus Christ's teaching on work echoes in the life of St. Paul and he expresses it in his letters. "Slaves, be obedient to those who are your earthly masters, with fear and trembling, in singleness of heart, as to Christ; not in the way of eye-service, as men-pleasers, but as servants of Christ, doing the will of God from the heart, rendering service with a good will as to the Lord and not to men" (Eph. 6:5-7).

4.1.2.5. Soharai

The Oraons are cultivators and they depend on cattle for agriculture in many ways: for ploughing, manure, transportation, etc. They consider cattle as an important part of their wealth. They celebrate the *Soharai*[583] feast in order to acknowledge the worth of cattle in their lives. On this occasion prayer and sacrifices are offered to the *gohardeota* (cattle-shed-spirit). This feast is again, disguised in the trappings of a spirit cult, an acknowledgement of God's goodness to each individual family, clan and tribe.[584]

4.1.2.5.1. Celebration

Soharai is celebrated in the month of October-November. In the evening of new the moon day in October or November, a number of earthen oil lamps are lit in the cattle shed and the places around it like the manure pit, kitchen garden, etc. As far as possible the lamps are kept burning during the entire night. At times incense is also burned in the cattle shed.[585] In each house special food is prepared with pulses for the cattle.

On the next morning, the cattle are bathed ritually and are brought back to the cattle shed. Then their legs are washed and rice beer is given them to drink and sprinkled on their hoofs. They also receive slices of the spiked tuber

[581] LE27.

[582] Cf. GS 35.

[583] The term *soharai* seems to have derived from *sohan* which means a sense of 'feeling beautiful.' Etymologically, it means to wrap from head to foot, to drape or adorn down to the ground. (A. TIRKEY, "Religious Dimension of Sohrai: The Uraon way", in *Sevartham*, 21 (1996), 129. For an Oraon *soharai* denotes plenty of crops, i.e. his field is full with flowers and fruits; when everything is plenty in his household he hopes to have a good harvest. (Cf. M. KUJUR, *Oraon Sanskriti*, op. cit., 257).

[584] Cf. A. A. KUJUR, *The Oraon Habitat*, op. cit., 182.

[585] Cf. S. C. ROY, *Oraon Religion and Customs,* op. cit., 190.

mixed with salt, together with the special food prepared out of the pluses. The foreheads, horns and hoofs are anointed with *sindhur* (vermilion) and oil. Then they are garlanded with marigold flowers.[586] In *soharai* a fowl or a pig is sacrificed to the cattle-shed spirit. After the cattle have been fed they are taken to the village pasture land. On this day the professional cattle herd as well as individual cattle herds are given a festal treat.[587]

4.1.2.5.2. Symbolism-Interpretation of Meaning

In *Soharai* the cattle shed and its surroundings are illumined with oil lamps. Burning lamps manifest the presence of the sacred. It also signifies the attitude of welcome. In Hindu tradition *Brahman* is understood like a flash of lighting. The *Upanishad* says "In the thunder-flash is the Truth" (*Kansitaki Upanishad*, IV, 2).[588] In Christianity, Jesus is the Light, who dispels the darkness: "I am the light of the world. Whoever follows me will never walk in darkness but will have the light of life" (Jn. 8:12). "As long as I am in the world, I am the light of the world" (Jn. 9:5). In all the liturgical celebrations of the Church the use of lighted lamps is very awe provoking; it reveals the presence of the Divine. The eucharistic presence of Jesus Christ is recognised by a lighted lamp in our Christian Churches. The Easter candle represents the risen Christ who is the winner over darkness, evil and its forces. By his death and resurrection Christ proclaims liberation from all malicious powers.[589] Therefore the use of lamps on this feast manifests the presence of the sacred who has the power to bless their cattle, to free them from the malicious spirits, and to provide abundance in everything good and useful.

The animals can be another symbol in this feast, the priced wealth of the Oraons. Animals are symbols of positive and negative forces. For instance the stone figures of animals like the lion and tiger etc. reveal the sovereign power of an authority, where as the sheep manifest the docility and submission of a person. Animals display the range and riches of God in creation (cf. Jb. 12:10), and He provides for each of them (cf. Ps. 36:6). At times some animals are pictured as images of God's anger and judgement (cf. Dt. 32:24; Jer. 15:3).

In paradise Adam (old) was among the animals (cf. Gen. 2:19-20). Jesus Christ, the new Adam, was born among the animals and lying in a manger (cf. Lk. 2:12). Jesus after his baptism led by the Spirit went into the desert and he was with the wild beasts (cf. Mk. 1:13). Jesus Christ is the Good Shepherd who gave his life for his sheep (cf. Jn. 10:11). He the innocent Lamb who took upon himself the sins and iniquities of the world (cf. Jn. 1:29) and humanity was redeemed by

---

[586] Cf. J. LAKRA *Tribal Cultural Anthropology*, op. cit., 54.

[587] J. LAKRA *Tribal Cultural. Anthropology*, op. cit., 52

[588] Quoted in M. ELIADE, *Images and Symbols: Studies in Religious Symbolism*, translated by P. MAIRET (London: Harvill Press, 1961), 75.

[589] Cf. S. ROSSO, "Elementi Naturali", in *NUOVO DIZIONARIO DI LITURGIA*, a cura di D. SARTORE e A. M. TRIACCA (Roma: Edizione Paoline, 1984), 436.

his precious blood (cf. 1Pt. 1:19).[590] It was on an ass that Christ entered Jerusalem before his passion (cf. Jn. 12:14-15).

The herdsman cares for his cattle. And in an Oraon community as we have already seen there are *panches*, catechists who are the immediate herdsmen for them. In a way the parable of the Good-Shepherd can be a lived experience for the Oraons. Christ is the Herdsman of his herd the Church. He is the good pastor who cares for the scattered ones and also goes after those who have left the flock. Today, there are priests, bishops who are the pastors ministering to the sheep of Christ.

4.1.2.5.3. Soharai in the Light of Christian Faith

Soharai, an agricultural feast yet disguised in the feast of the cattle, has some noteworthy elements which make sense to modern man. Among them the following seem to be outstanding:

- Sense of gratitude to God.
- Love for domestic animals.
- Awareness that animals are the creation of God.

We see a sense of gratitude for the benefits received form God. Without the help of cattle the Oraons are handicapped in their agricultural activities. Even though these are only animals, the Oraons express their thankfulness to them by giving them special food and the traditional respect and honour. This shows their care for their domestic animals.

God is the author of every kind of life. Hence it is right to give thanks to God and his creatures and to ask blessings upon our cattle. It is really meaningful to introduce this feast into Christianity. All the preparations for this feast can be done without any distinction of creed. Since there are two prominent symbols, light and animals, and both are relevant to the person of Jesus Christ: Christ the Light of the world (cf. Jn. 8:12), Christ the Good-Shepherd (cf. Jn. 10:1-15), Christ who is born in a manger (cf. Lk. 2:12), Christ who comes on an ass (cf. Mt. 23:37), who is the Lamb of God (cf. Jn. 1:29), etc. These are possible themes for a significant liturgy. Special prayers can be offered for the welfare of the cattle, bringing out the importance of the day.

Cattle can be brought in procession to the an open place led by their herdsmen in order to be blessed by the village catechist or elder by sprinkling them with holy water. Although God is the author of blessings his graces can be imparted by his representatives on earth.[591] Even though animals are speechless creatures, yet it is the responsibility of every human being to care for them, to

---

[590] Cf. M. LURKER, *Dizionario delle Immagini e dei Simboli Biblici*, op. cit., 14-15.

[591] Cf. A. MISTRORIGO, *Liturgia: Linee di Fondamento Theologico-Paastorale* (Vicenza: Favero Editore, 1969, 2 ed.), 355.

look after them, to preserve them, for they were created by God. As the crown of creation, man was entrusted with this duty by the creator God. This corresponds to the ecological awareness of man, and it displays man's love to the creator God. Jesus teaches us that the sovereignty of God is not domination, but love which gives life and creates beauty. Therefore God needs no steward, no monitor of creation, but friends among friends with the attitudes of a saintly mystic like Francis of Assisi.[592]

4.2. Rites of Passage of the Individuals

Rites of passage are a category of rituals that are performed in order to celebrate the passage of a person through the life cycle. This passage marks a transition from one social status to another or from one role to another which integrates human and cultural experience with a biological destiny: birth, marriage and death. These are also the three most important events in the life of an Oraon. The corresponding rites are initiatory and transformative in nature.[593] Certain religious ceremonies are associated with these social events. They are so important in the life of an Oraon because they make him a full member of the tribe, and entrust him with specific responsibilities for the good of the tribe as well as for his own good.[594]

4.2.1. Birth Rites

Birth rites are rather elaborate rites performed at different stages related to birth and childhood. Birth rites include the observances of various customs from the moment of conception like the *joda kamna* (cutting paternal links) sacrifice, determination of the sex of the unborn babies, painless delivery, cutting of the umbilical cord, purificatory rituals, sacrifices to the principle village spirits, *Dandakatta* ceremony, name giving ritual, etc. The following points will be discussed in detail.

4.2.1.1. Pre-natal and Post-natal Observances

The Oraons consider their children as gifts from God. Human life has a great value for them. Hence they care for their children from the very moment of conception. They express their love and care for them through various practices and rituals which apparently may seem ridiculous to an outsider.

According to the Oraons the expectant mother is more susceptible to supernatural influences, especially of the evil spirits. Therefore the mother needs

[592] Cf. P. PINTO, "Creation and Holistic Mission", in J. KAVUNKAL and F. HRANGKHUMA (ed.), *Bible and Mission in India Today* (Bombay: St. Pauls, 1993), 298.

[593] Cf. B. G. MYERHOFF and others, "Rites of Passage", in M. ELIADE (editor in chief), *The Encyclopedia of Religion*, Vol. 12 (New York: Macmillian Publishing Company, 1987), 380-381.

[594] Cf. B. TIRKEY, *Oraon Symbols*, op. cit., 43.

to observe certain precautions in order to protect herself as well as the baby.[595] She should not expose herself to thundering and lightening. "She must not be present at a cremation nor even touch a dead body."[596] She is expected to bring forth life and so she should not participate in anything that is contrary to life in the world. When an Oraon woman is with child for the first time *Jodakamna* ritual is celebrated. The woman given in marriage belongs to the family of her husband and bears children from his ancestor spirits. In order to separate her from the ancestry of her father this sacrifice is performed.[597]

It does not only cut off the woman's relations with her ancestor spirits but serves also to ensure protection to the mother and the baby in the womb from the evil attacks of the spirits. The sacrifice ends with a sumptuous meal with rice beer.[598] Everything is concluded with a feast.

The birth of the child is followed by several rituals. Either on the day of birth or within two to three days the father of the child goes to the village priest with a red coloured fowl, some pearl rice and copper coins to be offered to the principal village spirits and offers a libation of rice beer to the ancestor spirits. Then *Dandakatta* ceremony is performed asking God for his blessings upon the baby, to free him/her from all harm and dangers. *Dandakatta* is performed in all the important phases of life.[599]

4.2.1.2. Name Giving Ceremony

There is a custom among the Oraons centred on ancestral belief regarding the name giving ceremony. Usually the child is named soon after its birth according to the day of the week[600] on which he/she was born. However a formal name giving ceremony is held later. This rite is significant because it marks the admittance of the child into the community.

The Oraons believe in the re-birth of the ancestors and ancestresses in the same the family. In order to make sure who this reincarnated ancestor is, they resort to this religious ceremony in which the ancestors are invoked.[601] From

---

[595] Cf. J. LAKRA, *Tribal Cultural Anthropology*, op. cit., 30.

[596] S. C. ROY, *Oraon Religion and Customs,* op. cit., 83.

[597] The pregnant woman's father or uncle is invited to the house of her husband. A sacrifice of a pig or a female sheep is offered to the ancestor spirits of the pregnant woman. During sacrifice they pray "From this day, oh ancestor spirits, *deotas* (deities) and *bhuts* (spirits) of the pregnant woman's father have no concern whatsoever with her. Leave her ye ancestor spirits, deities and ghosts." (S. C. ROY, *Oraon Religionand Customs*, op. cit., 84).

[598] Cf. S. C. ROY, *Oraon Religionand Customs*, op. cit., 83-84.

[599] Cf. J. LAKRA, *Tribal Cultural Anthropology,* op. cit., 32.

[600] A child who is born on a Sunday is called Etwa if a male, and Etwaria if a female. Sunday is Etwar in *Sadri*, the lingua franca of Adivasis (Cf. S. C. ROY. *Oraon Religion and Customs*, op. cit., 93).

[601] Cf. E. CAMPION, *My Oraon Culture* (Ranchi: Catholic Press, Ranchi, 1980), 38.

among the many ancestors they choose the name of one. "The ancestor, whose name is given to the child, becomes the protector spirit of the child."[602]

Usually eight days after the birth of the child this simple but elaborate ritual is performed. On that day the hair of the child is shaved off leaving a tuft of hair on the crown of the head. The shaving is done by "any elderly man, preferably by the babe's grandfather."[603] The hair is then collected in a leaf cup and thrown into a stream or a bamboo grove.[604]

Then the child's name is selected. The father sits on a mat along with the village elders and other relatives. He takes two leaf cups one filled with water and the other one with some paddy. Either a village elder or the father of the child takes three grains of paddy, husks them in the hand and drops them one by one into the leaf cup full of water. As he drops the first grain he invokes the name of *Dharmes,* with the second grain the name of a village elder, and with the third grain the name of an ancestor. If these grains meet in the water or form a cluster the name of the ancestor pronounced then becomes the name of the new babe. If these grains do not meet then the process is repeated until they succeed to find a name for the child. This ritual is called *chhatti.*[605]

Once they find a name the father of the baby joyously announces the name of the child to the people gathered for the occasion. The child is then anointed with oil and turmeric paste and bathed in cold water. Then they begin with celebrations: eating, drinking and dancing. It is a family feast. Friends, relatives and important people of the village offer gifts to the new born baby. The money thus collected will be saved for the child for his/her marriage when he/she grows up.[606] The remaining paddy which is used for the *chhatti* ritual is also a capital invested in the name of the child for his/her marriage. It will be sown separately year after year in constant progression so that they could get a good income from it for the growing child.[607]

4.2.1.3. Christian Significance of Traditional Elements

We have discussed some of the practices of the Oraons during pregnancy and after birth. These practices have rich meanings behind them. The Oraons value their children, both male and female equally. They acknowledge that life is a gift from *Dharmes* and he is the author of life. These sentiments are very deep in them.

---

[602] L. KUJUR, The Sacramental Celebration of the Rites of Passage in the Uraon Culture (Rome: Pontificia Universitas Gregoriana, Extract of doctoral dissertation, 1993), 29.

[603] E. CAMPION, *My Oraon Culture,* op. cit., 38.

[604] Cf. S. C. ROY, *Oraon Religion and Customs,* op. cit., 93.

[605] Cf. L. KUJUR, *The Sacramental Celebration*, op. cit., 30; cf. E. CAMPION, *My Oraon Culture,* op. cit., 38-39.

[606] Cf. E. CAMPION, *My Oraon Culture,* op. cit., 39-40.

[607] Cf. P. DEHON, *Religion and Customs of the Oraons,* op. cit., 154.

"Though the father and mother are held directly responsible for the birth still the supreme Bonga, Dharmes or God is supposed to be the sole and ultimate authority. The birth of a child which satisfies the natural eagerness of parenthood is a joyful occasion for them, whether the child is male or female."[608]

They are aware that they need to protect and preserve this gift of life. Therefore every care is taken to protect the child from all dangers and evil spirits. A sacrifice is offered to ancestors and village spirits so that they may protect the life in the womb and the mother. The sacrificial victim is normally a female sheep or pig which according to the Oraons is a symbol of fertility. It also represents the mother and the child, a symbolic offering of themselves for their well-being in the days to come.[609]

During *chhatti* (the name giving ceremony) a particular ancestor is invoked, and the name that is revealed by this ritual is the true name of the child. Then this ancestor becomes the guardian or patron of the child. Remembering the dead ancestors is found to be a good practice among the Oraons. It is a way of acknowledging their goodness and greatness from whom they have received life and wealth. Even though the child is born within the tribe of his ancestors, the child is officially initiated and accepted as a member of the tribe only by this 'renaming' ceremony.

The name has a mysterious identity with its bearer. It can be considered as a substitute for the person. When God completed his creation, he gave the responsibility to man to name the creatures (cf. Gen. 2:19). The name of the first parents revealed their being: thus Adam meant man, and he named his wife Eve, because she was the mother of all the living (cf. Gen. 3:20).[610] The name characterises the person. A person's name is changed when a transformation takes place in his/her life. For instance Abram (exalted father) becomes Abraham (father of a host of nations) (cf. Gen. 17:5-6). Jacob's name was changed to Israel (contested with God) (cf. Gen. 32:29; 35:10).[611] Among the Israelites, it is God Himself who decides to name Himself. He reveals his name to Moses "I am He who is" (Ex. 3:13-16), and this name signifies that God is present among his people, he is Yahweh.[612] Jesus was given his name when he was circumcised and it means God saves (cf. Lk. 2:21). After his conversion Saul was called Paul (Acts 13:9) which denotes that he was set apart for the service of the gospel. When Jesus elected Simon as his apostle he named him Peter (cf. Mk. 3:16).

---

[608] L. P. VIDYARTHI and B. K. RAI, *The Tribal Culture of India* (New Delhi: Concept Publishing Company, 2nd ed. 1985), 291.

[609] Cf. B. TIRKEY, *Oraon Symbols,* op. cit., 44.

[610] Cf. M. LURKER, *Dizionario delle Immagini e dei Simboli Biblici*, op. cit., 131.

[611] Cf. G. J. POLAN, "Name", in C. STUHLMUELLER (ed.), *The Collegeville Pastoral Dictionary of Biblical Theology*, op. cit., 666.

[612] Cf. X. LEON-DUFOUR, (ed.) *Dictionary of Biblical Theology* (London: Geoffrey Chapman), 378.

It is an ancient belief that a name displays the destiny of its bearer ("nomen est omen").[613] This concept has some influence in Christianity when people take names of saints in baptism for their children, they seek the protection of the saint and the influence of the saint's virtues on their children. Thus change in name or acceptance of a new name has a profound effect on the person as it is considered as a rebirth by baptism. Therefore this renaming ceremony can be compared to Christian baptism. "Holy Baptism is the basis of the whole Christian life, ... we become members of Christ, are incorporated into the Church and made shares in her mission."[614] Baptism is important because it liberates human being from all forces of evil and sin and transfigures him/her into the likeness of Christ. It is an explicit way of proclaiming one's belonging to Christ. In other words one is born in Christ.[615] There is a new identity as a member of Christ's family, entrusted with a new responsibility, to follow the foot steps of Christ in imitation of his life.

This ritual is celebrated usually on the eight day after birth and is significant for the initiation into the tribe. In fact, eight is the number of a new beginning. The creation of seven days precedes the completeness of reality. The ark of Noah saved eight persons (cf. Gen. 6:18; 1Pt. 3:20). In this context the number eight is equally important for the Oraons as it was for Israel. According to the law of Moses Jesus was incorporated into his tribe on the eight day.

After eight days had passed, it was time to circumcise the child; and he was called Jesus, the name given by the angel before he was conceived in the womb. When the time came for their purification according to the law of Moses, they brought him up to Jerusalem to present him to the Lord (Lk. 2:21-22).

At any rate by this ritual the child is incorporated into the tribe, he is no more an outsider.[616]

Rice grain and water are used to select or divine the name of the child. Grain that sinks in the water is full with life. These grains stand for a community, a family of *Dharmes*, represented by the village elder, the mediator between *Dharmes* and his people, and the ancestor who has won the favour of *Dharmes*. They form a sacred communion to which each Oraon is supposed to accede by living according to the norms of the tribe. Water is a symbol of life. In the OT, water that falls on a dry land is not only the symbol of life, as it produces the plants to grow but it is considered as the expression of God's goodness and blessings (cf. Is. 35:6-8). The Prophet Ezekiel speaks of water that purifies the heart and liberates the person from the various types of evils (cf. Ez. 36:25-29).

---

[613] M. LURKER, *Dizionario delle Immagini e dei Simboli Biblici*, op. cit., 132.

[614] CATECHISM OF THE CATHOLIC CHURCH, para. 1213.

[615] Cf. A. KAVANAGH, "Gli avvenimenti nel ciclo della vita: riti civili e cristiani", in *Concilium,* edizione italiana, anno XIV, 2 (1978), 38-39.

[616] Cf. M. LURKER, *Dizionario delle Immagini e dei Simboli Biblici* (Milano: Edizioni Paoline, 1990), 72.

Jesus refers to this symbolism of water in a deeper way when he speaks to the Samaritan woman about the living water that gives eternal life (cf. Jn. 4:4). However this analogy is connected in a profound sense to the baptismal water for the remission of sins (cf. Lk. 3:3), and for the rebirth in the Spirit (cf. Jn. 3:5). Strictly speaking baptism is an immersion into the passion, death and resurrection of Jesus (cf. Rom. 6:4) thus to be purified by the precious blood of Christ, in order to live in Christ (cf. Jn. 19:30).[617] Through these simple and ordinary symbols the Oraons manifest their deeper aspirations of life. That is to be in the good company of *Dharmes* and ancestors, to live within the tribe, to have plenty of wealth and good children.[618]

In Christianity we talk of the communion of saints which results from our incorporation into the life of Christ through baptism, by which all the faithful both living and dead form a community; a communion. Thus it is not only a horizontal relationship that can be produced in this world, but also a constant union with those who have gone before us in the faith.[619]

"The term "communion of saints" has two closely linked meanings: communion "in holy things (sancta)," and "among holy persons (sancti)." Sancta sanctis! ("God's holy gifts for God's holy people") The faithful (sancti) are fed by Christ's holy body and blood (sancta) to grow in the communion of the Holy Spirit (koinonia) and to communicate it to the world."[620]

The Church is called to be an assembly of saints. Communion among them is rooted in the sacraments: "All the sacraments are sacred links uniting the faithful with one another and binding them to Jesus Christ."[621]

This name giving ceremony can be integrated to the Christian life as it displays some significant elements in Christianity. All the preliminary preparations: the shaving off the hair, giving a bath, anointing with oil and turmeric, etc. can be done according to the convenience of the people. This can be celebrated at home in the presence of a priest. The parents and the child should be seated on a clean mat. It can be taken as an occasion to bless the mother after her delivery.[622] When all the participants have assembled, the catechist begins the celebration with a prayer thanking God for the gift of the child and his / her parents also ask God's assistance and guidance. The priest after his catechetical instruction

---

[617] Cf. S. ROSSO, "Elementi Naturali", in *NUOVO DIZIONARIO DI LITURGIA*, a cura di D. SARTORE e A. M. TRIACCA (Roma: Edizione Paoline, 1984), 432-433.

[618] Cf. B. TIRKEY, *Oraon Symbols*, op. cit., 46.

[619] Cf. C. BURKE, "Communion of Saints", in R. SHAW (ed.), *Our Sunday Visitor's Encyclopedia of Catholic Doctrine* (Huntington: Our Sunday Visitor Publishing Division, 1997), 119.

[620] CATECHISM OF THE CATHOLIC CHURCH, para. 948.

[621] CATECHISM OF THE CATHOLIC CHURCH, para. 950.

[622] Cf. W. VON ARX, "La Benedizione della Madre dopo il Parto", in Concilium, edizione Italiana, anno XIV. 2 (1978), 106.

blesses the mother by sprinkling the holy water, he then sprinkles the holy water in different parts of the house, and on the participants that they may be cleansed from all impurities in order to welcome the new born into the family, into the tribe. Then the catechist takes three grains of paddy: one in the name of Jesus, the second grain in the name of the patron saint of the village, and the third grain in the name of the ancestor/ancestoress of the child, and drops it in the holy water which is kept in the leaf plate. Once they find out the name of the child, the priest blesses the child by making the sign of the cross on the forehead and makes the child to wear a scapular. Similarly the parents, the catechist, the village elders and all the participants bless the child by making the sign of the cross. This can be concluded by a meaningful hymn or prayer. All rejoice by sharing the meal and express their joy by the offering of gifts. Thus the child is brought into the tribe of God's people in a symbolic way, which will be actualised through baptism.

4.2.2. Marriage Customs

Marriage is a central event in the life of an Oraon. It is an unavoidable obligation for them, for the continuation of the clan and tribe is kept up through marriage. "For an Oraon the prime significance of marriage lies in its ability to bring forth children."[623]

An Oraon marriage is monogamous. They keep tribe endo-gamy, i.e. to marry within the tribe and clan exo-gamy, i.e. to marry out side of one's clan. Their main concern in marriage is to increase in number in order to maintain their tribal existence independent. Every tribe is divided into various *gotras* (clans), and the members of one clan are distinguished from the others by the name of their clan. The members of the same clan are considered to have descended from a common ancestor and are thus regarded as blood relatives. Within the Oraon tradition marriage is not permitted among blood relatives. Hence, no marriage is possible within the clan.[624]

There is no child marriage and "old bachelors and maidens are practically unknown in the tribe."[625] Marriages are patrilocal except in the case of *agharjis* or *ghar-damad*[626] marriage. There is no polyandry/polygyny. The widow/widower is allowed to remarry if they desire to do so. Widowhood is never considered as

---

623 D. BARA, "Oraon Marriage: Socio-Cultural Context", in *Sevartham*, 14 (1989), 63.

624 Cf. D. BARA, "Customary Matrimonial Law of the Oraons", in *Sevartham*, 13 (1988), 3-5.

625 S. C. ROY, *Oraon Religion and Customs*, op. cit., 99.

626 Couples who have no male heir may adopt a boy whom they accept as their prospective son-in-law. He may live in his wife's house as heir to all property of her parents.

a curse. There is no dowry[627] system. The bridegroom has to give *dali-dhiba*[628] (a special gift) to the bride's party in order to obtain a bride. Among the Oraons divorces are very rare.[629] Divorce is permitted by the *panches* in extreme cases.[630]

Usually marriages are held in the dry winter season when granaries are full. "The Oraons have no prescribed wedding garments, neither the bride nor the bridegroom."[631] "They use any kind of clothing but the corner of the clothing is always dipped in diluted turmeric."[632] Among the Oraons it is the duty of the parents to select brides for their sons and bridegrooms for their daughters, through an *agua*[633] (intermediary). The initiative has to be taken by the boy's parents or guardians. On their arrival at the girl's house, the purpose of their visit is expressed in some symbolic language.[634] Then the omens of their journey are examined.[635] If the omens are found to be positive, then the negotiation continues, otherwise it is terminated. The Oraon marriage customs are very elaborate and solemn.

---

[627] "The money, goods, or estate, which a woman brings to her husband in marriage." (WEBSTER'S COLLEGIATE DICTIONARY (Springfield, U.S.A.: G. & C. Merriam Co., Publishers, 1946), 303.

[628] At the time of marriage the bridegroom gives some gifts: rupees five, *maensari, dhoti* and *sari* (traditional clothes) to the bride's parents, grandparents, brothers, and sisters. It is a traditional custom and this gift remains the same even in this modern age. The amount is fixed by the village elders and not the bride's parents. (Cf. J. LAKRA, "Rewriting Tribal Anthropolgy", in *Sevartham*, 22 (1997), 18). It was interpreted as bride price by S. C. Roy. But today scholars like J. Lakra give the explanation that it is a gift by which the groom's party shares the expenses of the marriage.

[629] Cf. S. C. ROY, *Oraon Religion and Customs*, op. cit., 101-103.

[630] It may happen that the wife is barren or the husband is impotent, that either the husband or the wife is a lunatic, that she habitually runs away from her husband's place, that she has been caught in adultery, that she possesses the evil eye or she is a witch, etc. (Cf. S. C. ROY, *Oraon Religion and Customs*, op. cit.. 102).

[631] E. T. DALTON, *Descriptive Ethnology of Bengal*, op. cit., 259.

[632] A. A. KUJUR, *The Oraon Habitat*, op. cit., 198.

[633] *Agua* is a guide or a leader in a special sense, the friend who acts as messenger to arrange a match. (A. GRIGNARD, *Oraon English Dictionary*, (Vienna: St. Gabriel Mödling, Administration "Anthropos", 1924), 22.

[634] Here are a few examples: We have seen some edible leaves or vegetable in your garden, we have come to pluck it, or one of our heifer is lost and it entered just this house, therefore we have come to look for it. (Cf. J. LAKRA, *Tribal Cultural Anthropology*. op. cit., 33; cf. V. ROSNER "The Marriage Ceremonies of the Telia Nagesia of Jashpur, India", in *Anthropos*, 59 (1964), 403. According to S. C. Roy the boy's party ask for tobacco powder and lime as the Oraons are fond of chewing it. (Cf. S. C. ROY, *Oraon Religion and Customs*, op. cit., 103).

[635] Some of the omens deemed favorable for a proposed marriage are: the sight of a corpse, the sight of a cow suckling her calf, the sight of a full pitcher of water being carried on the way, hearing the call of a tiger or leopard or meeting them on the way. The bad omens for a marriage are: a branch falling from a tree, a jackal or a squirrel cutting across the way, a crow darting down to make a kill, seeing an empty pitcher of water, fading off a lighted lamp during the meal of the guests etc. (Cf. V. ROSNER, "The Marriage Ceremonies of the Telia Nagesia", op. cit., 403-404).

4.2.2.1. Betrothal Ceremony

Marriage, for the Oraons, is specifically a rite of deeper incorporation into the life of the community. Hence there are various moments of contract by which they start this new relationship. When both parties come to an agreement, the consent of the boy and girl is sought. This is the betrothal rite or *lota pani*. On a certain evening mutually agreed upon, the boy's party arrives at the girl's house. The number of people to form this party is fixed depending on the local customs, but within a maximum of twenty. The guests engage themselves in chit-chat, singing and dancing overnight. The following morning the whole village community, along with friends and relatives assemble in the courtyard of the girl's house. The ceremony begins with the boy and girl, each one with a companion, standing approximately at a six foot distance facing each other with pots filled with water. These pots are made of brass, may contain 1-1.5 litre water. The *panch* (village head) asks the boy and girl to move simultaneously one step forward as a sign of their consent. It is done thrice after which the boy and girl stand close to each other. Then the *panch* asks them thrice for their consent and this consent should be expressed loud enough to be heard by all who are present. Finally the *panch* asks them to exchange their pots of water as an affirmation of their consent. The ceremony ends with the festal meal and with much rejoicing.[636]

"In traditional societies relationships take precedence over structural order. ...Marriages are more than a personal covenant between two persons; they are alliances between kinship groups that take years to negotiate."[637] After the betrothal ceremony there are a series of celebrations which would help both the parties to deepen their relationship. In this relationship ceremonies, all the other important formalities of the marriage like further visits of the parties, the date of marriage, the *dali-dhiba*, etc. are discussed and fixed. This is the economic side of the marriage contract. The *dali-dhiba* is five rupees and four mounds of grain.[638]

The bridegroom's party goes in great rejoicing to the bride's house. The girl's party comes out in procession and welcomes the bridegroom and his people by sprinkling water on them using mango leaves. The bridegroom is carried to the bride's house by one of the close relatives of the bride. Both bride and bridegroom are anointed with oil and turmeric. This is a purificatory rite.[639]

4.2.2.2. Principal Rite of Marriage

Marriage is celebrated in the house of the bride. A village elder explains the seriousness and implication of the ceremony. He says "what is joined in flesh is

---

[636] Cf. E. CAMPION, *My Oraon Culture,* op. cit., 42.

[637] P. G. HIEBERT, *Anthropological Reflections on Missiological Issues* (Grand Rapids, Michigan: Baker Books, 1994), 141.

[638] Cf. L. KUJUR, *The Sacramental Celebration*, op. cit., 38.

[639] Cf. E. CAMPION, *My Oraon Culture,* op. cit., 46.

indissoluble (life long), what is joined in iron is breakable. During the life time of the husband and wife, none of the party is free to marry. But if one of the party dies the other party is free to marry."[640]

The central ceremony of marriage is the final consent of the bride and bridegroom which they express by the reciprocal exchange of *sindhur* (vermilion). The place for marriage called *marwa* (marriage pavilion) is made ready with all the necessary things for marriage. A mat is spread on the ground. A yoke is placed over it and covered with three or five bundles of straw or *sabai* grass (straw like grass). A curry stone is placed near it.[641]

The bride and bridegroom are led in solemnly, either carried or escorted by a close relative, to this place. They are made to stand on this curry stone, the left toe of the bridegroom touching the heel of the left foot of the bride and the right toe touching the heel of the right foot. As they are in this position they exchange *sindhur* (vermilion). The bride applies the *sindhur* on the forehead of the bridegroom and the bridegroom does the same on the forehead and on the parting line of hair of the bride. As soon as the *sindhur* is exchanged women sprinkle or pour water on them as a sign of blessing.[642] During this ceremony the couple are screened in on all sides with a piece of cloth. A few relatives remain inside the screen. This is to ward off the evil eye and evil spirits.

4.2.2.3. Chuman/Sabha (Offering of Gifts) and Farewell

The newly wedded pair are carried to the centre of the *marwa* (marriage pavilion) and seated there facing the east. Friends, relatives, family members and villagers bring their gifts to the couple and congratulate them. They give them a present according to each one's capacity. Each gift, however small it may be, is recorded and announced with the sound of the drum.[643] After the marriage one of the elders of the family gives some advise to the new couple concerning married life and its responsibilities. It is an exhortation on family life to remain in fidelity and love supporting each other and fulfilling their responsibility towards the tribe by producing children. For an Oraon marriage is indissoluble.[644]

When all the ceremonies are complete the marriage party is given a ceremonial farewell. The elder brother of the bride carries her in his arms up to the boundary of the village and then hands her over to the bridegroom. The father

---

[640] E. CAMPION, *My Oraon Culture,* op. cit., 47.

[641] Cf. J. LAKRA. *Tribal Cultural Anthropology,* op. cit., 37. The curry stone is used to grind the ingredients for making curry.

[642] Cf. E. CAMPION, *My Oraon Culture*, op. cit., 50.

[643] Cf. J. LAKRA, *Tribal Cultural Antropology*, op. cit., 38.

[644] Cf. A. A. KUJUR, *The Oraon Habitat*, op. cit., 202-203.

of the bride bids her farewell in a special way.[645] Then the party moves on.[646] On their arrival at the groom's house the bride's feet are washed as a sign of welcome by female members of the family. Rice beer is offered to her. During this drink a broom and a winnowing shovel is handed to her symbolising her authority in the house. When all the marriage rites are completed the *Dandakatta* ceremony is performed in both houses in order to ask God's blessings on the newly wedded pair.[647]

Though the marriage is a contract between two individuals it is the concern of the whole village. A new relationship has been established between the families of the new couple. The whole village of the both parties take active part in all the needed preparation as well as the marriage ceremonies. The village elders have a very important role to play in any marriage. The approval and guidance of the village elders is sought in all the important events connected with marriage. All the people in the village from children to the old people have specific roles allotted to them and everyone participates in the celebrations wholeheartedly.[648]

4.2.2.4. Christian Significance of Traditional Elements

"Marriage is the greatest occasion in the life of an Adivasi."[649] and it comprises many rituals with a lengthy process. Thanks to marriage the couple is incorporated fully into the tribe, and permitted to shoulder the responsibilities for the good of the tribe, clan and family.

Rice beer is an indispensable element of an Oraon celebration. It is their favourite beverage. They consider it a symbol of life and union. According to the creation myth rice beer has played an important role for the continuation of the tribe.

"Before instituting the marriage proper, God taught the first human beings how to brew rice beer. The couple drank it and behaved like husband and wife. Tribals consider this plan of God as the institution of marriage and the beginning of procreation. Since both institution and procreation were designed by God and carried out by the first couple through the instrumentality of the rice beer, the latter stands as the symbol of life and union. Hence tribals not only offer rice beer to God and the spirits, but also conclude all the important events and works with the same life giving spirit."[650]

---

645 The bride is given a sari, some amount of money and an arrow with an iron arrow head. The gift of an arrow is one of the oldest traditions which shows that once upon a time the Oraons were hunters. This arrow is used by the boy. (Cf. A. A. KUJUR, *The Oraon Habitat,* op. cit., 205).

646 Cf. J. LAKRA *Tribal Cultural Anthropology,* op. cit., 39.

647 Cf. E. CAMPION, *My Oraon Culture*, op. cit., 52-54.

648 Cf. L. KUJUR, *The Sacramental Celebration*, op. cit., 39.

649 P. EKKA, "Adivasi Riti Rivaj", op. cit., 21.

650 P. KULLU, "Tribal Spirituality: An Integrated Life with Belief", in *Sevartham*, 21 (1996), 112.

The bridegroom and bride express their final consent in standing. Standing symbolises a pilgrim's action. A pilgrim is ready to move ahead, in spite of the difficulties, because he has a definite goal to reach. Here in this ritual, standing manifests that the new couple is stepping forward in life; a new stage in their life comes up and they need to walk together. The bridegroom's standing pressing the heel of the bride with his toes signifies the submission of the wife to her husband.[651] Such a ceremony reminds Christians of St. Paul's words: "Be subject to one another out of reverence for Christ. Wives, be subject to your husbands, as to the Lord"(Eph. 5:21-22). This also manifest reverence towards the Supreme Being and to one another.

Marriage means to form a family, to make a home. For the Oraons the yoke, grinding stone and straw are symbolic expressions of it. They use all these items in their daily life, for their happy living. The yoke represents the main occupation of the Oraons. They are farmers, and the yoke is used to plough the field to cultivate. In the Bible the yoke is the symbol of submission to Yahweh (cf. Jer. 2:20) and an obligation of the law (cf. Gal. 5:1). Thus a yoke can be identified as a sign of their new commitment in life, commitment to each other and to society.[652]

It is said that a precious stone, diamond, is used to manifest the depth of love, because stone is durable by nature. Stone is a sign of divine presence and power (cf. Gen. 28:11-19). In biblical language the image of a stone also reveals the hardness of heart (cf. Ez. 11:19; Jb. 41:16).[653] Therefore here a grinding stone is the symbol of a life-long love and faithfulness. In Chotanagpur a house is thatched by means of straw or grass. Though these are simple ordinary things they contain rich meanings.[654] Through these symbols they express that marriage is permanent and indissoluble, as it also corresponds to the biblical conviction: "Therefore a man leaves his father and his mother and clings to his wife and they become one flesh" (Gn. 2:24).

The most important gesture in the Oraon marriage ceremony is the exchange of *sindhur* (vermilion). *Sindhur* has the colour of blood and hence symbolises life. Thus it is a sign of the couple's new life in full union and fidelity. "The *sindhur* is prepared in oil in view of the marriage. Leftover would be considered as *juta*, 'touched' and could not be used for any other purpose. *Sindhur* indeed, always stands for blood and blood is life."[655]

The sprinkling of water is considered as a symbol of fertility. Children are the wealth of their parents. To multiply in number is one of the aspirations of the tribe. Water is poured or sprinkled by means of mango leaves. Green leaves are a sign of hope and prosperity, and the Oraons hope for good and healthy children.

---

[651] Cf. M. LURKER, *Dizionario delle Immagini e dei Simboli Biblici,* op. cit., 156.

[652] Cf. J. L. McKENZIE, *Dictionary of the Bible*, op. cit., 945.

[653] Cf. E. URECH, *Dizionario dei Simboli Cristiani*, op. cit., 26.

[654] Cf. B. TIRKEY, *Oraon Symbols,* op. cit., 47-48.

[655] A. VAN EXEM, *The Religious System of the Munda Tribe*, op. cit., 235.

Anointing the bride and bridegroom with turmeric and oil signifies an act of purification. They need to be purified ritually in order to be fully and totally incorporated into the tribe. Through marriage the boy and girl have the obligation to preserve and perpetuate the purity of the tribe.[656] "Turmeric symbolises purity and stability that should exist in a marriage relationship."[657]

During marriage too, there is a moment to remember the village spirits and the ancestors of the newly-weds. It is a sign of communion with them so that they may protect the couple from all harm. When all ceremonies are done, finally the *Dandakatta* ritual is performed to thank God for all his benefits, since he has made it possible for them to establish this new relationship.

In fact the Oraons have a very noble concept of marriage. They believe that marriage is instituted by *Dharmes* and it is indissoluble. The couple needs to live in love and fidelity and bring forth new members for the tribe.

Marriage is a concern of the whole community and never a private affair. The consent is expressed in words and actions always in the presence of a community. In spite of the fact that marriages are arranged by parents there is a lot of freedom possible for each one of the future couple to express approval or disapproval. The exhortations of the village elder serve as a wise counsel to the newly wedded pair about their duties as husband and wife, as parents, as members of the community. After the marriage the elder brother entrusts the bride (his sister) to the bridegroom. The new husband is expected to provide all the protection and care needed for her.

In the emerging Christian concept, marriage is a vocation and a sacrament. "Marriage is the vocation of a baptised man and woman to that state consecrated by the Sacrament of Matrimony, devoted to the service of a new life in Christ, which involves the specific spiritual perfection of the spouses as a way of life."[658] St. Paul in his teachings uses the symbol of marriage for Christ's union with the Church (cf. Eph. 5:22-24). It has a profound effect on Christian thought, elevating and purifying the conception of marriage. For a Christian marriage is more than a social institution, it is a 'holy estate.'[659] "For God himself is the author of marriage."[660] By instituting marriage he gave meaning to it. The solemnisation of marriage by a religious ceremony is not new to Christian tradition alone, as it is common at all times and in all countries. On the other hand, the form of our liturgical services, the ministerial benediction, and the clear expression of

---

[656] Cf. B. TIRKEY, *Oraon Symbols*, op. cit., 49.

[657] S. RITA, "The Chamar Marrige Customs and their Meaning", in *Sevartham*, 3 (1978), 59.

[658] H. V. SATTLER, "Marriage (Theology of)", in NEW CATHOLIC ENCYCLOPEDIA, Vol. IX (New York, St. Louis: McGraw Hill Book Company, 1967), 265.

[659] Cf. W. M. FOLEY, "Marriage (Christian)", in J. HASTINGS (ed.), *Encyclopaedia of Religion and Ethics*, Vol.VIII (Edinburgh: T. & T. CLARK, 1915), 434.

[660] GS 48.

Christian doctrine in prayers and exhortations have helped to preserve the sanctity of marriage.[661]

Marriage is, in the first place, an affair of the family. The Church is a spiritual family who is concerned with the welfare of her members. Therefore no member of this spiritual family ought to enter upon so important a step in life as the contract of matrimony without the witnessing approval of its members. In this respect a Christian marriage, even though the spouses themselves are the ministers, it is fitting that they should seal their consent by uniting themselves in the context of the Eucharistic Sacrifice of Christ, which is an offering of Christ for his Church. By the reception of the Body and Blood of Christ they may form but "one body" in Christ (cf. 1Cor. 10:17).[662] Thus the official witness of marriage is the priest, who is the visible presence of Christ, the third partner of the marriage who enriches the spouses with his grace. "Inasmuch as it is a sacramental action of sanctification, the liturgical celebration of marriage ...must be, per se, valid, worthy, and fruitful."[663] Traditional Oraon marriage is not a sacrament but a social institution, but it clearly shows a "transcendent" orientation too.

4.2.3. Funeral Rituals

The Oraons believe in the immortality of the soul and in heaven where the souls of their ancestors rest. It is the duty of each Oraon to treat the dead with due respect and reverence and to offer them sacrifices at regular intervals. "Burial ceremonies manifest faith in the after-life."[664] When a death occurs in an Oraon family the female members of the family cry and weep loudly in order to make known the death to the whole village. Women let loose their unkempt hair as a sign of their grief.[665]

The Oraons follow two customs in disposing of the dead bodies, burial or cremation. If one dies after the new paddy seedlings have sprouted, then he is buried. When death occurs after the harvest and before the sprouting of the new paddy plants, the body is cremated. But nowadays they mostly bury their dead.

After death the body of the deceased is washed and anointed with turmeric and oil, and covered with a new piece of cloth. If the wife would die when her husband is still alive, he anoints her dead body with *sindhur* (vermilion) mixed in oil. The body is then placed in the courtyard with its head to the south and feet to the north.[666] This has a symbolic meaning, i.e. "leaving Rohtasgarh[667] behind

---

[661] Cf. W. M. FOLEY, "Marriage (Christian)," op. cit., 435.

[662] Cf. CATECHISM OF THE CATHOLIC CHURCH, para. 1621.

[663] FC 67.

[664] P. EKKA, "Adivasi Riti Rivaj", op. cit., 26.

[665] Cf. E. T. DALTON, *Descriptive Ethnology,* op. cit., 268.

[666] Cf. S. C. ROY, *Oraon Religion and Customs*, op. cit., 125.

[667] Rohtasgarh was the fortified kingdom of the Oraons which they lost due to the jealousy and cunning of a milk-maid who betrayed them into the hands of powerful enemies.

and marching towards Chotanagpur."[668] As soon as the dead body is taken out of the room, ashes are spread on the floor and the door is shut.

4.2.3.1. Cremation and Burial

The corpse is carried to the *masan* (cremation ground) in procession. All the relatives and villagers participate in this funeral procession. For an aged person the procession is accompanied by music. Boiled rice, some oil and copper coins are taken to the cremation ground and all is placed near the head of the corpse. Some copper coins, *usna rice*[669] and rice beer are put into the mouth of the deceased by the women saying "Take, eat. Now you have given us up. Now you have seen your way. Go taking (with you) all our sickness and sins."[670]

The dead body is placed on the pile of wood in direction of south-north, head southwards and feet northwards. The son of the deceased or in his absence the nearest male relative sets fire to the pyre. When the corpse is reduced to ashes both men and women undergo a ceremonial purification.[671]

If one has to be buried, a pit is dug in a north to south direction. Various shapes of branches cover the bottom of the grave so that the body which is wrapped only in a white cloth does not touch the ground. Before lowering the corpse down into the pit, it is carried around the pit three times. All the things needed for daily use are provided for the deceased. An earthenware jar filled with water is left at the grave and holes are made for the water to drip close to the head of the corpse. The grave is sprinkled with turmeric powder mixed in water. The funeral party undergoes the ceremonial purification as said above. After the rainy season the grave is opened, the bones are collected and burned in the normal manner.[672]

Women go to the cremation ground and gather the parts that are left after the cremation. They wash these bones and collect them in a new piece of cloth, anoint them with turmeric paste and put them in a new earthenware jar which is buried later. Some copper coins are placed in the jar. This jar is suspended on the post near the residence of the deceased till the second burial. Three leaf plates with half boiled rice are also placed at the cremation spot. Then the place is cleaned with cow-dung diluted in water.[673]

---

[668] E. CAMPION, *My Oraon Culture*, op. cit., 61.

[669] *Usna* rice: Rice which is parboiled before husking. (Cf. S. C. ROY, *Oraon Religion and Customs,*op. cit., 126).

[670] S. C. ROY, *Oraon Religion and Customs,* op. cit., 126.

[671] The participants of a funeral ceremony take a bath in a stream or a tank. A part of the courtyard is cleaned with cowdung diluted in water. A quantity of grain -husks has been piled. On return of the funeral party, this chaff is set fire to and oil poured on it so that it emits smoke. Over this smoke every one places the palms by way of ceremonial purification.Then turmeric oil is rubbed on some parts of the body. (Cf. S. C. ROY, *Oraon Religion and Customs,* op. cit., 126-127).

[672] Cf. S. C. ROY, *Oraon Religion and Customs*, op. cit., 128.

[673] Cf. ibid., 130.

In order to bring back the spirit of the deceased, about half way to the cemetery, three twigs of a *Sal* tree are planted in the form of a hut and straw is placed like thatch. Then the straw is set on fire. The women shout thrice taking the name of the deceased "come, your house is burning". Then they return home in great silence.

On arriving at the house of the deceased they see the doors closed. They knock at the door and shout `open the door'. Then they hear a voice from inside: "What have you brought for us? Happiness or sorrow?" They reply: "Happiness." They enter the house and examine the flame of the lamp. If the flame is seen wavering then it is believed that the shade is a manifestation of the spirit of the dead back in the house.[674]

4.2.3.2. Kaman

The Oraons believe that their dead join the ancestors only when all the obsequies are completed. Ritual grieving comes to an end a few days after the burial or cremation of the corpse with the celebration of *kaman. Kaman* is observed by sacrificing a pig and offering libation for the ancestors of the defunct. They plead with the ancestors to admit the dead into their company.[675] It is an occasion to show gratitude to all those who participated in the funeral. During the ceremony the life-history of the dead man is chanted. For ten days, they offer water and tooth brush to the dead person, also food materials like rice and *dal* (phaseolus mungo, a kind of beans). On the tenth day all the relatives and friends are invited and prayers and sacrifices are offered to admit the spirit of the deceased into the company of the ancestors. The tribals believe that till then the spirit of the deceased remains around the house looking for a place to rest.[676]

4.2.3.3. Final Ceremonies

In the months of December-January the final obsequies for all the deceased are completed. This is the celebration of the final burial of the bones of the dead of each clan in the *kundi* (family grave).[677] The bones that are in the earthen vessel are carried by women in procession accompanied by relatives, friends and villagers to the family grave. The bones are buried there and *pulkhi* (a memorial stone) is erected which indicates the clan to which the deceased belonged. This is done amidst singing and dancing. Women anoint the memorial stone with *sindhur.* The village priest sprinkles turmeric powder dissolved in water on it. Half cooked rice is kept on the stone block. Then they say: "We have completed all the rites for you. Everything is done and we are going home."[678]

---

[674] Cf. P. EKKA, "Adivasi Riti Rivaj". op. cit., 23; A. A. KUJUR, *The Oraon Habitat*, op. cit., 210.

[675] Cf. B. TIRKEY, *The Smiling Oraon*, op. cit., 27.

[676] Cf. L. KUJUR, *The Sacramental Celebration*, op. cit., 42.

[677] It is a deep pit. Each family has its own sepulchral spot near a stream or a pond.

[678] J. LAKRA, *Tribal Cultural Anthropology*, op. cit., 43.

Then all the participants take a purificatory bath. They go to the house of the *pahan* and the purificatory ceremony is repeated. Later they return to their respective houses to celebrate this occasion with a festal meal. With the burial of the bones the dead are considered to be fully incorporated among the ancestors.[679]

4.2.3.4. Christian Significance of Traditional Elements

The Oraons invoke the memory of their ancestors in their daily life. It is the duty of an Oraon to drop a handful of rice and curry on the ground in memory of his deceased ancestors.[680] The Oraons belief in life after death. These rituals are not expressions of separation but ways of incorporation into the communion of the dead ancestors. This communion is the final destiny of each Oraon. Ancestors are benevolent people who protect and guard their descendants. Hence they are remembered and prayed to, even as *Dharmes* is remembered in every phase of life.[681]

For the Oraons death is a transformation of life and not an end. Hence, they attribute the highest homage to the dead. They treat their dead with great respect washing and anointing the corpses with turmeric and oil, and giving them all necessities of life (rice grains, new cloth, copper coins etc.). Normally turmeric is used for purificatory rites but it is also used as a sign of new life. The yellow colour of the turmeric gives an impression that they have been tested by fire, yet remain alive. It has a biblical significance: "For gold is tested in the fire and acceptable men in the furnace of humiliation" (Sir. 2:5).[682] Cremation of the body signifies transformation through fire, assimilation to *Dharmes*. For *Dharmes* entered into the *Asur*'s fire and came out of it with an immortal body, thus revealing his divine glory. Similarly the dead by being consumed by fire, assume a new body, which is the sign of their new life with *Dharmes*.

Moses had a vision of God in the midst of a burning bush, and Moses experienced a transition towards a new life (cf. Ex. 3:2ff). The book of kings speaks of a chariot of fire and horses of fire which separated Elijah the prophet, from Elisha, and Elijah was taken to heaven in a whirlwind; he was transformed and received a new life (cf. 2Kg. 2:11-12). Thus fire, which is symbol of God himself, brings a change to the human body converting it to immortality. The Oraons express their mourning by abstaining from meat and fish for about a week. *Kaman* is celebrated to make an offering to their ancestors and to manifest their gratitude to all those who shared their sorrow.[683] The bones of the dead are reburied in the family grave. Sacrifices are offered to the ancestor spirits, thus seeking their intercession to include the dead into their community. This they

---

[679] Cf. A. A. KUJUR, *The Oraon Habitat*, op. cit., 211.

[680] Cf. S. C. ROY, *The Oraons of Chotanagpur*, op. cit., 212.

[681] Cf. B. TIRKEY, *Oraon Symbols*, op. cit., 50-51; cf. P. EKKA, "Adivasi Riti Rivaj", op. cit., 22

[682] Cf. P. KULLU, "Tribal Culture-Religion in Practice", op. cit., 29

[683] Cf. B. TIRKEY, *Oraon Symbols*, op. cit., 51

call *konha benja* (great marriage). Marriage incorporates them fully into the tribe, so this great marriage initiates the dead into the company of the ancestors and to a transformed state of life.[684] "Life is no longer a continued existence of the innocent in the visible presence of God; it has become limited and time-bound: only by dying can one enter into a mode of existence where God is met face to face."[685]

The dead body is placed in north-south direction, that is head towards south and feet towards north. The exact significance of this is difficult to find. According to E. Campion it is a remembrance of their flight from Rohtasgarh, a kingdom which the Oraons fortified before their settlement in Chotanagpur.[686] It is a reminder that human life is a pilgrimage. "The north-south burial reminds the human being of his true and eternal abode. His face is turned toward the East so as to enable the dead continuously to look at God."[687] This again signifies the new life the dead is supposed to attain. One who faces *Dharmes*, (for East symbolises the sun and at times the Oraons compare *Dharmes* with the sun) will be illumined like him, freed from all sorts of darkness and attain a new life.

The dead body is carried three times around the pit before burial. Three is an important number in many religious traditions.[688] In the religion of the Oraons *Dharmes* was in the furnace for three days and three nights. On the third day he rose in glory and splendour loaded with gold and silver, shining brightly, as manifestation of his victory over the evil powers.[689] The final destiny of every Oraon is to be in the company of the ancestors who have won the favour of *Dharmes*.

In Christianity the Holy Trinity is the union of three persons, Father, Son and Spirit. By Baptism one is incorporated into the company of the Holy Trinity and by death one enjoys the beatific vision of this divine community. The Father made the Son to rise from the dead on the third day. He rose from the dead triumphantly overcoming the evil of sin and other evil forces. Thus there is a similarity in both traditions, victory over evil through the self-immolation

---

[684] Cf. B. TIRKEY, *Oraon Symbols*, op. cit., 51; J. LAKRA, *Tribal Cultural Anthropology*, op. cit., 42-43

[685] A. VAN EXEM, "The New Dispensation in Sarna Religion: A Theological Interpretation" in *Sevartham*, 10 (1985), 78.

[686] Cf. E. CAMPION, *My Oraon Culture*, op. cit., 61.

[687] P. KULLU, "Tribal Spirituality: An Integrated Life with Belief", in *Sevartham* 21 (1996), 111.

[688] *Sat-Cit-Ananda* (being, knowledge, bliss) is a common triad in Indian thought. Buddhism conceives of *triloka* (three worlds) and of *trikaya* (three bodies of the Buddha), and Islam distinguishes between *islam* (surrender), *iman* (faith), and *ihsan* (acting perfectly beautifully). (Cf. A. SCHIMMEL, "Numbers: An Overview", in M. ELIADE (editor in chief), *The Encyclopedia of Religion*, Vol. 11 (New York: Macmillian Publishing Company, 1987), 14.

[689] Cf. S. K KUJUR, "Tribal Concept of the Divine: A Trinitarian Perspective", in *Sevartham* 21 (1996), 117.

of the Divine, thereby manifesting the glorification, and effectuating a total transformation of the old self. Therefore the custom of carrying the dead body three times around the pit reminds one of the resurrection of Lord Jesus Christ. The immortal soul enters into life with the risen Lord. "Indeed they cannot die anymore, because they are like angels and are children of God, being children of the resurrection" (Lk. 20:36). Jesus said: "I am the resurrection and the life. Those who believe in me, even though they die, will live and everyone who lives and believes in me will never die" (Jn. 11:25-26). Christ did not remain in the tomb (cf. Lk. 24:1-12).

In a Christian context, one speaks of life with the risen Christ. Since Christians are united with Christ in baptism and it is through the Spirit, that they share in his resurrection. The resurrection of the faithful constitutes the core of Christian faith. God's creative power will transform what we know as the material body into a spiritual one.[690] This theme receives an excellent elaboration in St. Paul's letter to the Corinthians (cf. 1Cor. 15). Christians are dead only in so far as they are in the state of death and lack a living body. The resurrection of Jesus and the future resurrection of the Christian are a testimonial that a Christian is liberated from sin.[691] Christ, the life-giving Adam, is the first born from the dead, and Christians will be raised by him, even though they are dead due to their union with the life-taking Adam. Therefore, the resurrection of the faithful completes the victory of Christ over sin and death, and Christ has become the life-giving, spiritual Adam who communicates new life.[692]

The re-burial of the bones again reflects new life, incorporating the dead ones into the life of the Supreme Being. In the Christian understanding, these bones can be taken as relics of the dead persons. It is the veneration of those Christians, who through death are believed to be more closely united with Christ. The Church has encouraged the use of relics of the saints as a means to obtain graces from God. This is due to the conviction that they have restored the image of Christ in them by their holy and virtuous life, and after death they enjoy the beatific vision of God. Therefore they can continue in communion with their fellow Christians on earth through Christ.[693]

---

[690] Cf. P. PERKINS, "Resurrection", in C. in C. STUHLMULLER (ed.), *The Collegeville Pastoral Dictionary of Biblical Theology* (Minnesota:The Liturgical Press, 1996), 838.

[691] Cf. F. W. GROSHEIDE, *The New International Commentary on the New Testament: The First Epistle to the Corinthians* (Grand Rapids, Michigan: WM. B. Eerdmans Publishing Company, 1953), 381.

[692] Cf. J. L. McKENZIE, *Dictionary of the Bible,* op. cit., 734.

[693] Cf. S. LASH, "Relics, Theology of", in A. RICHARDSON AND J. BOWDEN (ed.), *The Westminster Dictionary of Christian Theology* (Pennsylvania: Philadelphia, The Westminster Press, 1983), 495-496.

Chapter Summary

The study on the various festivals and rituals with religious connotations has revealed the richness of the culture and religion of the Oraons. The analysis and interpretation of symbols which they use to express the different realities of their culture are very meaningful and inspiring. In fact these symbols (water, fire, food, tree, etc.) bear numerous references to represent the sacred and transcendental realities.

It is significant to note that the basic concern of the Oraons in life is *Dharmes* himself. There is dependence and total surrender only to *Dharmes* and this is publicly acknowledged and symbolically manifested in their life. *Dharmes* is constantly remembered and proper worship is rendered to him on all important occasions of life, above all during festivals that are connected with their life's occupations with various phases in their personal existence as members of the community. Along with the worship of *Dharmes* they offer due respect and veneration to their ancestors from whom they have inherited their life and wealth. The values that are communicated through symbolic ritual actions can be purified, perfected and incorporated into Christian life to promote an effective evangelisation of the Oraons.

They see their entire life permeated by religious connotations, which might at least partly be identified as precious roads towards a better understanding of the Christian faith. Such a process will be gradual and needs a certain time before it will arrive at fully developed Christian convictions. It requires of the missionaries, be they foreigners or local faithful, much patience, hard work, above all a thorough knowledge of the traditional culture as well as of the central issues in Christianity.

CONCLUSION

Inculturation of the Gospel and the evangelisation of a culture is a new challenge that the Christian faith is faced with. It demands courage, to encounter the unknown when it meets new cultures and wants to purify them. Such interactions are necessary for the emergence of a new Christian community. Religion and culture are inter-related and this inter-relatedness is so obvious in an Oraon traditional religion. According to P. Kullu a scholar in *sarna* religion "the tribal (Oraon) religion is nothing else but beliefs expressed culturally, and tribal culture is nothing else but beliefs being lived out, religion in practice."[694]

After having made a study on the religion and culture of the Oraons, we arrive at a conclusion that the Oraon traditional religion is in many ways close to Christianity and has even some traits of a Christian tradition. Evangelisation of the Oraon culture is possible through the incarnation of the Gospel. This in turn will help the people to change their belief systems by which they have enslaved themselves. This is what we see in the evangelising activities of Fr. Constant Lievens, S.J., who preached the liberative message of Jesus Christ at an opportune time when the Oraons were eager to accept it.

"For the Church, evangelising means bringing the Good News into all the strata of humanity, and through its influence transforming humanity from within and making it new."[695] "Behold, I make all things new" (Rev. 21:5; cf. 2 Cor. 5:17; Gal. 6:15). Even though evangelisation is a multidimensional reality, in this context inculturation of the Oraon culture is a way for the evangelisation of this particular traditional religion, in order to bring about a radical transformation in the life patters and belief systems of the Oraons.

After having made a survey of the traditional religion of the Oraons we have jotted out some of the prominent values this religion, both positive and negative in character.

1. *Dharmes* is the Supreme Being, the creator God who has given them freedom.

---

[694] P. KULLU, "Religion in Practice," op. cit., 15.

[695] EN 18.

2. The Oraons experience the presence of the supernatural forces everywhere in the nature.
3. Appeasement of the spirits is done through occult practices.
4. Only women are accused as witches.
5. Man is the central figure of creation.
6. Man is created as a co-creator and a co-operating being endowed with the power to enter into relationship with God and with one another.
7. Marriage is instituted by *Dharmes* and it is indissoluble.
8. The Oraons are *Dharmes*' own people, *Dharmes* is the founder of the tribe.
9. *Dharmes* determines the occupation for the Oraons.
10. *Dharmes* is the Unique Being, who is worshipped with a unique cult.
11. Observances of ascetical practices, such as fasting, praying, observance of purity, is in view of encountering the divine.
12. No promise is found of a personal Saviour, but its foretaste is found in the myth of the *Asurs*.
13. Reconciliation is founded on human judgement regard as salvation.
14. *Pahan* is accepted as the representative of *Dharmes.* Usually a married person is chosen for this purpose and vests white dress for his office.
15. There is a sense of solidarity or community in all spheres of life.
16. They believe in the ancestors as their intercessors or patrons.
17. They have a concept of common ownership of the land, without denying private property.
18. The religion of the Oraons is not founded on sacred books nor on ritual books; They have no special places to offer sacrifices and have no written moral codes either.
19. Celebration of festivals as communitarian expression of religiosity.

These findings could serve as a base for an effective evangelization. Belief in *Dharmes*, other supernatural spirits, ancestral spirits, and life after death are the key elements of the Oraon traditional religion. *Dharmes* is also addressed by relational names as 'Old one or Grandfather' which helps them to imagine him anthropomorphically. However, in actual life this Supreme being is considered as a far away God. A really personal God seems to be out of their mind. They are more occupied with the placation of the spirits whom they address 'gods and deities' who are ambivalent in character, so that they may obtain prosperity in all spheres. Even though they claim themselves to be monotheistic persons their everyday reality displays confusion (as they worship these 'gods and deities' in actual life). The difference is that these spirits and gods are lower than the Supreme Being and they denote them with a small 'g or d.'[696] This explanation is insufficient.

[696] Cf. V. P. BARJO, "The Religious Life of the *Sarna* Tribes," in *Indian Missiological Review*, 19 (1994), 44.

"God is seen as far away and basically unconcerned with humans, though positive toward them."[697] Transformation of this conceptualisation alone would be a fruitful starting point in effective evangelisation. Missionaries need to have an adequate knowledge of the cultural traditions and religious expressions by which they would help the people to re-evaluate and re-interpret their religious beliefs in the light of the Gospel (cf. Acts. 17: 22ff).[698] Christianity gives us a God who is not only our Creator but also one who loves and cares for each one of us, who is our Father, who gives us adoptive sonship in Jesus Christ. The understanding of God as a loving, caring and forgiving Father must be made explicit to the Oraons by the missionary through his/her way of witnessing life, adequate catechetical instruction and pastoral care.

The Oraon concept of God as all good, virtuous and just is an edifying point to help them to discern and to find meaning in time of sickness, suffering and such other calamities in life. "For God so loved the world that he gave his only Son, that whoever believes in him should not perish but have eternal life" (Jn. 3:16). These words spoken by Jesus Christ to Nicodemus not only introduce us into the very heart of God's salvific work but also express the very essence of Christian soteriology. Salvation means liberation from all evil, and this is achieved by the only begotten Son through his suffering. And in this, the unconditional love of both the Father and the Son is manifested; the Father by giving his only Son to the world and the Son by willingly accepting the Cross which is his Father's will. Even though Christ has won victory over all evil by his death and resurrection it does not eliminate suffering from the life of humans.[699] Thus, suffering is part of human life and it is for our sanctification.

"If one becomes a sharer in the sufferings of Christ, this happens because Christ has opened His suffering to man, because He Himself in His redemptive suffering has become, in a certain sense, a sharer in all human sufferings. Man, discovering through faith the redemptive suffering of Christ, also discovers in it his own sufferings; he rediscovers them, through faith, enriched with a new content and new meaning."[700]

Therefore the evangeliser should help the Oraons to find meaning in their difficulties by communicating to them the value of the Cross in their life. This is possible only by cultivating in them a deep faith in a loving God who in turn helps them to get rid of their fear of spirits. In this respect the missionary should accompany the people in their faith life assisting them to start a personal relationship with God and also to deepen it through daily prayers, through the

---

[697] C. H. KRAFT, *Christianity in Culture A study in Dynamic Biblical Theologizing in Cross-Cultural Perspective* (Maryknoll, New York: Orbis books 1980), 363.

[698] Cf. R. J. SCHREITER, *Constructing Local Theologies* (Maryknoll, New York: Orbis books, 1985), 21.

[699] Cf.SD 14.

[700] SD 20.

practice of popular devotions, through the use of sacramentals, and through adequate catechesis. It is the community who is the agent of inculturation and the missionary is only a guide who points out the path.

The sense of solidarity and a sense of community feeling in the Oraon society is another element to be considered. This concept is mainly because of their understanding of *Dharmes* as the author of the tribe. Unfortunately these sentiments of solidarity and community feeling are not extended beyond the limits of tribe. It is a fact that Oraons are victims of exploitation by the non-tribals and it is naturally human to have such limitations. However, it is here that the messages of Christ should make an impact, for as children of the same father we are called to become images of him in the world by our very life. "For if you love those who love you, what reward have you? Do not even the tax collectors do the same? And if you salute only your brethren, what more are you doing than others? Do not even the Gentiles do the same? You, therefore, must be perfect, as your heavenly Father is perfect" (Mt 5: 46-48). Thus, this is a noteworthy element which needs to be purified and emphasised. Christian understanding of community should help them to appreciate and accept individual persons as brothers and sisters of the same family (the Church).

Inculturation of the Gospel and evangelisation of the Oraon culture aim at having a local community of believers who would worship their God in their own cultural patterns, without losing their identity as Oraons as well as Christians. This is possible only when the Gospel is preached in the cultural 'language' of the people. In other words, the proclamation of the Word, the participation in worship, and the specific forms of communication, fellowship service and organisation should be attuned to the cultural garb of the people thereby they can develop an Oraon Christian theology which is closely connected to the understanding and practice of their culture.[701]

Oraons did not base their religion on any sacred books, but on myths, legends and folklores, which are passed on through oral tradition. "Myth is the central pillar of their tribal life around which all the rest is structured. It is the memory of their origins, by which the members of the tribe know their identity and their place in the world. The myth enfolds, sustains, guides and protects them, provides their upbringing. With its strange symbolism, the myth hides its secret from outsiders and reveals it to those who belong to the household."[702]

The Christian Oraons should be encouraged and helped to find their central pillar of Christian life in the Bible which is the major deposit of Christian faith. The missionary should present the Word of God in such a way that it would be interesting to the hearers; through bible classes, through storytelling, through a chalk talk method, through an incarnational approach for the meditation on the Word of God, etc. Oraons love song, dance and joyful community celebrations,

[701] Cf. L. J. LUZBETAK, *The Church and Cultures*, op. cit., 375.

[702] C. MAESTERS, "Indian Myths and the Old Testament," in *Sedos* Bulletin 24 (1992), 67-68.

and so integration of these cultural elements in prayers, in the presentation of Gospel, even in liturgical and para-liturgical celebrations, and popular devotions are worth considering.

As Oraon sacrifices constitute a number of symbols (water, fire, incense, flowers, *aruva chaval* (pearl rice), green leaves and trees), the use of such in the expressions of their worship would be meaningful to them especially in the celebration of festivals and other important phases in life. "Religion is never divorced from ritual. This is, of course, particularly true of the Christian faith. Ritual fortifies belief as belief fortifies ritual."[703]

The Oraon traditional religion displays their worship in sacred rites which are dramatisations of their beliefs, and this is communicated in a tangible way. Thus, it becomes more experiential than mere actions performed. All the five senses have to take part in the sacred rites. Therefore, the sacred rites should be effective and experiential like the sounds of melodies, songs, clinging of cymbals, musical instruments, clapping of hands; experienced by seeing and smelling as the fragrance of incense rising up to heaven, lighting of the lamps, offering of flowers and other cultural objects; experienced by feeling, by the sprinkling of the holy water, by the washing of feet as a sign of welcome and acceptance; also experienced in bodily gestures and postures such as the sign of the cross, devotional dancing, prostration, removal of footwear, etc. Thus, they could feel at home with their worship, at home with their faith without loosing their identity.[704]

"Evangelization calls upon every culture to transcend itself by opening up to the absolute. This is the liberation of man announced by the Gospel."[705] "It cannot be contained in the simple and restricted dimension of economics, politics, social or cultural life; it must envisage the whole man, in all his aspects, right up to and including his openness to the absolute, even the divine Absolute."[706]

Thus, incarnation of the Gospel and evangelisation of the culture aims at the discernment of the cultural values, to reach out to the very soul of a living culture, helping them to respond to the Christian faith through the power of the Gospel. This is the deeper dimension of the discernment, a change-metanoia. In this respect, the purification of a given culture brings a death and resurrection experience.

Christian faith in Chotanagpur is a century old. Although, the Church is self-sufficient except for the financial situation, the Christian faith has not permeated to the soul of the Oraons. For instance even today we find appeasement of the spirits by the Christian Oraons. Likewise, witchcraft is still performed. A witch is often a poor widow, who has no strong support in the community which

---

[703] L. J. LUZBETAK, *The Church and Cultures*, op. cit., 382.

[704] Cf. ibid., 382.

[705] P. POUPARD, *The Church and Culture Challenge and Confrontation* (St. Louis: Central Bureau CCVA, 1994), 25.

[706] EN 33.

not only accuses her, but maltreats her and if opportunity even allows to stone her to death. In such cases Christianity stands spell bound. Occult practices are seen even in developed cultures. This should be a consoling and comforting answer to church leaders. The Gospel that Jesus proclaimed brings salvation to all. It is a Gospel of the kingdom of God (cf. Is. 52:7) that announces peace, justice, goodness and salvation. In other words a total liberation of the person from all sorts of evils thereby establishing a right relationship with God and with one another. The actualisation of this integral liberation is in Jesus Christ who is the king of the universe and the defender of the widow, the poor, the orphan, the marginalised and who grants justice to them.[707]

The Oraon experience is the presence of evil forces all over nature in their traditional religion. But this realisation blocks them to deepen their faith in the power of a Supreme Being-*Dharmes*. Instead, there is lot of fear and this fear makes them victims of occult practices. They do not find a reason for the causes of sickness, calamities, bad crops, etc. Therefore, they attribute it to 'evil eye and evil mouth' and other malicious forces. This is a challenge to Christianity. Pastors should guide the people to rectify their wrong notions. A sense of the sacred should be transformed by Christian faith, that persons are images of God, and that they are sacred because they are consecrated to God by baptism and so they are temples of the Holy Spirit. This would help them to respect the dignity of every individual also to keep the right relationship.[708] This is possible only through a surrendering faith in God. "Christianity should aim at influencing the whole of life and producing integrated persons, rather than have people live parallel lives, at different levels."[709]

Like the Israelites in their relationship to Yahweh, the Oraons too believe that they are *Dharmes*' own people and their place in the world is determined by *Dharmes*. Therefore, there are very few non-farmers. Most of the Oraons refuse to accept other occupations even when their economic conditions fail to support them. This is a wrong conception of God's will for humanity, and here Christianity should take action. This is where corrective secularisation in a positive sense is needed.

Ascetical practices like fasting, prayer and keeping abstinence are noteworthy requirements for the traditional offering of sacrifices. More emphasis should be given to the spirit of such practices than to the ritual observances. Purity is a needed requisite in all the sacrifices. This attitude and practice could be further developed, not by the observation of bodily cleanliness or cleanliness of the objects or place but in a deeper sense that it is purity of heart (cf. Ez. 36:24-30). And true

---

[707] Cf. G. ODASSO, *Regno di Dio, Signoria di Cristo e Missione della Chiesa*, Class notes (Roma: Pontificia Universitá Urbaniana, 1998), 1-2.

[708] F. ARINZE, "The Present-Day Challenge of Bringing Christ to the People of Traditional Religions", op. cit., 35.

[709] Ibid., 29.

inculturation would help the people to have a change of heart, which would be translated in their actions.

In the context of reconciliation some observations are needed. Reconciliation is always a community celebration and judgement is given by the village elders who impose the punishment on human grounds, which is used for agape-meal to conclude the process of reconciliation. At times, the reconciliation ceremony consists in paying a certain amount of money, which may demolish the basic sense of the mercy and goodness of God, who waits for the return of the prodigal sons and daughters. "Inculturation is not just expressing the Jesus-event in and through the religious and cultural traditions of the place, but also when this is necessary to redeem these inhuman elements."[710] God's mercy is boundless. The acceptance of sinfulness is thus a corresponding repentance and is the only requirement God wants. "I will arise and go to my father, and I will say to him, Father, I have sinned against heaven and before you. And he arose and came to his father. But while he was yet at a distance, his father saw him and had compassion, and ran and embraced him and kissed him" (Lk. 15:18, 20). The values of Christ need to be rooted in the hearts of the people which would help them to correct themselves of their wrong understanding of traditional values. "A tradition can be meaningfully preserved only by being creatively reinterpreted."[711]

The study on Oraon Christian's Life; Interaction of Faith and Culture is worth discussing; however it is a delicate matter. There exist very few written records and this has brought a limitation to the research possibilities based on sources available. However, I must admit that my present study has helped me to find out the richness of the Oraon traditional religion, and I am deeply convinced that inculturation is relevant for the effective evangelisation of the Oraons of Chotanagpur. They have experienced the transforming power of the Gospel from the very beginning of their Christian existence through the missionary efforts of Fr. Constant Lievens. Acceptance of faith means to worship now, the Supreme Being whom they call *Dharmes*, with the new confidence of his own children who experience his fatherly love and care in their hearts as well as in their lives. And they express this awareness with the assimilated, transformed, rectified elements typical of their traditional culture, whereby they may feel at home with the riches of the Gospel message and its existential meanings and values.

Whenever Gospel encounters a culture there is the experience of a paschal mystery, the death and resurrection of Jesus. Both, Gospel and culture have to shed off their embodiment in order to rise up to a new creation (cf. Jn. 12:24). Inculturation is not a finished product, or a once-for-all event or a definite achievement. It should be and always remain dynamic. Such an on-going inculturation is necessary to safeguard the very identity of both the Gospel and

---

[710] S. ANAND, "Inculturation in India: Yesterday, Today and Tomorrow," in *Indian Missiological Review*, 19 (1997), 22.

[711] Ibid., 27.

culture.[712] Therefore, attempts to insert the local feasts into the liturgy should be taken seriously as these communitarian celebrations play an important role in the life of the Oraons.

In the course of the past hundred and thirty four years, Christianity has influenced the people to a great extent. Missionaries introduced the Oraons to school and to many development projects. Today, one can notice a lot of differences between a Christian and a non-Christian Oraon or a literate and a non-literate Oraon. There is a tendency among the educated Oraon Christians to look down at the non-educated Oraons. Thus, the progress and development are good but it should lessen the existing social gaps rather than creating more. Pastors should take care that in the name of religion, the Oraons are not be detribalised or alienated from their socio-cultural roots. Proper inculturation would enhance their good traditional values and give them a precious sense of identity.

Challenges have to be faced and changes have to be made. One needs the courage to jump into deep waters to get the pearls. Such a search is also represented by this study. However, modest its outcome may be, I am proud of having undertaken the present work as it has increased my interest in the people of Chotanagpur, especially the Oraons. This study has deepened my knowledge and widened my vision and thus has helped me to nourish my zeal as an evangeliser and to identify myself with the people I serve, among whom I live.

---

[712] Cf. S. RAYAN, "Inculturation and People's Struggles," in *Indian Missiological Review*, 19 (1997), 36.

GLOSSARY

Achrael	The guardian spirit of the women
Adivasi	The original settlers in the land; dwellers from the beginning etc.
Agharjis	An adopted son-in-law.
Agni	God of the fire in Hindu religion
Agria	Left out or extra.
Agrialohar	The extra blacksmith.
Agua	A guide or a leader in a special sense, the friend who acts as a messenger to arrange a match.
Ahir	Herdsman.
Akhra	Village dancing place.
Aruvachaval	White rice that is prepared from paddy without parboiling.
Asur women	Wives of *Asur* brothers.
Asurs	Legendary people who smelted iron day and night, who disobeyed *Dharmes.*
Ayo Sangat	Mothers' Sodality.
Baba	Father.
Bahin	Sister.
Bai-bhak	Evil-mouth.
Baiga	Village priest.
Ban	Forest.
Baranda pachcho	A household spirit to which sacrifices are offered on behalf of individual families.
Bariso	Rain down.

Beth begari	Compulsory labour with out payment to be rendered by the tenants to the landlords.
Bhag	Tiger.
Bhaghout	The spirits of persons bitten to death by tigers.
Bhagwan	Hindu name for God.
Bhaiya	Brother.
Bhakh Khandna	An alternative name for the *Dandakatta* ceremony. It means warding off evil word.
Bhakti	Devotion to a personal God.
Bhelwa	Semicarpus anacardium. A tree commonly found in Chotanagpur to which the Oraons attribute the power to bring blindness in persons.
Bhelwa Phari	An alternative name for the *Dandakatta* ceremony. It means *bhelwa* twig splitting.
Bhuinhar	The original clearer and owner of the land.
Bhut	A Hindi word for spirit
Biri-Belas	The name used by the Oraons to refer to God. It means Sun.
Bonga	A Mundari word for spirit.
Burhia	Old lady
Chandi	The spirit of hunting and war propitiated by young men.
Chatursima	Boundaries of the village.
Chaval	Rice.
Chhatti.	A ceremony for the new born child which is held usually on the eight day after birth to divine the child's name and to welcome him/her to the tribe.
Chiuda	Beaten rice.
Chulha nad	Spirit of the hearth.
Chuman	A meeting held in honour of the newly married couple in order to congratulate and to offer gifts them.
Churil	The spirit of a woman who dies in pregnancy or child birth.
Dain	Witch
Dal	Phaseolus mungo, a kind of beans.
Dali-dhiba	A special gift given by the bridegroom to the family of bride before marriage.

Dand	Tooth.
Danda Rengna	An alternative name for the *Dandakatta* ceremony. It means dragging the twig, waving the wand.
Dandakatta	The Oraon ceremony to ward off evil. It means tooth-splitting or breaking.
Dangra nad	A spirit to which bullocks are periodically offered.
Deonra	Soothsayer.
Deota	Deity.
Des	Nation.
Dhanbuni	An Oraon agricultural feast celebrated when the Oraons sow the paddy seeds.
Dhangar	Servant.
Dharmes	The name of the God of Oraons.
Dharti	Earth.
Dhorha	Streams.
Diwani	Tribute paying district.
Garha	Rivers.
Ghar-damad	An adopted son-in-law.
Goensli nad	A tutelary spirit.
Gohar	Cattle shed.
Gohardeota	Cattle-shed spirit.
Gorait	A village drudge.
Gotar	Exogamous, patrilineal, totemic clans among the Oraons.
Harbora	bone burial ceremony to incorporate the recently dead into the company of the ancestors to give them *Pachbalar* status.
Hariari	An Oraon agricultural feast celebrated when the paddy plants are green in colour after the initial growth.
Jagirdar	One who holds a lease granted by the chief of Chotanagpur to his foreign agents for services rendered.
Jamadar	One who is in charge of the Police station.
Jammudeep	The Island of Jammu.
Jethraiyats	A sub division of the non-*bhuinhars* of the village.
Jharkhand	Forest Tract, ancient name of Chotanagpur.

Joda kamna	A ceremony that is performed when the new bride has conceived for the first time, in order to severe all connection with the spirits of her father's household.
Juta	Something that is touched or used.
Kala Pani	The Andaman Isles.
Kamna	To make
Karam festival	A festival celebrated for productivity and fertility.
Karam tree	Nauclea Parvifolia. A tree which is found in Chotanagpur to which the Oraons assign the power to give good fortune, whose branches are used in *karam* festival.
Keond	Drospyros melanoxylon. A tree to which the Oraons attribute some destructive powers.
Khalihani	An Oraon agricultural feast celebrated when the crops are ready to be threshed.
Khana	To eat, food.
Khunt	Lineage, Clan
Khuntbhut	Clan spirit.
Khuntkatti lands	The ancestral lands of the descendants of the original Munda settlers.
Kisan	Farmer.
Klkilia	King fisher.
Konha benja	Great marriage. The bone drowning ceremony in order to incorporate the recently dead into the company of the ancestors.
Kumhar	Potter.
Kuri	A handful of pearl rice is placed on *sal* leaf plates in the name of different spirits.
Kurukh	The name by which Oraons call themselves and their language.
Lohar	Blacksmith.
Lota	Jug.
Lotapani	Water in a brass or any other jug.
Maghe	The name of the month. An Oraon festival in honour of the servants.
Mahto	Village leader.
Malguzar	Tributary.

Malik	Owner.
Manitabhuts	Family spirits.
Marwa	Marriage pavilion.
Masan	Cremation ground.
Mati	An exorcist.
Merkha	Heaven.
Mua	The spirit of persons dying of hunger or starvation or of strangulation or hanging or any other violence.
Munshi	A kind of a parish clerk.
Nad	An Oraon word for spirit.
Najar-gujar	The evil eye.
Nasan	A magic bundle that is placed in a small earthen jar.
Naya	New
Nayakhani	Festival of eating the first fruits especially the new rice.
Pachbalar	Ancestor spirits.
Pahan	Village priest.
Pahari	Hill dwellers.
Palkusna	An alternative name for the Dandakatta ceremony. It means destroying evil tooth.
Panbhara	The village priest's assistant.
Panch	The leader of the village. This also means five.
Panchayat	A body of five village elders who are responsible for bringing law and order in the village.
Panchayati-Raj	A decentralised system of administration.
Pani	Water
Parha	Federation of Oraon villages.
Parha Panchayat	The administrative body of the *parha*.
Patalpur	Subterranean world.
Phagua	One of the forest festivals which is celebrated in the month of *Phagun* in order to mark the end of an year for Oraons.
Pugi-Nad	Private bad spirit.
Pujar	*Pahan's* assistant.
Pulkhi stone	A memorial stone erected to indicate the clan to which the deceased belong.

Put	Son, Children.
Raiyats	A tenant, a farmer or a peasant.
Raja	King
Sabha	Meeting of people.
Sakhri nad	Spirit of the hearth.
Sakti	Power.
Samachar	News.
Sarhul	The principal forest festival of the Oraons, celebrated when the *sal* trees begin to blossom.
Sarnadanri	Village spring.
Sat bahini	Seven sisters.
Sat-pati-raji	Seven strips of land, signifying the totality of land or the whole world.
Semar	Bombax malabaricum. It is a tree which stands for death and destruction in Oraon culture.
Sindhur	Vermilion
Sirjana	To create
Sirpanch	Head leader.
Soharai	Some thing beautiful. It is a festival which is celebrated in honour of the cattle.
Sokha	A non-Oraon witch diviner or a soothsayer.
Soop	Winnowing basket
Su	Good.
Susamachar	Good News
Tana	To pull out.
Thana	Police station.
Thikedar	Lease-holder.
Usnarice	Rice that is made out of boiled paddy.
Vanvasi	Inhabitants of the forest.
Zamindar	A landlord.

BIBLIOGRAPHY

1. MAGISTERIUM

A. Documents of Vatican II

Sacrosanctum Concilium, 4 December 1963, AAS, 56 (15 February 1964), 97-138 (English version from FLANNERY, A. (ed.), Council Vatican II, Dublin: Dominican Publications, new revised edition, 1992).

Lumen Gentium, 21 November 1964, AAS, 57 (30 January 1965), 5-75 (English version from FLANNERY, A. (ed.), Council Vatican II, Dublin: Dominican Publications, new revised edition, 1992).

Nostra aetate, 28 October 1965, AAS, 58 (24 October 1966), 745-749 (English version from FLANNERY, A. (ed.), Council Vatican II, Dublin: Dominican Publications, new revised edition, 1992).

Ad Gentes Divinitus, 7 December 1965, AAS, 58 (30 December 1966), 947-990 (English version from FLANNERY, A. (ed.), Council Vatican II, Dublin: Dominican Publications, new revised edition, 1992).

Gaudium et Spes, 7 December 1965, AAS, 58 (7 December 1966), 1025 - 1120 English version from FLANNERY, A. (ed.), Council Vatican II, Dublin: Dominican Publications, new revised edition,1992).

B. Papal Encyclicals and Apostolic Exhortations

BENEDICT XV, Encyclical letter, *Maximum Illud*, 30 November 1919, AAS, 11 (1 December 1919), 440-455.

PIUS XI, Encyclical letter, *Rerum Ecclesiae*, 29 February 1926, AAS, 18 (1 March 1926), 65-83.

PIUS XII, Encyclical letter, *Evangelii Praecones*, 2 June 1951, AAS, 43 (6 July 1951), 497-528.

__________, Encyclical letter, *Fidei Donum*, 21 April 1957, AAS, 49 (18 May 1957), 225-248.

JOHN XXIII, Encyclical letter, *Princeps Pastorum*, 28 November 1959, AAS, 51 (10 December 1959), 833- 864.

PAUL VI, Encyclical letter, *Ecclesium Suam*, 6 August 1964, AAS, 56 (20 August 1964), 609-659.

_________, Apostolic Exhortation, *Evangelii Nuntiandi*, on Evangelization in the Modern World, 8th December 1975, AAS 68 (31 January 1976), 6-76.

JOHN PAUL II, Apostolic Exhortation, *Catechesi Tradendae*, on Catechesis in Our Time, 16 October 1979, AAS 71 (31 October 1979), 1277-1340.

_________, Encyclical letter, *Dives in Misericordia*, 30 November 1980, AAS, 72 (29 December 1980), 1177-1232.

_________, Encyclical letter, *Laborem Exercens*, On Human Work, On the Ninetieth Anniversary of Rerum Novarum, 14 September 1981, AAS, 73 (5 November 1981), 577-647.

_________, Apostolic Exhortation, *Familiaris Consortio*, The Role of the Christian Family in the Modern World, 22 November 1981, AAS, 74 (3 February 1982), 81-91.

_________, Apostolic Letter, *Salvifici Doloris*, On the Christian Meaning of Human Suffering, 11 February 1984, AAS, 76 (1 March 1984), 201-250.

_________, Post Synodal Apostolic Exhortation, *Reconciliatio et Paenitentia*, 2 December 1984, AAS, 77 (4 March 1985), 185-275.

_________, Encyclical letter, *Redemptoris Mater*, Mother of the Redeemer, March 25 1987, AAS, 79 (2 April 1987), 361-433.

_________, Encyclical Letter, *Redemptoris Missio,* On the permanent validity of the Church's Missionary mandate, 7 December 1990, AAS, 83 (8 April 1991), 249-340.

C. Other Papal Teachings

PAUL VI, *Address to the Vatican II Council Fathers*, 1963, AAS, 55 (1963), 581-583.

JHON PAUL II, *Speeech on Radio Veritas to the people of Asia*, 1981, AAS, 73 (391-398).

_________, "Letter to Cardinal Agostino Casaroli", Secretary of State, 20 May 1982, in *L'Osservatore Romano* (English weekly edition 28 June 1982), 7-8.

_________, 'Ad limina Apostolorum': Episcopal Conference of Zaire, 22 November 1996, "Inculturation is a Movement towards full evangelization", in *L'Osservatore Romano* (English weekly edition 4 December 1996), 5-6.

D. Other Ecclesial Documents and Episcopal Conferences

CATECHISM OF THE CATHOLIC CHURCH (Translated from the Latin, English translation for United Kingdom, London: Geoffrey-Chapman, 1994).

SYNOD OF BISHOPS' SPECIAL ASSEMBLY FOR ASIA, *Lineamenta* (Vatican City:1996).

CONGREGATION FOR THE DOCTRINE OF FAITH, *Litterae Communionis notio ad Catholicae Ecclesiae Episcopos de aliquibus aspectibus Ecclesiae prout est Communio*, Rome: 28 May 1992, AAS, 85 (1993), 838-850.

FEDERATION OF ASIAN BISHOPS' CONFERENCE, "His Gospel to Our Peoples...", Book one: Before Taipei, TEJIDO, M. (ed.), Manila, 1975.

FEDERATION OF ASIAN BISHOPS' CONFERENCE, "His Gospel to Our Peoples...", Book Two: Taipei, DACANAY, D.C. (ed.), Manila, 1976.

CATHOLIC BISHOPS' CONFERENCE OF INDIA, *National Catechetical Directory of India* (C.B.C.I. Commission for Christian Life and N.B.C.L.C., Bangalore, 1990).

E. Studies Prepared by Commisions

INTERNATIONAL THEOLOGICAL COMMISSION, *Faith and Inculturation*, (A document prepared by I.T.C., during its plenary session of December 1987, broadly approved in October 1988, and published with the placet of Cardinal Joseph Ratzinger).

DIVAKAR, P. R., "Reflections on the Problem of Inculturation", In *The Encounter of the Gospel with Culture: A Short Symposium,* F.A.B.C. Papers, No. 7. (Hong Kong: F.A.B.C. Central Secretariat, 1976).

HARDAWIRYANA, H. R., "A Pastoral Primer on Christian Inculturation", in *Bulding the Church of Christ in a Pluricultural Situation,* F.A.B.C. Papers No. 41. (Hong Kong: F.A.B.C. Central Secretariat, 1985).

ROSALES, B. G., and AREVALO, C. G. (ed.), *For all the Peoples of Asia,* F.A.B.C. Documents from 1970-1991, (Quezon city: Claretian Publications, 1992).

THEOLOGICAL ADVISORY COMMISSION OF THE F.A.B.C. *Theses on the Local Church: A Theological Reflection in the Asian Context,* F.A.B.C. Papers, No 60 (Hong Kong: F.A.B.C. Central Secretariat, 1991).

2. STUDIES

A. On Oraons (Tribals) and Chotanagpur

AMALADOSS, M., "Theologizing in a Tribal Context: Some Methodological Observations", in *Sevartham,* 9 (1984), 3-9.

AREEPARAMPIL, M., *Tribals of Jharkhand: Victims of Development* (New Delhi: Indian Social Institute, 1995).

ARTURO, M., *Libin Saheb*, Collezione Lega Missionaria Studenti (Roma: 1933).

BANERJEE, M., *An Historical Outline of Pre-British Chotanagpur* (Ranchi: Educational Publications,1989).

BARA, D., "Customary Matrimonial Law of the Oraons", in *Sevartham*, 13 (1988), 3-13.

_________, "Oraon Marriage: Socio-Cultural Context", in *Sevartham*, 14 (1989), 63-73.

BARJO, V. P., "The Religious Life of the Sarna Tribes", in *Indian Missiological Review*, 19 (1994), 42-56.

BHAT, V. A., "Priestly Functions among the Hos", in *Sevartham*, 5 (1980), 89-93.

BIASUTTI, R., "Oraon", in *Enciclopedia Italiana*, Vol. XXV (Roma: Istituti della Enciclopedia Italiana Fondata da Giovanni Treccani, 1935), 429.

BOGAERT, M.V., *The Tribal: My Brother* (Ranchi: Xavier Institute of Social Service, 1983).

BONA, B., "Co-Operation", in FLEMING, A., *Golden Harvest* (Rourkela: Bishop's House, 1958), 17-18.

BOWEN, J. F., *Father Constant Lievens S.J. The Apostle of Chotanagpur* (London: 1936).

BRUGGEMAN, A., "Worship: Sarna and Christian Theological Reflections on the Munda Ba-Parab", in *Sevartham*, 7 (1982), 45-63.

CAMPION, E., *My Oraon Culture* (Ranchi: Satya Bharati, 1980).

CELESIANO, T., *Il Picolo Saverio - P. Constante Lievens S.J.* (Venezia, Ser. 3-I Missionari, 6, 1933).

CHACKO, E. O., "Santal Sacrifice and Festival", in *Sevartham*, 12 (1987), 115-125.

CHEENATH, R., "The Catholic Church in Orissa", in KANJAMALA, A. (ed.), *Integral Mission Dynamics* (New Delhi: Intercultural Publications, 1995), 273-287.

CHOWDHURY, B., "Tribes and Development", in PATNAIK, S. R. (ed.), *Orissa Today* (Bhubaneswar: Eastern Media Limited, 1996), 43-51.

CLARYSEE, L., "Lievens and the Zemindari System", in *Sevartham,* 5 (1980), 5-17.

_________., "Lievens The Missionary", in *Indian Missiological Review* 7 (January 1986), 19-31.

_________., *Father Constant Lievens S.J.* (Ranchi: Satya Bharati, 1984).

COELHO, E., "Ancestor Veneration Among the Hos", in *Sevartham*, 5 (1980), 94-99.

D'SOUZA, L., "Religious Decline or Return: A Appraisal of the Secularization Process", in *Indian Missiological Review*, 19 (1997), 77-85.

DALTON, E. T., *Descriptive Ethnology of Bengal* (Calcutta: Studies Indian, 1973).

DAS, C., "The Santal Creation myth", in *Sevartham*, 11 (1986), 113-127.

DAS, S. T., *Indian Tribes - Life Style-Locational Practice* (New Delhi: Gian Publishing House, 1989).

DE MEULDER, E., *They have not Spoken Yet* (Raigarh: Catholic Ashram, 1963).

DE SA, F., *Crisis in Chotanagpur* (Bangalore: Redemptorist Publications, 1975).

DEHON, P., "Religion and Customs of the Uraons", in *Memoirs of the Asiatic Society of Bengal,* Vol.1 (Calcutta: The Asiatic Society, 1906), 121-181.

DHAN, R. O., *These are my Tribesmen: the Oraons* (Ranchi: G.E.L. Church Press, 1967).

DOONGDOONG, A., "The Kharias: Where do they come from?", in *Sevartham,* 6 (1981), 100-110.

DULLARD, M., "Ignatian Spirituality and Chotanagpur Mission", in *Indian Missiological Review,* 7 (1985), 6-17.

DUNG DUNG, M., "Kharia Pramukh Pradhayem aur Ulsav", in *Sevartham,* 5 (1980), 45-54.

EKKA, P., "Adivasi Riti Rivaj", in *Sevartham,* 1 (1976), 86-95.

_________., "Adivasi Riti Rivaj", in *Sevartham,* 2 (1977), 20-25.

_________., "Messianic Movements among the Chota Nagpur Tribes", in *Sevartham,* 4 (1979), 21-33.

_________., "Tribals and Inculturated Liturgy", in *Indian Missiological Review,* 7 (April 1985), 145-151.

_________., *The Mundas and Oroans of Chotanagpur, A Comparative Ethnological Survey,* Unpublished, B. Litt. Thesis Submitted to Campion Hall, (Oxford: 1960).

_________., *Catholic Adaptation of Adivasi Customs,* A Summary of the talk given at the Missionary meeting at Archbishop's House (Ranchi: 1967).

EKKA, X., "Theological Insights in Tribal Songs", in *Sevartham,* 3 (1978), 108-122.

FLEMING, A. (ed.), *Golden Harvest* (Rourkela: Bishop's House, 1958).

FRANKLIN, D., "Impact of Christianity on the Status of Women from the Socio-Cultural Point of View", in *Religion and Society,* 32 (June 1985), 43-55.

FUCHS, S., "Concept of Salvation in Tribal Religions," in *Indian Missiological Review,* 2 (1982), 361-371.

_________., "Messianic and Chiliastic Movements among Indian Aboriginals", in AAVV, *Hinduism,* Studia Missionalia, XIII (Romae: Pontificiae Universitatis Gregorianae, 1963), 85-103.

_________., "Culture in the Service of Evangelization in India", in *Indian Missiological Review,* 3 (January 1981), 4-18.

_________., "Liberation Movements among the Tribals of India", in PUTHANANGADY, P. (ed.), *Towards an Indian Theology of Liberation* (Bangalore: N.B.C.L.C., 1986), 199-218.

_________., "The Conversion of the Tribals", in *Indian Missiological Review*, 8 (April 1986), 103-114.

_________., *The Rebellious Prophets: A Study of the Messianic Movements in Indian Religions* (Bombay: SVD Anthropological Institute, 1965).

_________., *The Aboriginal Tribes of India* (New Delhi: Inter-India Publications, 1992).

GRIGNARD, F. A., "The Oraons and Mundas from the time of their settlement in India", in *Anthropos*, IV (1909),1-19.

_________., *Oraon-English Dictionary* (Vienna: St. Gabriel, Administration of "Anthropos", 1924).

HAHN, F. and CROOKE, W., "Oraons", in HASTINGS, J. (ed.), *Encyclopaedia of Religion and Ethics,* Vol. 9 (New York: T. & T. Clark, 1917), 501-510.

HAHN, F., *Grammar of the Kurukh Language* (Delhi: Mittal Publications, 1986).

HEDLUND, R. E., Missiological issues in the study of Christianity in Tribal areas", in *Ishavani Documentation and Mission Digest,* XV (1997), 94-107.

HOFFMANN, J., *Encyclopedia Mundarica* (Patna, Bihar and Orissa: Super Intendent Government Printing, 1930).

IVERN, F., *Chotanagpur Survey* (New Delhi: *Indian Social Institute*, 1969).

JOSSON, H., *The Mission of West Bengal or The Archdiocese of Calcutta: Belgian Province of the Soicety of Jesus,* translated from the French by L. Clarysee (Ranchi: Catholic Press, 1993).

KANJAMALA, A., "The Future of the Mission in the Hindi Belt", in *Vidyajyoti,* 5 (1992), 261-278.

_________., *Religion and Modernization of India: A Case Study of Northern Orissa* (Steyler Verlag, St. Augustin / Ishvani, Pune / Satprakashan, Indore, 1981).

KUJUR, M., *Oraon Sanskriti* (Ranchi: Catholic Press, 1993).

KUJUR, A. A., *The Oraon Habitat: A Study in Cultural Geography* (Ranchi: The Daughters of St. Ann,1989).

KUJUR, L., *The Sacramental Celebration of the Rites of Passage in the Uraon Culture* (Rome: Pontificia Universitas Gregoriana, Extract of doctoral dissertation, 1993).

KUJUR, R., *Liberative Evangelization in the Light of Evangelii Nuntiandi*, doctoral dissertation (Rome, Pontificia Universitas Urbaniana, 1985).

KUJUR, S. K., "Tribal Concept of the Divine: A Trinitarian Perspective", in *Sevartham*, 21 (1996), 115-122.

KULLU, P., "Tribal Religion and Culture", in *Jeevadhara*, XXIV (1994), 89-109.

_________., "Tribal Culture-Religion in Practice", in *Sevartham*, 18 (1993), 15-33.

_________., "Tribal Culture-Religion in Practice", in *Sevartham*, 19 (1994), 49-71.

_________., "Figures of Christ in Kharia Religion", in *Sevartham*, 11 (1986), 97-111.

_________., "Tribal Culture and its Importance for Liturgy: Catechesis and Biblical Apostolate", in *Word and Worship,* 26 (February 1993), 50-56.

_________., "Tribal Culture and its Importance for Liturgy: Catechesis and Biblical Apostolate", in *Word and Worship,* 26 (March 1993), 112-115.

_________., "Tribal Spirituality: An Integrated Life with Belief", in *Sevartham*, 21 (1996), 105-113.

LAKRA, C., "Christianity and Tribal Identity", in *Religion and Society*, Vol. 34 (1989), 30-39.

LAKRA, J., "The Genesis of man: the Uraon Myth", in *Sevartham*, 9 (1984), 33-55.

_________., "Genesis of Spirits-The Uraon Myth", in *Sevartham*, 11 (1986), 45-57.

_________., "Rewriting Tribal Anthropolgy", in *Sevartham*, 22 (1997), 11-28.

_________., "Seasonal Songs of Chota Nagpur", in *Sevartham,* 8 (1983), 67-76.

_________., *Adivasi Missa Samgrah* (Ranchi: Catholic Press, 1982).

_________., *Tribal Cultural Anthropology*, Unpublished class notes (Ranchi: St. Albert's college, 1996).

MALLICK, K. W., "The Integrity of the Variegated Creation: A Tribal Point of View", in *Religion and Society*, 37 (January 1990), 85-87.

MATTHIJS, F., "The Contribution of the Chota Nagpur Church and its Impact", in *Indian Missiological Review*, 7 (January 1985), 55-63.

MINJ, N., "Mission in the context of Diversity: Mission in Tribal Context", in *Religion and Society,* 36 (March 1989), 5-21.

_________., "A Theological Interpretation of the Tribal Reality in India", in *Religion and Society*, XXXIV (1987), 71-85.

_________., *A Responsible Christian Task For Lok Mukti in Chotanagpur* (Ranchi: Sudarshan Press, 1988).

MUNDA, R. D., "The Bases of Cultural Identity of Chota Nagpur", in *Religion and Society*, 36 (June 1989), 24-39.

NADER, A., *The Ignatian Land* (Archdiocese of Calcutta: A. B. Cusack, 1925).

PALATTY, V., "The Religious World-View of the Oraons", in *Sevartham,* 19 (1994), 101-119.

_________., *The Concept of God in Sarna Religion of the Oraons and the Christian Concept of God*, Extract of doctoral dissertation (Rome: Pontificia Universitas Gregoriana, 1997).

PARAPULLIL, A., "Tribal Theology", in *Sevartham,* 2 (1977), 27-52.

PONETTE, P. (ed.), *The Munda World: Hoffmann Commemoration Volume* (Ranchi: Catholic Press, 1978).

_________., "Ranchi Mission: Before and After Lievens", in *Indian Missiological Review,* 7 (1985), 32-54.

_________., "Spirituality of the Mundas", in *Sevartham* 9 (1984), 69-78.

_________., "The Ethics of the Mundas", in *Sevartham* 4 (1979), 112-133.

_________., "The Evolution of the Munda Tribe", in *Sevartham* 7 (1982), 3-24.

PRASAD, N., *Land and people of Tribal Bihar* (Ranchi: Bihar Tribal Research Institute, 1961).

PULLOPPILLIL, T., "The Values that Undergird a Tribal Theology", in *Vidyajyoti,* 61 (March 1997), 187-191.

RAJ, S. L., "People's Power through Panchayati Raj", editorial, in *Social Action,* Vol. 47 (1997), I-VI.

RITA, S., "The Chamar Marrige Customs and their Meaning", in *Sevartham,* 3 (1978), 40-76.

ROSNER, V. "The Marriage Ceremonies of the Telia Nagesia of Jashpur, India", *Anthropos,* 59 (1964), 398-425.

_________., "An Adivasi Drum", in *Anthropos,* 57 (1962), 89-120.

_________., "Flora of Chota Nagpur in Tribal Worship and Witchcraft", in *Sevartham,* 6 (1981), 85-93.

_________., "Myths from Chota Nagpur as Retold by V. Rosner, S.J.", in *Sevartham,* 17 (1992), 11-131.

_________., "Pahan, Cult-Priest of the Munda", in *Sevartham,* 4 (1979), 57-71.

_________., "Some Observations on the Soul Concept and the Evil Eye among the Adivasis of Chotanagpur", in *Anthropos,* 57 (1962), 85-93.

_________., "The Impact of Modern Forces on the Oraons of Samtoli", in *Anthropos,* 63 (1968), 177-186.

_________., *Flying Horse of Dharmes* (Ranchi: Sathya Bharati Publications, 1982).

ROY CHOUDHURY, P. C., *Inside Bihar* (Calcutta: Bookland Private Limited, no date).

ROY, S. C., *Oraon Religion and Customs* (Calcutta: Editions Indian 1928, reprinted 1972).

_________., *The Mundas and Their Country* (Ranchi: Man in India Office, 1912, reprinted 1995).

_________., *The Oraons of Chota Nagpur, Their History, Economic Life and Social Organization* (Satprakashan, Ranchi, 1915, reprinted 1984).

RYAN, J., *A Padre Sabih on the Ranchi Hills, Fr. Constant Lievens* (Trichinapol: Indian Catholic Truth Society, 1928).

SHOURIE, A., *Missionaries in India* (New Delhi: ASA Publications, 1994).

SOARES PRABHU, G. M., "Anti-Greed and Anti-Pride", in *Jeevadhara,* XXIV (1994), 130-150.

_________., "Tribal Values in India", in *Jeevadhara,* XXIV (1994), 84-88.

SURIN, S. N., "Customary Law among the Tribals", in *Religion and Society* 36 (June 1989), 49-55.

TANGHE, O., "Father Constant Lievens, Apostle of the Adibasis of Chotanagpur (India)", in *Omnis Terra* (English edition, Nov. 1993), 453-463.

TETE, P. (ed.), *To Chotanagpur With Love and Service: Pioneers in the Ranchi Jesuit Province* (Ranchi: Ranchi Jesuit Society, 1991).

_________. (ed.), *They Still Speak to Us: Pioneers in the Ranchi Jesuit Province* (Ranchi: Ranchi Jesuit Society, 1993).

_________., *A Missionary Social Worker in India, J.B. Hoffmann, The Chota Nagpur Tenancy Act and the Catholic Co-operatives 1893-1928,* Documenta Missionalia 18 (Roma: 1984).

_________., Catholic Mission in the Chotanagpur Region, in. A. KANJAMALA, (ed.), *Integral Mission Dynamics,* (New Delhi: Intercultural Publications, 1995), 208-223.

THURUTHUMALIL, A., "The Poetry of the Indian Tribals", in *Journal of Dharma,* 17 (April-June 1992), 110-121.

TIRKEY, A., "An Oraon Myth of Redemption", in *Vidyajyoti,* LI (October 1987), 484-492.

_________., "Father Constant Lievens, S.J., The Missionary", in *Indian Missiological Review,* 7 (April 1985), 109-144.

_________., "Hariari: the Festival of Green Paddy Plants", in *Sevartham,* 15 (1990), 65-74.

_________., "Khalihani: Ritual and Myth", in *Sevartham,* 13 (1988), 17-25.

_________., "Religious Dimension of Sohrai: The Uraon Way", in *Sevartham,* 21 (1996), 123-131.

_________., "Sarhul and Kathori: Two Festivals", in *Sevartham,* 16 (1991), 73-79.

_________., "Symbolic Activities", in *Sevartham,* 8 (1983), 83-103.

_________., "The Karam Festival Myth", in *Sevartham,* 11 (1986), 3-22.

_________., "The Origin of Evil Spirits", in *Sevartham,* 18 (1993), 35-39.

TIRKEY, B., "Oraon Approaches to God and Spirits", in *Sevartham,* 7 (1982), 25-43.

_________., "Oraon Ethical Values," in *Sevartham,* 9 (1984), 25-43.

_________., "Theologizing in Oraon Context", in *Vidyajyoti,* 44 (1980), 1-11.

_________., *Oraon Symbols* (Delhi: Vidyajyoti, 1980).

_________., *The Smiling Oraon* (Patna: Navajyoti Niketan, 1989).

TOPNO, M., "Funeral Rites of the Mundas on the Ranchi Plateau", in *Anthropos,* 50 (1955), 715-733.

_________., "Pati and Parha: Social Structure of the Munda", in *Sevartham*, 16 (1991), 3-19.

_________, "Spirits in the Life and Belief of the Mundas", in *Sevartham*, 3 (1978), 5-26.

TOPPO, R., *The Role of Oraons in the Work of Evangelization in Chotanagpur,* Doctoral Dissertation (Roma: Pontificia Università Urbaniana, 1987).

TOPPO, S. K., "Totemism (Gotra Pratha) in Chotanagpur", in *Sevartham*, 4 (1979).

TROISI, J., "Hindu - Tribal Religious Interaction", in *Sevartham*, 5 (1980), 115-144.

TROY, J. V., "The Pre-History of the Coming of the Mundas to the Ranchi Plateau: A Review", in *Sevartham*, 15 (1990), 27-38.

VADAKKUMCHERY, J., "Religion in the Tribal Eco-System", in *Journal of Dharma* 17 (Bangalore: 1992) 85-97.

VAN DEN BOGAERT, M., "Communication, Community and Tribals", in *Sevartham*, 15 (1990), 43-55.

_________., "Social Transformation of a Tribal Society: Fall out of Evangelization in Chotanagpur", in *Sevartham*, 10 (1986), 19-37.

VAN EXEM, A., "The New Dispensation in Sarna Religion", in *Sevartham*, 10 (1985), 75-90.

_________., "The Sacrifice and Meal", in *Vidyajyoti*, LII (1988), 122-136.

_________., "The Tribe: God's Own People A Theological perspective", in *Sevartham*, 12 (1987), 45-64.

_________., "Tribal for ever. The Eschatology of Sarna", in *Sevartham*, 13 (1988), 27-41.

_________., "Creation and Fall in Sarna Religion", in *Sevartham*, 9 (1984), 11-31.

_________., "Crisis and the Sarna", *Sevartham*, 3 (1978) 27-45.

_________., "Genesis 1-11 as a Living Tradition", in *Sevartham*, 21 (1996), 3-29.

_________., "Man and His Imperceptible self: The Munda Philosophy of Man", in *Sevartham*, 5 (1980), 63-88.

_________., "Sin and Salvation in Sarna Religion", in *Vidyajyoti*, 47 (1983), 297-309.

_________., "The Gospel to the Sarna Tribal", in *Bible Bhashyam* XVII, 4 (1991), 242-260.

_________., "The self understanding of the Sarna Man", in *Sevartham*, 11 (1986), 59-72.

_________., "Christian Tribals and Tribal Community", in *Indian Missiological Review,* 8 (April 1986), 91-99.

_________., "Evangelization in Chota Nagpur: Past, Present and Future", in *Indian Missiological Review*, 7 (January 1985), 65-73.

_________., "Genesis Read by Chotanagpur Tribals", in *Bible Bhashyam,* XII (December 1986), 263-278.

_________., "Genesis Read by Chotanagpur Tribals", in *Bible Bhashyam,* XIII (March 1987), 42-56.

_________., "The Tribe, a Link with Singbonga", in *Sevartham*, 4 (1979), 90-111.

_________., "Cultural Liquidation of the Tribe and therefore Need of Inculturation", in *Sevartham*, 15 (1990), 57-63.

_________., "Inculturating the Liturgy: the Tribal Way", in *Word and Worship*, 26 (February 1993), 57-62.

_________., "Munda Sacrifice and Festival", in *Sevartham*, 7 (1982), 81-116.

_________., *Basic Socio-Economic Attitudes of Chota Nagpur Tribals* (Ranchi: The Catholic Co-operative Society, 1992, 2 ed.).

_________., *Evangelisation Today, A Local Church Reflects* (Ranchi: Ranchi Jesuit Society, 1975).

_________., *The Religious System of the Munda Tribe: An Essay on Religious Anthropology*, (Collectanea Instituti Anthropos, Vol. 28, St. Augustin, Germany, 1982).

VERRIER, E., *Tribal myths of Orissa* (Bombay: Oxford University Press, Geoffrey Cumerlege, 1954).

VIDYARTHI, L. P. and RAI, B. K., *The Tribal Culture of India* (New Delhi: Concept Publishing Company, 2nd edition, 1985).

B. Theological Resources

AAVV., *The New Interpreter's Bible,* Vol. 5 (Nashville, Abingdon Press, 1994).

_________., *Inculturation: Its Meaning and Urgency*, (Kampala: Uganda, St. Paul Publications, 1986).

ABEYASINGHA, N., *A Theological Evaluation Of Non-Christian Rites* (Bangalore: Theological Publications in India, 1979).

AMALADOSS M., "Inculturation: Theological Perspectives", in *Jeevadhara* 6 (1976), 296-297.

_________., "Inculturation and Tasks of Mission", in *East Asian Pastoral Review*, XVII (1980), 117-125.

_________., "Challenges of Mission Today", in JENKINSON, W., and O'SULLIAN, H. (ed.), *Trends in Mission* (Maryknoll: New York, Orbis Books, 1991), 359-397.

_________., *Becoming Indian: The Process of Inculturation* (Bangalore: Dharmaram Publications, 1992).

__________., *Do Sacraments Change* (Bangalore: Theological Publications, 1979).

__________., *Mission Today, Reflections from an Ignatian Perspective* (Anand: Gujarat Sahitya Prakash, 1989).

AMALORPAVADASS, D. S., *Gospel and Culture* (Bangalore: N.B.C.L.C., 1978).

__________., *Efforts made in the Roman Catholic Church Toward Indigenisation* (Bangalore: N.B.C.L.C. 1971).

__________., *Main Problems in Preaching the Gospel* Today, (Bangalore: N.B.C.L.C., 1973).

__________. (ed.), *Report of the IVth All-Indian Liturgical Meeting* (2nd to 8th December 1973), (Bangalore: N.B.C.L.C., 1976).

__________., *The Theology of Indirect Evangelization*, (Bangalore: N.B.C.L.C., 1969).

__________., *Theology of Evangelization in the Indian Context* (Bangalore: N.B.C.L.C., 1971).

__________., *Towards Indigenisation in the Liturgy* (Bangalore: N.B.C.L.C., 1973) no date.

__________. (ed.), *Report of the Vth All-India Liturgical Meeting,* 11th to 16th December 1976 (Bangalore: N.B.C.L.C., 1977).

__________., *Official meeting of the C.B.C.I. Commission for Liturgy* (Bangalore: National Liturgical Centre, 1978), 111-136.

ANAND, S., "Inculturation in India: Yesterday, Today and Tomorrow", in *Indian Missiological Review*, 19 (1997), 19-34.

ARBUCKLE, G., *Earthing the Gospel: An Inculturation Handbook for Pastoral Workers* (London: Geoffrey-Chapman, 1990).

ARINZE, F., "The Present-Day challenge of Bringing Christ to people of Traditional Religions", in *Indian Missiological Review,* 15 (1993), 23-36.

AZEVEDO, M., "Challenges to Inculturated Evangelization", in JENKINSON, W., and O'SULLIAN, H. (ed.), *Trends in Mission* (Maryknoll: New York, Orbis Books, 1991), 134-142.

BAROFFIO, B., "Sacerdozio", in *Nuovo Dizionzrio di Liturgia,* a cura di SARTORE, D., e. TRIACCA, A. M. (Roma: Edizione Paoline, 1984),1233-1253.

BARTOLI, L., *La Chiave per la Comprensione del Simbolismo e dei Segninel Sacro,* (Trieste: Edizioni Lint Trieste, 1982).

BEAUCHAMP, P., *Bible and Inculturation* (Rome, Pontifical Gregorian University, 1983).

BIERNATZKI, W. E., "Roots of Acceptance: The intercultural Communication of Religious meanings", in *Inculturation,* Working papers on living faith and Cultures, XIII (Roma: Centre "Cultures and Religions", Pontifical Gregorian University, 1991).

BISWAS, J., "Man in Genesis Chapters 1-11", in *Jeevadhara*, 26 (1975), 114-125.

BOROBIO, D., "I 'Quattro Sacramenti' della Religiosita Popolare: Una Critica", in *Concilium*, edizione Italiano, XIV, 2 (1978), 101-114

BOUESSE, H., "Glory of God", in RAHNER, K. (ed.), *Encyclopaedia of Theology, The Concise Sacramentum Mundi,* Vol. 2 (London: Burns and Oates, 1975, reprinted 1986), 401-403.

BROVELLI, F., "Esequie", in *Nuovo Dizionario di Liturgia*, a cura di SARTORE, D., e TRIACCA, A. M. (Roma: Edizione Paoline, 1984), 463-476.

BURKE, C., "Inculturation: John Paul II and the Third World", in *East Asian Pastoral Review*, 32 (1995), 276-291.

CARVALHO AZEVEDO, M., *Inculturation and Challenges of Modernity* (Rome, Centre "Culture and Religions" Pontifical Gregorian University, 1982).

CASTELLANO, J., "Religiosita Popolare e Liturgia", in *Nuovo Dizionario di Liturgia*, a cura di SARTORE, D., e TRIACCA, A. M. (Roma: Edizione Paoline, 1984), 1168-1187.

CASTI, J., "Inculturation in Asia: Religious and Cultural Aspects", in *Indian Missiological Review* 7 (1985), 217-253.

CHUPUNGCO, A. J., *Cultural Adaptation of the Liturgy* (New York: Paulist Press, 1982).

_________., *Liturgies of the Future, the Process and Methods of Inculturation* (New York: Paulist Press, 1984).

COLOMBO, G., "Matrimonio", in *Nuovo Dizionario di Liturgia*, a cura di SARTORE, D., e TRIACCA, A. M. (Roma: Edizione Paoline, 1984), 809-820.

_________., "Unzione degli infermi", in *Nuovo Dizionario di Liturgia*, a cura di SARTORE, D., e TRIACCA, A. M. (Roma: Edizione Paoline, 1984), 1539-1552.

CROLLIUS, A. R., "Inculturation", Working papers on Living Faith and Cultures, in CROLLIUS, A. R. (ed.), *Building Church in Pluricultural Asia*, Centre " Cultures and Religions" Vol. VII (Rome: Pontifical Gregorian University, 1986).

_________., *What is new about Inculturation* (Rome: Pontifical Gregorian University, 1984).

DINH DUC DAO, J., "Present-Day Situations of the Mission "ad gentes" at the Service of the Poor", in *Omnis Terra* (English edition, April 1993), 287-293.

_________., Evangelization and Culture in Asia: Problems and Prospects", in *Omnis Terra* (Eng. ed., February 1994), 70-80.

_________., *Preghiera Rinnovata per una Nuova Era Missionaria in Asia* Inculturation: Testi di lavoro su Fede e Culture XV, a cura di A.R.

CROLLIUS, 'Centro Culture e Religioni' (Roma: Editrice Pontificia Universita Gregoriana, 1994).

DOERFLINGER, R., "Human Life, Dignity and Sanctity of", in R. SHAW (ed.), *Our Sunday Visitor's Encyclopedia of Catholic Doctrine* (Huntington: Our Sunday Visitor Publishing Division, 1997), 303-307.

DONAHUE, R., "The God and Father of Our Lord Jesus Christ", in C. STUHLMUELLER (ed.), *The Collegeville Pastoral Dictionary of Biblical Theology*. (Minnesota: The Liturgical press, 1996), 387-389.

DOURNES, J., *God in Vietnam: A Christian Mission on the Plateaux of Vietnam (*London: Geoffrey-Chapman, 1966).

DUJARIER, M., *The Rites of Christian Initiation* (New York, N.Y.: Sadlier, A Division of William H. Sadlier,1979).

ELIADE, M., *Images and Symbols: Studies in Religious Symbolism*, translated by P. Mairet (London: Harvill Press, 1961).

__________., *The Sacred and the Profane*, Translated from the French by W. R.Trask (New York: Harcourt, Brace & World, Inc. 1959).

ELUVATHINGAL, S., *Inculturation and Christian Art* (Roma: Urbaniana University Press, 1990).

ESQUERDA BIFET, J., *Pastoral for a Missionary Church* (Rome: Urbaniana University Press, 1993).

FENTON, J. C., "Salvation", in RICHRDSON, A., and BOWDEN, J. (ed.), *The Westminster Dictionary of Christian Theology* (Pennsylvania: Philadelphia, The Westminster Press, 1983), 519-521.

FICHTNER, J. A., "Anthropology, Theological", in *New Catholic Encyclopedia*, Vol. 1 (New York: McGraw-Hill Book Co., 1967), 613.

FISCHER, A., "God", in STUHLMULLER, C. (ed.), *The Collegeville Pastoral Dictionary of Biblical Theology* (Minnesota: The Liturgical press, 1996), 381-386.

FRESE, P. R., and GRAY, S.J.M., "Trees," in ELIADE, M. (editor in chief), *The Encyclopedia of Religion,* Vol. 15 (New York: Macmillan Publishing Company, 1987), 26-33.

FUELLENBACH, J., *The Kingdom of God* (Indore: Satprakashan Sanchar Kendra, 1994), 207.

GEERTZ, C., *The Interpretation of cultures* (New York, N.Y.: Basic Books, A Division of Harper collins Publishers, 1973).

GEORGE, F. E., *Inculturation and Ecclesial Communion, Culture and Church in the Teaching of Pope John Paul II* (Rome: Urbaniana University Press, 1990).

GIGLIONI, P., "Inculturazione e Missione", in *Chiesa Locale e Inculturazione* (Roma: Urbaniana University Press, 1987), 76-130.

_________., *Inculturation and non-Christian Religions* (Roma: The P.M.U. International Secretariat, 1983).

GITTINS, A., *Gifts and Strangers: Meeting the Challenge of Inculturation* (New York: Paulist Press, 1989).

GROSHEIDE, F. W., *The New International Commentary on the New Testament: The First Epistle to the Corinthians* (Grand Rapids, Michigan: WM. B. Eerdmans Publishing Company, 1953).

GUENON, R., *Simboli delle Scienza Sacra* (Milano: Adelphi edizioni S.P.A., 1975).

HAYDEN, T., *An Anthropological Methodology for Research in a Theology of Inculturation,* Faculty Lecture Series, (Nairobi: Catholic University of Eastern Africa, 1993).

HAYES, Z., "Judgement: Pastoral-Liturgical Tradition", in C. STUHLMUELLER (ed.), *The Collegeville Pastoral Dictionary of Biblical Theology* (Minnesota: The Liturgical press, 1996), 509-510.

HELMING, D., "Angels," in SHAW, R. (ed.), *Our Sunday Visitor's Encyclopedia of Catholic Doctrine* (Huntington: Our Sunday Visitor Publishing Division, 1997), 9-10.

HIEBERT, P.G., *Anthropological Reflections on Missiological Issues* (Grand Rapids, Michigan: Baker Books, 1994).

_________., *Cultural Anthropology* (Grand Rapids, Michigan: Baker Book house, 1983).

HUNT, I., "Excursus: Israel and her Neighbours", in BROWN, E.R. and others (ed.), Jerome Biblical Commentary, Vol. 1 (London: Geoffrey-Chapman,1968), 201-222.

KALATHIL, M., "Inculturation a Sociologist's Reflection", in *Jeevadhara*, 6 (1976), 312-323.

KANJAMALA, A. (ed.), *Paths of Mission in India Today* (Mumbai: St. Pauls, 1996).

KAROTEMPREL, S., "Inculturation and Missionary Formation", in *Indian Missiological Review*, 7 (1985).

_________., (ed.), *Following Christ in Mission* (Bombay: Pauline Publications, 1995).

_________., "Jesus Christ at the Centre of Evangelization", in *Omnis Terra* (English edition, February 1993), 73-85.

KAVUNKAL, J., and HRANGKHUMA, F. (ed.), *Bible and Mission in India* Today (Bombay: St Pauls, 1993).

_________., "Mission without the Church", in *Jeevadhara*, Vol. XXIV (1984), 282-292.

__________., *The Abba Experience of Jesus: Model and Motive for Mission in Asia* (Indore: Satprakashan Sanchar Kendra, 1995).

KOCHUPARAMPIL, X., *Evangelisation in India* (Kottayam: Oriental Institute of Religious studies India Publications, 1993).

KRAFT, C. H., *Christianity in Culture A study in Dynamic Biblical Theologizing in Cross-Cultural Perspective* (Maryknoll, New York: Orbis books 1980), 363.

KUNNUMPURAM, K., "Inculturation in Vatican II", in *Jeevadhara*, 6 (1976), 283-292.

__________., "Inculturation and Ecclesiology", in *Indian Missiological Review*, 19 (1997), 46-55.

LASH, S., "Relics, Theology of", in RICHARDSON, A. and BOWDEN, J. (ed.), *The Westminster Dictionary of Christian Theology* (Philadelphia Pennsylvania:, The Westminster Press, 1983), 495-497.

LaVERDIERE, E., "The Eucharist, Sacrament of the Transformation of the World", in *Omnis Terra*, (English edition, May 1994), 381-385.

LAWLER, R. D., "Beatific vision", in SHAW, R. (ed.), *Our Sunday Visitor's Encyclopedia of Catholic Doctrine* (Huntington: Our Sunday Visitor Publishing Division, 1997), 50-51.

LEGRAND, L., "Inculturation and Hermeneutics: The Example of St. paul", in *Indian Missiological Review*, 19 (1997), 5-16.

LEON-DUFOUR, X. (ed.), *Dictionary of Biblical Theology* (London: Geoffrey Chapman, 1969).

LOURDUSAMY, D. S., *The Liturgy and Adaptation* (Bangalore: St. Mary's Press, 1965).

LOVELEY, E., "Creation", in *New Catholic Encyclopedia*, Vol.1 (New York: McGraw-Hill Book Co., 1967), 417-419.

LURKER, M., *Dizionario delle Immagini e dei Simboli Biblici* (Milano: Edizioni Paoline, 1990).

LUZBETAK, L. J., *The Church and Cultures, New Perspective in Missiological anthropology* (Maryknoll: New York, Orbis Books, 1988).

MATTAM, A., *Inculturation of the Liturgy in the Indian Context* (Oriental Institute of Religious Studies, India Publications, (Kottayam: Kerala, 1991.

MATTAM, J., and KIM, S. (ed.), *Dimensions of Mission in India* (Mumbai, St. Pauls, 1995).

__________., (ed.), *Mission and Conversion: A Reappraisal* (Mumbai, St. Pauls, 1996).

McKENZIE, J. L., *Dictionary of the Bible* (Bangalore: Asian Trading Corporation 1984).

MENAMPARAMPIL, T., "Cultures and Evangelisation" in *Evangelisation in India* (Shillong: Pastoral Centre, 1987), 11-19.

_________., *Thoughts on Evangelization* (Mumbai: St. Pauls, 1997).

MISTRORIGO, A., *Liturgia: Linee di Fondamento Theologico-Pastorale* (Vicenza: Favero Editore,1969, 2 ed.),

_________., *Dizionario Liturgico-Pastorale: Dai Documenti del Concilio Vaticano II e dagli altri documenti Ufficiali fino al 1977* (Paduva: Edizioni Messaggero, 1977).

MULLUR, A., *Faith and Culture: India Today Perspectives*, (Kerala, Jyotir Dara Publications, 1991).

NKERAMIHIGO T., "Inculturation and the Specificity of Christian Faith", in A. R. CROLLIUS, *Inculturation, Working Papers on Living Faith and Cultures* (Rome: Pontifical Gregorian University, 1984).

ODASSO, G., *Regno di Dio, Signoria di Cristo e Missione della Chiesa*, Class notes (Roma: Pontificia Universitá Urbaniana, 1998).

PATHRAPANKAL, J., "Salvation in Christianity: A Biblical Approach", in *Indian Missiological Review,* 4 (1982), 332-369.

PEDRO, A., "Fr. P. Arrup's Letter on Inculturation to the whole Society of Jesus", *in Indian Missiological Review,* 1 (1979), 87-95.

PERKINS, P.,"Resurrection", in STUHLMULLER, C. (ed.), *The Collegeville Pastoral Dictionary of Biblical Theology* (Minnesota: The Liturgical Press, 1996), 838.

PINTO, J. P., *Inculturation Through Basic Communities* (Bangalore: Asian Trading Corporation, 1985).

_________.,"Creation and Holistic Mission", in KAVUNKAL, J. and HRANGKHUMA, F. (ed.), *Bible and Mission in India Today* (Bombay. St. Pauls, 1993), 286-308.

POLAN, G.J., "Name", in STUHLMUELLER, C. (ed.), *The Collegeville Pastoral Dictionary of Biblical Theology* (Minnesota: The Liturgical Press, 1996), 665-667.

POUPARD, P., *The Church and Culture Challenge and Confrontation* (St. Louis: Central Bureau CCVA, 1994).

PUTHANANGADY, P., "Inculturation in Spirituality and Worship", in *Jeevadhara*, 6 (1976), 302-311.

_________., "Inculturation of Liturgy in India", in *Word and Worship* 23 (1990), 188-198.

_________., "A Missionary Approach to Liturgy", in *Indian Missiological Review,* 1 (July 1979), 137-246.

_________., *Initiation to Christian Worship* (St. Peter's Seminary, Bangalore :Theological Publications in India, , 1979).

RAYAN, S., "Flesh of India's Flesh", in *Jeevadhara*, VI (1976), 259-267.

_________., "Inculturation and People's Struggles", in *Indian Missiological Review*, 19 (1997), 35-45.

REBELLO, A., "Inculturation and Education", in *Euntes Docete,* XLVII (1994), 167-176.

RHEENEN VAN, G., *Communicating Christ in Animistic Contexts* (Grand Rapids, Michigan: Baker Book House, 1991).

RYAN R., "Healing: Patoral-Liturgical Tradition", in STUHLMUELLER, C. (ed.), *The Collegeville Pastoral Dictionary of Biblical Theology* (Minnesota: The Liturgical press, 1996), 420-422.

S.P.U.C., *In Quibus Rerum Circumstantiis* On Admitting other Christians to Eucharistic Communion in the Catholic Church (1 June 1972).

SAHI, J., "Popular Spirituality", in JENKINSON, W., and O'SULLIAN, H. (ed.), *Trends in Mission* (Maryknoll: New York, Orbis Books, 1991), 87-95.

_________., *Stepping Stones: Reflections on the Theology of Indian Christian Culture* (Bangalore: Asian Trading Corporation, 1986).

SALDANHA, J., "A Fresh Impulse for Evangelization in our Times", in *Indian Missiological Review*, 1 (1979), 23-43.

_________., *Inculturation* (Bandra: Bombay, St. Paul Publications, 1987).

_________., "The Teaching of Pope John Paul II on Evangelization", in *Indian Missiological Review,* 5 (1985), 358-369.

SARIVA, M., *Missione e Cultura*, (Roma: Pontificia Università Urbanianan (1986).

SATTLER, H.V., "Marriage (Theology of)," in *New Catholic Encyclopedia*, Vol. IX (New York, St. Louis: McGraw Hillbook Company,1967), 265-267.

SCHIMMEL, A., "Numbers: An Overview", in ELIADE, M. (editor in chief), *The Encyclopedia of Religion*, Vol.11 (New York: Macmillian Publishing Company, 1987), 13-21.

SCHINELLER, P., *A Handbook on Inculturation* (Mahwah, New York: Paulist Press, 1990).

SCHLETTE, H.R., "The Plurality of Religions," in RAHNER, K. (ed.), *Sacramentum Mundi, an Encyclopedia of Theology*, V (London: Burns & Oates,1970), 282-284.

SCHMAUS, M., *God and Creation: The Foundations of Christology,* Dogma, Vol. 2 (Kansas City: Sheed & Ward, 1969).

SCHREITER, R. J., *Constructing Local Theologies* (Maryknoll, New York: Orbis books, 1985).

SEASOLTZ, R.K., "Priest Pastoral-Liturgical Tradition", in STUHLMUELLER, C. (ed.), *The Collegeville Pastoral Dictionary of Biblical Theology* (Minnesota: The Liturgical press, 1996), 779-781.

SHORTER, A., *Toward a Theology of Inculturation* (London: Geoffrey-Chapman, 1988).

SOARES PRABHU, G.M., "The New Testament as a Model of Inculturation", in *Jeevadhara*, 6 (1976), 268-282.

_________., "The Church as Mission", in *Jeevadhara*, Vol. XXIV (1984), 271-281.

SODI, M., "Benedizione", in *Nuovo Dizionario di Liturgia*, a cura di SARTORE, D., e TRIACCA, A.M. (Roma: Edizione Paoline, 1984), 157-175.

TEJIDO, M., (ed.), *The communication from C. B. C. I. to the Synod of Bishops in Rome submitted to and approved by the general assembly on January 14, 1974* (Manila: 1975).

TOPEL, J. T., *The Way to Peace, Liberation Trough the Bible* (Maryknoll, New York: Orbis Books, 1979).

UPKONG, S. P., "Inculturation and Evangelization", in *Vidyajyoti*, 58 (1994), 298-307.

URECH, E., *Dizionario dei Simboli Cristiani* (Roma: Edizioni Arkeioes, 1995).

VADAKUMPADAN, P., "Gospel-Culture Encounter", in *Indian Missiological Review*, 19 (1997), 69-76.

VANDANA, "Water Symbolism in the Gospel of St. John in the Light of Indian Spirituality," in SUGIRTHARAJAH, R.S., and HARGREAVES, C., *Readings in Indian Christian Theology*, Vol. 1 (London: SPCK Holy Trinity Church, 1993), 200-213.

VANHOYE, A., "The New Testament and Inculturation", in *Indian Missioogical Review*, 7 (1985), 198-216.

WARD B., "Saints, Cult of the", in RICHARDSON, A., and BOWDEN, J. (ed.), *The Westminster Dictionary of Christian Theology* (Pennsylvania: Philadelphia, The Westminster Press, 1983), 518-519.

WENHAM, G.J., *Word Biblical Commentary*, Vol 1 (Waco, Texas: Word Books Publisher, 1987).

C. Related Works

AMALADOSS, M., "Festivals and their Significance", in *Jeevadhara*, 6 (1976), 435-444.

_________., "Mission in the 1990's", in *Tripod* (March-April 1991), 11-16.

_________., "Music as Sadhana", in *Journal of Dharma*, 7 (1982),181-188.

_________., "Religious rite as Symbol", in *Jeevadhara*, 29 (1975), 319-328.

AMALORPAVADASS, D. S., "Socio-Economic Development as an Integral part of Evangelisation in India", in *Indian Missiological Review*, 6 (1984), 214-220.

_________., *Indian Christian Spirituality* (Bangalore: N.B.C.L.C., 1982).

BARBOZA, F., "Christian Themes through Bharatanatyam", in *Journal of Dharma*, 7 (1982), 189-201.

BOLLE, K.W., "Myth and Mythology", in GOETZ, P. W. (ed.), *The New Encyclopaedia Britannica*, Micropaedia, Vol. XI (Chicago: University of Chicago, 1981), 793-804.

CHEENATH, R., "Participative leadership in the Church in India", in A. KANJAMALA (ed.), *Integral Mission Dynamics* (New Delhi: Intercultural Publications, 1995), 344-354.

CHERUVALEL, L., "Liturgy in the Missions", in *Indian Missiological Review* 1(1979), 189-201.

_________., "Liturgy in the Missions", in *Indian Missiological Review*, 3 (1981), 187-195.

CHETHIMATTAM, J., "Man and Feast", in *Jeevadhara*, 6 (1976), 405-417.

_________., "Symbolism and Cult in World Religions", in *Jeevadhara*, 29 (1975), 329-344.

CROOKE, W., "Death and Disposal of the Dead" (Indian, non-Aryan), in HASTINGS, J. (ed.), *Encyclopaedia of Religion and Ethics*, Vol. IX (New York: T. & T. Clark, 1914), 479-484.

_________., "Death; Death Rites; Methods of Disposal of the Dead among the Dravidian and other non-Aryan Tribes of India", in *Anthropos*, IV (1909), 457-476.

D'ALVIELLA, G., "Intiation" (Introductory and Primitive), in HASTINGS, J. (ed.), *Encyclopaedia of Religion and Ethics*, Vol. VII (New York: T. & T. Clark, 1914), 314-319.

De LUBAC, H., *Aspects du Boudhisme* (Paris: 1951).

DES PLACES, E., "Anthropomorphism", in *New Catholic Encyclopedia*, Vol.1 (New York: McGraw-Hill Book Co., 1967), 613-614.

DHAVAMONY, M., *Phnomenology of Religion*, Documenta Missionaria, 7 (Roma, Università Gregoriana Editrice, 1973).

DINH DUC DAO, J., "Spiritualita e Santita, Fonte, Via e Campo di Evangelizzazione", in *Euntes Docete*, XLIX (1996), 63-78.

FOLEY, W.M., "Marriage (Christian)," in HASTINGS, J. (ed.), *Encyclopaedia of Religion and Ethics*, Vol. VIII (Edinburgh: T. & T. CLARK, 1915), 433-443.

FREDERICKSEN, L., "Feast and Festival", in *The New Encyclopaedia Britannica*, Macropaedia, Vol. 7 (1974), 197-202.

FUCHS S., "Primitive Cultures", in *The New Review*, XVIII (Calcutta, 1943), 105-121.

_________., *Anthropology for the Missions* (Allahabad: St. Paul Publications, 1979).

GONDA, J., "The Hindu Trinity", in *Anthropos*, Vol. 63/64 (1968-1969), 212-226.

GROTTANELLI, V. L., *Dinamica Culturale e Dialettica Etnologica* (Roma: Urbaniana University Press, 1964).

HEISING, J.W., "Symbolism", in ELIADE, M. (editor in chief), *The Encyclopedia of Religion*, Vol. 14 (New York: Macmillian Publishing Company, 1987), 198-208.

IRUDAYARAJ, X., "Flowers as Religious Symbols", in *Word and Worship*, X (1977), 330-333.

_________.,"Jesus Means Truth-that Sets Men Free", in *Jeevadhara*, 5 (1975), 209-218.

JACOB, T., "Man in the Preaching of Jesus", in *Jeevadhara*, 6 (1976), 126-134.

KANJAMALA, A. (ed.), *Integral Mission Dynamics* (New Delhi: Intercultural Publications, 1995).

KAVANAGH, A., "Gli Avvenimenti nel Ciclo della Vita: Riti Civili e Cristiani", in *Concilium,* edizione italiana, XIV, 2 (1978).

KNOBEL, S.P., "Rites of Passage: Jewish Rites", in ELIADE, M. (editor in chief), *The Encyclopedia of Religion*, Vol. 12 (New York: Macmillian Publishing Company, 1987), 392-398.

KUNNUMPURAM, K., and FERNANDO, L. (ed.), *Quest for an Indian Church, An exploration of the possibilities opened up by Vatican II* (Anand: Gujarat Sahitya Prakash, 1993).

KUNNUMPURAM, K., "The Church of my dreams", in KANJAMALA, A.(ed.), *Integral Mission Dynamics* (New Delhi: Intercultural Publications, 1995) 403-422.

LOURDUSAMY, L., "Inculturation at Christmas", in *Word India*, Vol.12 (1998), 8-9.

LUKE, K., Puja: its Origin and Significance", in *Jeevadhara*, 29 (1975), 345-365.

MAESTERS, C., "Indian Myths and the Old Testament," in *Sedos Bulletin* 24 (1992), 67-68.

MALAYALA MANORAMA COMPANY LTD, *Manorama Year Book 1992* (Kottayam: Kerala, 1992).

McGAVRAN, D.A., *Ethnic Realities and the Church, Lessons from India* (Pasadena, California: William Carey Library, 1979).

McMULLEN, O.C. (ed.), *Rituals and Sacraments in Indian Religions* (Delhi: I.S.P.C.K., The Christian Institute of Sikh Studies, 1979).

MYERHOFF, B. G., and others, "Rites of Passage: An Overview", in ELIADE, M. (editor in chief), *The Encyclopedia of Religion*, Vol. 12 (New York: Macmillian Publishing Company, 1987), 380-386.

No Author, "Tribe", in GOETZ, P. W. (ed.), *The New Encyclopaedia Britannica*, Micropaedia, Vol. XI (Chicago: University of Chicago, 1985), 918-919.

OGASAWARA, M., "The Family and the Last Things: Family Ties and Christian Faith in the Resurrection of the Body as seen against the Background of "Ancestor Worship", in *Japan Mission Journal*, 47 (1993), 18-31.

PADILLA, C.R., "The Relevance of the Jubilee in Today's World", in *Mission Studies, Journal of IAMS*, XIII (1996), 12-31.

PROKSH, G., "Music, Dance and Inculturation", in *Indian Missiological Review*, 5 (1988), 187-200.

PUTHANANGADY, P., "The Evolution of the Feasts of Roman Rites", in *Jeevadhara*, 6 (1976), 445-457.

_________.,"Symbolism of Fire in Indian Worship", in *Word and Worship*, X (1997).

REISS, P. J., "Marriage", in *New Catholic Encyclopedia*, Vol. IX (New York: McGraw-Hill Book Co., 1967), 258-265.

RIVERS, W. H. R., "Marriage" (Introductory and Primitive), in HASTINGS, J. (ed.), *Encyclopaedia of Religion and Ethics*, Vol. VIII (New York: T. & T. Clark, 1914), 423-432.

ROUILLARD, P., "La Liturgia della Morte Come Rito di Passaggio", in *Concilium*, edizione Itatiana, XIV, 2 (1978), 115-128.

SAHI, J., "Dance in the Wilderness", in CHOO LAK, Y., and ENGLAND, C.J. (ed.), *Doing Theology with People's Symbols & Images* (Singapore: Vive Lithographers Pte Ltd, 1989), 51-71.

_________., "Mammon and Myth: The Market Pictured as a Monster", in *Mission Studies, Journal of IAMS*, XIII (1996), 268-280.

_________, "Thoughts on Village Religion and Culture", in *Vidyajyoti*, XLI (February 1997), 68-73.

SCHEER, A., "La Veglia Pasquale, Rito di Passaggio?", in *Concilium*, edizione Itatiana, XIV, 2 (1978), 85-100.

SOARES PRABHU, G.M.,"From Alienation to Inculturation", in T.K. JOHN (ed.), *Bread and Breath: Essays in Honour of Samuel Rayan* (Anand: Gujarat Sahitya Prakash, 1991), 55-99.

SULLIVAN, L.E., "Supreme Beings", in ELIADE, M. (editor in chief), *The Encyclopedia of Religion*, 14 (New York: Macmillian Publishing Company, 1987), 167-181.

VON ARX, W., "La Benedizione della Madre dopo il Parto", in *Concilium*, edizione Italiana, XIV, 2 (1978), 101-114.

WEBSTER'S COLLEGIATE DICTIONARY (Springfield, U.S.A: G.&C. Merriam Co., Publishers, 1946).

YVON, A.,"Culture: Liberating or Alienating?," in *Jeevadhara*, 22 (1992), 26-32.